The Years of
Our Friendship

The Years of Our Friendship

Robert Lowell and Allen Tate

William Doreski

University Press of Mississippi
Jackson

Paperback Edition 2010

The paper in this book meets the guidelines for perma-
nence and durability of the Committee on Production
Guidelines for Book Longevity of the Council on Library
Resources. ∞

Library of Congress Cataloging-in-Publication Data

Doreski, William.

   The years of our friendship / William Doreski.

     p.   cm.

   Includes bibliographical references.

   ISBN: 978-1-60473-510-9

   1. Lowell, Robert, 1917–1977—Criticism and interpretation.
2. Lowell, Robert, 1917–1977—Friends and associates. 3. Tate,
Allen, 1899——Friends and associates. 4. Tate, Allen, 1899——
Influence—Lowell. 5. Poets, American—20th century—
Biography.

   I. Title.

   PS3523.089Z65   1990

   811'.52—dc20

   [B]   89-49308

                                           CIP

British Library Cataloguing-in-Publication data available

ACKNOWLEDGEMENTS AND PERMISSIONS

I would like to thank Don Keck Dupree, James Randall, A. Walton Litz, Louis D. Rubin, Jr., and Carole Doreski for their suggestions, information, and encouragement. A grant from the Whiting Foundation and a summer stipend from the National Endowment for the Humanities helped fund my research and travel.

Sections of chapters 1 and 2 appeared in somewhat different form in the *Southern Literary Journal*. I am grateful to Louis D. Rubin, Jr., for publishing this material and for permission to reprint.

Special acknowledgement is made to the following libraries for the use of material from their collections: Houghton Library, Harvard University; Firestone Library, Princeton University; Harry N. Ransom Humanities Center, University of Texas at Austin.

Previously unpublished material by Robert Lowell, copyright © 1990 by Caroline Lowell, Harriet Lowell, and Sheridan Lowell, is used by permission of Frank Bidart, literary executor for the estate of Robert Lowell.

Previously unpublished material by Allen Tate, copyright © 1990 by Helen H. Tate, is used by permission of Helen H. Tate, literary executor for the estate of Allen Tate.

Previously unpublished material by Jean Stafford, copyright ©1990 by Josephine Monsell, is used by permission of Russell & Volkening, Inc., agent for the estate of Jean Stafford.

The following material is reprinted by permission of Farrar,

Acknowledgements and Permissions

Straus and Giroux, Inc.: selections from *Collected Prose* by Robert Lowell, copyright © 1987 by Caroline Lowell, Harriet Lowell, and Sheridan Lowell; selections from *Day by Day* by Robert Lowell, copyright © 1975, 1976, 1977 by Robert Lowell; selections from *The Dolphin* by Robert Lowell, copyright © 1973 by Robert Lowell; selections from *For the Union Dead* by Robert Lowell, copyright © 1956, 1960, 1961, 1962, 1963, 1964 by Robert Lowell; selections from *History* by Robert Lowell, copyright © 1967, 1968, 1969, 1970, 1973 by Robert Lowell; selections from *Imitations* by Robert Lowell, copyright © 1958, 1959, 1960, 1961 by Robert Lowell; selections from *Notebook 1967–1968* by Robert Lowell, copyright © 1967, 1968, 1969 by Robert Lowell; selections from *Phaedra* translated by Robert Lowell, translation copyright © 1960, 1961 by Robert Lowell; selections from *Selected Poems* by Robert Lowell, copyright © 1944, 1946, 1947, 1950, 1951, 1956, 1959, 1960, 1961, 1962, 1963, 1964, 1965, 1966, 1967, 1968, 1969, 1970, 1973, 1976, and renewal copyright © 1972, 1974, 1975 by Robert Lowell; selections from *Collected Poems* by Allen Tate, copyright © 1952, 1953, 1970, 1977, and renewal copyright 1959, 1960, 1965 by Allen Tate.

The following material is reprinted by permission of Harcourt, Brace, Jovanovich, Inc.: excerpts from "Christmas in Black Rock," "The Quaker Graveyard in Nantucket," "Christmas Eve under Hooker's Statue," "At the Indian Killer's Grave," and "The Crucifix" from *Lord Weary's Castle*, copyright © 1946, 1974 by Robert Lowell; excerpt from "Mother Marie Therese" from *The Mills of the Kavanaughs*, copyright © 1946, 1947, 1950, 1951, 1974, 1975 by Robert Lowell.

Passages from *The Poetry Reviews of Allen Tate, 1924–1944*, edited by Ashley Brown and Frances Neel Chaney, are reprinted by permission of Louisiana State University Press, copyright © 1983 by Louisiana State University Press.

The years of our friendship seemed to roll through me the other night as the hours went and I hope my sobriety didn't hide my strong feelings. . . .

Robert Lowell to Allen Tate
7 November 1961

CONTENTS

The Years of
Our Friendship

Introduction

In the winter of 1942–43, Allen Tate, Caroline Gordon, Robert Lowell, and Jean Stafford lived and worked together at Monteagle, Tennessee, a mountain resort near Sewanee. The house, named Immokalee, had three stories and room for four working writers. Caroline Gordon was writing her novel *The Women on the Porch*, and Tate was working on various new poems and a translation of the *Pervigilium Veneris*. Both were established professional writers. Tate had taught at Princeton for the last three years and, although not invited back, was happy to give up academia for a stint of uninterrupted writing. He had by then published nine books, including four collections of poetry, and Gordon had published five novels. They were reasonably and justly confident in their talent and skills.

Their housemates were still relative beginners. Lowell had published two poems in the *Kenyon Review* and several others in school magazines, but he was still struggling with the focus and voice of his poetry. Jean Stafford had written a number of short stories and was attempting her first novel. As Gordon reported, Stafford had had her novel "torn to pieces by fiends in the guise of friends," with all three of her fellow writers offering their criticism.[1] However Stafford felt about it, the criticism may have been of benefit; *Boston Adventure* would be a best-seller and a book of acknowledged literary value. Her marriage to Lowell would not survive the book's success or the other tensions already growing between them, but this winter at Monteagle, for both Stafford and her husband, would be a crucial point in their literary lives.

The friendship of the Tates and the Lowells began with their mutual dedication to their art. In particular, the friendship of Allen Tate and Robert Lowell, the subject of this study, affected their literary lives in profound and subtle ways. Although Lowell was, during the first decade of the association, the apprentice and Tate the established poet, their relationship became by the late 1940s that of two accomplished peers who offered each other criticism, support, and a common understanding precious to them both. In the 1950s, they saw less of each other, and their distance produced some signs of mutual suspicion. Lowell became a more successful, better-known literary figure, and Tate's response was occasionally resentful, especially as it found expression in letters to other literary people. Lowell, however, remained impressed with Tate's poetry, and some of his best work responds to work Tate had written years before. "For the Union Dead" is a belated response to "Ode to the Confederate Dead"; *Life Studies* more immediately responds to the autobiographical impulse of Tate's "Buried Lake" trilogy; "Those Before Us" answers "To the Romantic Traditionalists"; Tate's "Mother and Son" is echoed in several of the poems in *Lord Weary's Castle*. Examples abound even though other influences also shaped Lowell's work: Eliot, Crane, Pound, Williams, and other poets left their imprint, but Tate had a special place in his life, and a sensibility that, however distinct from Lowell's, still embodied attitudes toward art and life that Lowell shared or wanted to share.

Those attitudes were by no means coincident in every respect, nor were their social and cultural backgrounds especially similar. For example, among the complicating factors in their intellectual and aesthetic interchange is their respective regionalism. On the surface, Lowell's poetry, most often set in urban Boston or rural Maine (except for his last two books), seems more regional than

Introduction

Tate's. If this seems an unexpected point to make, it is because American literary historians tend to see southern writers as regionalists (a view sometimes calculatingly fostered by the writers themselves), while granting New England writers (except obvious "local-color" writers like Walter Hard) ungrudging consideration as cosmopolites. Frost, Robinson, and Jewett, all dependent on strongly localized settings, have been rehabilitated from regional status and placed in the mainstream of our national literature. Of course Faulkner, Flannery O'Connor, and other major southern writers have attained this status also, but our national literature, to a great extent, has been defined by such writers as Hawthorne, Thoreau, Emerson, and Dickinson, who were born in, or worked in (like Melville), or were associated with (like T. S. Eliot) New England, and this linkage tends to exclude such writers as John Pendleton Kennedy, one of several fine and neglected southern authors who are no more narrowly regional in significance than Hawthorne.

Lowell immediately recognized that Tate was a sophisticated, European-oriented poet with a firm sense of his native soil. This combination characterizes many fine American writers, including those like Thoreau, to whom Tate otherwise bears little resemblance. Tate's specific concerns for the South, expressed in his criticism and fiction, lend his career a misleading air of regionalism; while even in his unfinished essay "New England and Further," Lowell looks beyond his region to an ideal of literary internationalism. It is here that he and Tate found common ground: not in adherence to their respective regions but to the republic of letters to which both of them properly belonged. Yet each respected the other's allegiance to his region and the role it played in his work. Lowell's poetry explicitly anchors itself in his region because, like Hart Crane and William Carlos Williams, he adheres to an aesthetic hierarchy that values specificity of place. Tate, in his poetic (and here he and Lowell differ in emphasis rather than in larger outlook), values the detached symbolism of Mallarmé over the place-specific image. Lowell's late poem "Shifting Colors" longs for a Mallarméan detachment; Tate achieves it—at least in some of his poetry.

Introduction

Although their mutual commitment to poetry was the basis of their friendship, they shared other areas of common interest. For instance, both took a sometime ironic pride in family background, a personal issue closely linked to the question of regionalism. Lowell's *Life Studies* was not the first literary manifestation of this pride. In the early 1930s, Tate planned, and even outlined in some detail, a book on his own ancestry, intended to explicate the social and cultural forces that produced such disparate examples of southern character as his brother Ben and himself. He never wrote this potentially interesting book, but in planning it, he laid much of the conceptual foundation of his fine novel *The Fathers*. Tate may have envied Lowell's more famous name, and this envy may have influenced his response to *Life Studies*. Both poets were family-aware, but not always family-proud, and this implicit acknowledgement of the importance of ancestry was one more common bond.

Friendship is a complex issue. Lowell and Tate supported and encouraged each other, but each exacted a price. Lowell retained an adolescent's right to tease his elder, and when Tate reacted, Lowell dismissed the offense as a triviality. Tate, on the other hand, reserved the elder's privilege of lecturing his protégé, even though doing so sometimes seemed pompous. This mock child-parent relationship, entered into at their earliest acquaintance, strained against their growing equality in literary affairs. In his poetic maturity, Lowell was fully Tate's equal, but at times, their correspondence fails to reflect their similar status as Lowell reverts to a reverential tone and Tate willingly assumes the role of master.

Regardless of subsequent developments, when Lowell met Tate in Tennessee, they entered into a deep personal friendship that would survive each other's broken marriages, imagined and actual slights and insults, and a development of Lowell's poetry that would take him far afield from some of the aesthetic notions he learned from Tate. Considering how widely their poetics came to diverge (some of Lowell's later imitations of Tate poems come close to parody), Tate was remarkably responsive to Lowell's work (except *Life Studies*, the book that most grieved him), and he was frightened and disturbed by Lowell's repeated attacks of mania—

the first bad attack directly touched Tate's life. Their relationship—shaped in part by the very experiences that might seem to an outsider to have threatened it—survived that distancing madness, and to the end of Lowell's life, Tate would remain one of his soundest critics and most supportive friends.

The psychological complexities of relationships based on both personal attraction and professional commonality give literary friendships enduring interest. As poetry brought Tate and Lowell together, so it sustained them through major and minor trials. Tate's respect for good writing was so profound that he could have forgiven far more of Lowell than he was ever asked, and Lowell found the fellowship of writers to be the basis of nearly every important friendship—and even his three marriages. Dark undertones, small quarrels, and jealousies seem to spice as much as to mar relations among writers. What Tate and Lowell forgave of each other was not remarkable. Although they were in many ways extraordinary people, they were not Verlaine and Rimbaud, whose professional and private lives became so enmeshed that they nearly destroyed each other. Lowell and Tate's friendship was far from the ideal that Thoreau envisioned, but it was powerful and healthy enough to shape Lowell's writing life and influence Tate's (both emotionally and professionally) by assuring them that someone of empathetic intellectual and emotional makeup was there to offer thoughtful and impassioned response.

This study is neither a full-scale critical discussion of their poetry nor a critical biography; it is a more limited and focused attempt to trace the sometimes faint tracks of Tate's influence and inspiration in Lowell's work and to note some of the stresses and exasperations that mark their lengthy friendship. Such a study raises more questions than it can answer. Placing the life of and work of a poet in this kind of focus, as Harold Bloom has amply and brilliantly demonstrated, both illuminates and distorts. Lowell did not live entirely under Tate's eye, nor was Tate unusually obsessed with Lowell and his career. The influence of Tate's poetry on Lowell's is considerable and more or less familiar to their readers. Biographies are always incomplete, and critical studies are always tentative, but the varied methods of critics, historians, and biographers offer not merely a recasting of fact but a rethinking of the lives under scrutiny, and such reexperiencing can actually, in some way, change their subjects.

The relationship between the important generations of modernist American poets, from Stevens through Ashbery, awaits full exploration. It is a larger issue than the friendship between Tate and Lowell, but extracted from the particular lives of poets, such abstractions as modernism and influence—even poetry itself—hardly exist. Reader-response criticism has taught us to pay close attention to the act of reading and reminds us that the literary work exists only in the act of transmission. By studying how poets transmit the idea of the literary act to the following generation, we may learn something fresh about the elusive ontology of the text. By considering particular acts of transmission, we may better understand how poetry adapts to its cultural climate and go beyond Harold Bloom's invaluable psychological theories of influence into an understanding of how culture itself evolves.

The shape of the relationship between Tate and Lowell is that of the younger poet's attempts to master the older poet's revision of Eliot's characteristically modernist idiom and then to escape its shadow and return to the lyric a traditional, frankly personal voice. Eliot's most influential tenets before 1940 were those of poetic impersonality and adherence to the idea, if not the specific precepts, of the Hebraic-Graeco-Roman-English literary tradition. His best-known essay, "Tradition and the Individual Talent," is a key text behind the more prescriptive criticism of I. A. Richards and William Empson which led to the development of the New Criticism of Tate's generation. Eliot's arguments about poetic impersonality, however, did not adequately describe his own work. The poems of his first three or four volumes had an autobiographical significance that only now, in light of the publication of *The Waste Land* manuscript and Lyndall Gordon's two-volume biography, seems clear enough to call into question his emphasis in *The Sacred Wood* on the poem as object and the "extinction," rather than the fuller realization, of the poet's personality in his work.

8

Introduction

Tate became an early admirer of Eliot, vehemently defending *The Waste Land* against John Crowe Ransom's deprecating view of it. Lowell, too, felt drawn to Eliot and, in 1944, reviewed *Four Quartets* with enthusiasm and insight. Contrary to critical practice that, by the 1950s, would become nearly dogmatic, the review begins by noting the autobiographical and religious significance of the poem rather than any aspect of its aesthetic quality. Although he duly states that "every line is symbolic,"[2] it is clear that the importance of Eliot's poem for him is its relation to experience and its religious profundity. He defends its aesthetic qualities, but what makes the *Quartets* exceptional, he says, is that "it is one of the very few great poems in which craftsmanship and religious depth are equal."[3]

The story of Lowell's career is his attempt to move poetry as close as possible to experience. Lowell invokes Eliot as a source of freedom from technique rather than as a model for its preeminence, as some writers described him. "I feel Eliot's less tied to form than a lot of people he's influenced," Lowell argues, "and there's a freedom of the twenties in his work that I find very sympathetic."[4] Craftsmanship, though never neglected, seems less significant with each of Lowell's published collections until *Day by Day* prompts questions concerning both imaginative writing and the kind of writing that is too close to life, "the threadbare art of [the] eye."[5]

Eliot, in the 1940s, reconsidered the impersonality he had earlier advocated, and Tate, in his last great poems, also would acknowledge more frankly the personal basis of his art. In 1940, Eliot argued that one of the sources of the power of Yeats's poetry was its "greater expression of personality."[6] Eliot's understanding of his own concept of impersonality was more complex than many of his readers then took it to be. Even though he modified the concept to more fully accommodate the obviously personal basis of lyric poetry, he maintained that the poetic art transformed the personal into something more general and symbolic—that is, something impersonal and objective. Although the "particularity of . . . experience" finds an essential place in the poem,[7] that very

Introduction

particularity may, in the overdetermined context of the poem, conceal more than it reveals. The autobiographical or confessional poem, by moving closer to experience, neither attempts to reveal nor conceal factual or historical matter but to render more firmly an experiential matrix in which a symbolic language might flourish.

Lowell acknowledges this point in his own way when, in his interview with Frederick Seidel, he argues, "Almost the whole problem of writing poetry is to bring it back to what you really feel, and that takes an awful lot of maneuvering. You may feel the doorknob more strongly than some big personal event, and the doorknob will open into something that you can use as your own. A lot of poetry seems to me very good in the tradition but just doesn't move me very much because it doesn't have personal vibrance to it."[8] When Lowell made this comment in 1961, he had published, just two years previously, his major effort to reintroduce "personal vibrance" into American poetry. To Allen Tate, it was an attempt that seemed to go too far, even though he had been writing his own more personal poems and had encouraged Lowell to do the same.

The recurring attempt to bring poetry closer to experience—either the experience of the mind or of society—is an established part of the history and tradition of poetry. For Allen Tate, Hart Crane, and other poets of their generation, the manipulation of impersonal voices and the use of traditional literary and religious symbols, inherited in part from their reading of Eliot's early work, were essential elements in their aesthetic. Lowell began by accepting their methods and remained attracted to them because of their respect for craftsmanship and their faith in poetry as a culturally central form of knowledge. Following Tate's example rather than specific precepts, and guided by a later and more revisionary view of Eliot, he evolved an aesthetic distinct from that of Tate, Crane, and Ransom. Tate's negative reaction to *Life Studies* may be that of the master whose apprentice has unexpectedly declared independence, but Lowell never completely rejected Tate's literary values. Rather, he came to understand them in a more flexible manner than Tate himself did.

10

Introduction

Lowell abandoned the symbol as he had used it in *Lord Weary's Castle* and followed Yeats in evolving a more personal, though less hierarchical, poetry in which symbols crystallize in particular contexts, rather than entering the poem burdened with previously established values. Even in his late poetry, Tate retained an allegiance to the allusive literary or religious symbol, and in no way did this hamper him: the received symbol was for him a natural means of expression. For Lowell, although he would not realize it for some years, the received symbol was inadequate to his more experience-oriented aesthetic.

As this book follows Lowell's emergence from Tate's nourishing shadow and his evolution into the representative poet of the early postmodern period, the presence of the elder poet fades, but as Lowell never felt he had outgrown Tate, so it would be wrong to think that he supersedes his father-figure poet in any way. The viability of Tate's work today is as great as ever, and his reputation, if literary history is just, will survive mere changes in fashion. The evolution from Eliot to Tate to Lowell represents a reinterpretation of modernism that poets initiated long before the critics noticed. In recent years, some of our best critical minds have turned to broad rereadings of the modernist movement and its legacy. In a small and local way, it is hoped that this study will contribute something toward the larger task.

Tate and Lowell in the Thirties

By 1942, when the Tates and Lowells shared a house for the winter, Robert Lowell had already known Allen Tate for five years. They had met in 1937 when Lowell drove over from Nashville to Benfolly, Tate's house overlooking the Cumberland River. When Lowell crashed into Tate's "frail agrarian mailbox post" that April, he entered a world of commitment to art and culture that the more established but rigidly stratified society of Boston and Harvard could no longer offer.[1] Lowell had not yet shown signs of producing the poetry for which he later became famous; he was an untested beginner who had published only a few poems in school magazines. Tate, on the other hand, was an established poet at the peak of his creative powers and near the peak of his reputation. Perhaps of equal importance to Lowell at this time, Tate was a member of a recognized group of writers whose dedication and craftsmanship already had won them wide respect and an audience of at least modest dimensions.

The Great Depression had hardly touched the Lowells. Their

trust funds remained intact; none of their friends had to stand in soup lines. Lowell's early work shows little awareness of the social and economic pressures that were crushing those in less privileged situations. Tate also suffered less than many although he and Gordon were cash poor and found entertaining numerous guests a serious strain on their resources. Even though Tate's poetry of the 1930s avoids direct confrontation with social issues, his prose demonstrates concern for the future of the South and seriously considers some of its economic and social problems, but he only glancingly touches on the problem of the status of black Americans, a concern that his brother Fugitive Robert Penn Warren would eventually address. In the future, the issue of race would touch Lowell's poetry, most brilliantly in "For the Union Dead," but in the 1930s, neither he nor Tate shared the passionate concern for social justice exhibited by such writers as John Cornford, Christopher Caudwell, John Steinbeck, W. H. Auden, Langston Hughes, and Zora Neal Hurston. Unlike Hart Crane or even Vachel Lindsay, whose poetry suggests at least a passing acquaintance with the Harlem Renaissance, both Tate and Lowell adhered for some years to an ideal of art that prescribed aloofness (though not necessarily indifference) toward the immediate issues of the day.

Tate was one of the leading figures among the Fugitives, the now-famous group that gathered at Vanderbilt during World War I and continued to meet though the early 1920s. The Fugitives had begun by meeting informally at the house of Sidney Hirsch in 1915 and had later published an influential journal in which many of the best early poems of John Crowe Ransom, Donald Davidson, Merrill Moore, Laura Riding, and Tate had appeared. The Fugitives were bright and well educated, and they agreed that poetry, philosophy, and the other arts were more important than modern industrial society apparently realized. Tate has best described the ethos of the group:

> I would call the Fugitives an intensive and historical group as opposed to the eclectic and cosmopolitan groups that flourished in the

13

The Years of Our Friendship

East. There was a sort of unity of feeling, of which we were not then very much aware, which came out of—to give it a big name—a common historical myth; and its use for the dramatic and lyric arts, I believe, is that it expresses itself in the simple ritual of greeting a friend in the street. Although we disagreed, and at times quarreled, we had, in addition to the peculiar solidarity of artists everywhere, a deep understanding that gave even the quarrels a special intensity and form.[2]

Their quarrels were carried out on common and familiar ground; all of the Fugitives were southerners, but the significance of region and its relationship to an aesthetic program varied among them. Tate, who joined the group as an undergraduate in 1921, was the most aggressively modernist in his poetics, but he was already concerned with the history and modern status of his region. When he wrote his biographies of Stonewall Jackson and Jefferson Davis (1928 and 1929), he became haunted by a vision of an agrarian, preindustrial South—a vision he critically considered rather than passionately embraced. He was a bit skeptical of the possibility of keeping agriculture at the center of the South's economy and communal life, but he joined with Ransom, Robert Penn Warren, Andrew Lytle, and others—some former Fugitives, some not—in producing *I'll Take my Stand* (1932), a collection of more or less reactionary essays that stirred considerable controversy and even some formal public debate between agrarians and the southern progressives who wanted the region to industrialize.

More important than economic issues, however, were culture and its traditions. Several of the Fugitives were poets, and the discussion of poetry and its publication was the earliest of their endeavors. This crucial shared interest brought Tate into the Fugitive circle. The only undergraduate admitted to the group, he developed quickly as a poet, justifying the confidence and interest of the elder members by writing publishable poems such as the following, which first appeared in an early issue of *The Fugitive:*

NON OMNIS MORIAR

I ask you: Has the Singer sung
   The drear quintessence of the Song?

14

Tate and Lowell in the Thirties

John Ford knew more than I of death,
  John Ford to death has passed along.

I ask you: Has the Singer said
  Wherefore his greatness is not dust?
Marlowe went muttering to death
  When he had done with song and lust.

And so I speak no other word,
  Nor ask where to go the jaunty throng,
For laughter frames the lips of death—
  Death frames the Singer and the Song.

Tate thought of himself as classical, detached, and modernist-objective. Certainly this poem owes a great deal to Eliot, his most important early model; but it owes at least as much to Ernest Dowson, indicated not merely by the Latin title but by the cool and jaunty (to use a word from the poem) attitude toward death, an echo in tone and spirit of Dowson's "Vanitas":

The crown and victor's token:
  How are they worth to-day?
The one word left unspoken,
  It were late now to say:
But cast the palm away!

Contemporary literary historians have demonstrated that modernist reaction to the moralist-Arnoldian dilution of high romanticism retains and even revitalizes certain romantic attitudes and values. Tate's poetry owes nothing to Keats, the "pictorial Poet,"[3] as he called him, but owes much to the empathy that Hazlitt taught Keats to appreciate in Shakespeare. Like Baudelaire, Tate commonly empathizes with landscape rather than with character, going beyond personification into momentary identification of seasonal nature with the speaking self:

Ambitious November with the humors of the year,
With a particular zeal for every slab,
Staining the uncomfortable angels that rot
On the slabs, a wing chipped here, an arm there. . . .
                              ("Ode to the Confederate Dead")

15

The Years of Our Friendship

And now the winter sea:
Within her hollow rind
What sleek facility
Of sea-conceited scop
To plumb the nether mind!

("Seasons of the Soul")

"Last Days of Alice" demonstrates his faith in negative capability, if not necessarily his ability to carry it through to Shakespearean effect. Of course, little in Tate is specifically Keatsian. Tate, under the spell of Eliot, found the French symbolists, particularly Rimbaud and Baudelaire, the representative poets of modern society, along with Blake and Poe: "Blake's 'hapless soldier's sigh,' Poe's 'tell-tale heart,' Rimbaud's nature careening in a 'drunken boat,' Eliot's woman 'pulling her long black hair,' are qualities of the life of Baudelaire's *formillante cite*, the secularism of the swarm, of which we are the present citizens."[4]

Tate translated Baudelaire's "Correspondences" in 1922, and in 1924, he argued that "Baudelaire's Theory of Correspondences—that an idea out of one class of experience may be dressed up in the vocabulary of another—is at once the backbone of modernist poetic diction and the character which distinguishes it from both the English tradition and free verse."[5] In 1940, looking back on his early reading in Eliot and other modern poets, he commented, "I began to connect with the modern world what I had already learned from Baudelaire, first through Arthur Symons, then from Baudelaire himself."[6] Given the central place in modern poetics and personal development assigned to him, it is not surprising that many of Tate's poems suggest or echo Baudelaire in their use of imagery drawn from the quotidian but contain that intensity that Eliot associates with French symbolism, as in this passage from "The Meaning of Death":

Although at evening clouds infest the sky
Broken at base from which the lemon sun
Pours acid of winter on a useful view—
Four water-towers, two churches, and a river:
These are the sights I give in to at night

When the long covers loose the roving eye
To find the horror of the day a shape
Of life: we would have more than living sight.
Past delusions are seen as if it all
Were yesterday flooded with lemon light,
Vice and virtue, hard sacrifice and crime
In the cold vanity of time.

The "lemon sun" and "acid of winter" catch not only the intensity of vision but the suggestion of evil that Baudelaire so often discovers in ordinary landscape. This Baudelairean imagery is only one facet of the poem. The colorfully poisoned symbolist landscape only momentarily engages the speaker. Following this passage, the poem relaxes into a mimicry of Latin hyperbole and ends with a line echoing Eliot's "Hollow Men," appropriately invoking his even greater ability to amalgamate disparate aspects of literary tradition into a fresh entity. For Tate, as for Eliot, literary tradition is a stay against secularized, valueless anti-intellectual modern society, and for this reason, traditional literary or religious symbols for both poets have special value. By their presence, these symbols not only link the poem to a larger literary and cultural tradition but suggest the continuity of certain prized values. Tate's invocation of other poets is as deliberate as Eliot's. In his best poems, a seamless flexible voice finds allusion a natural form of expression.

Lowell does not follow Tate and Eliot's lead, does not often construct the poem of calculated allusion ("The Quaker Graveyard" is a major exception), but through Tate's influence, he does echo many of his mentor's alter voices. He also found Baudelaire's poetry central to the very idea of modernism, but when he echoes the French poet, he is more likely to do so through the quasi-translation he came to call imitation. Some critics have found Lowell's poetry decidedly Baudelairean in its sensibility and strategies, and a number of reviewers especially praised his 1961 collection *Imitations* for its lively and intense rewritings of Baudelaire's most famous poems. Tate admired this method, as we shall see later in his comments on Lowell's *Imitations* and in "Translation or Imitation?" in which Tate singles out Lowell's version of "Au Lecteur" for special consideration.

17

Although its sensibility is modernist, Tate's poetry sometimes is directly shaped by his experience with the major English romantics. The famous "Ode to the Confederate Dead," for example, owes something to Shelley's "Ode to the West Wind." This does not make Tate a latterday romantic, however. Even his earliest tastes are catholic: "Red Stains," the earliest poem in his *Collected Poems*, written when he was twenty, owes more to Baudelaire than to the English romantics. This ability to assimilate quickly the rhetoric, imagery, and voice of a variety of poets contributed to his rapid development toward poetic maturity and had a central influence on Lowell's own vision of his place in literature. The cacophony of voices in Lowell's *History*—voices of Du Bellay, Dante, Baudelaire, Ovid, and many other poets—indicates that poetry is not a solitary art for him but an ongoing tradition in which the dead retain their living voices.

The source of Tate's poetic maturity is, however, not only in his choice, conscious or otherwise, of aesthetic models, but in the powerful historical sense that shapes all of his best poems. Tate was profoundly aware of the role of region, nation, and era in the making of poets and poems. His essay "The Profession of Letters in the South" demonstrates the seriousness with which he contemplated the importance of place and time in the making of literature: "Where, as in the Old South, there were high forms, but no deep realization of the spirit was achieved, we must ask questions. (The right questions: not why the South refused to believe in Progress, or why it did not experiment with 'ideas.') Was the structure of society favorable to a great literature? Suppose it to have been favorable: Was there something wrong with the intellectual life for which the social order cannot be blamed?"[7]

He was equally aware of the value of history and locale in the poem itself. "The Mediterranean," written during the European trip of 1932 and the title poem of the volume that Tate presented to Lowell in 1937, opens with a broad awareness of place and time. Its sweep of imagery subsumes both the modern and the ancient world:

Where we went in the boat was a long bay
A slingshot wide, walled in by towering stone—

18

Peaked margin of antiquity's delay,
And we went there out of time's monotone:

Where we went in the black hull no light moved
But a gull white-winged along the feckless wave,
The breeze, unseen but fierce as a body loved,
That boat drove onward like a willing slave. . . .

As numerous critics have pointed out, the voice of Virgil haunts this poem; Homeric phrases ("Feckless wave," "black hull") lend a powerful sense of continuity. The most striking aspect of these opening lines is the brooding sense of timelessness, as though the speaker had sailed into the past, not merely into a bay. "The Mediterranean" has something of the tone of Pound's "The Seafarer," but it is more closely linked to personal experience:

Where we feasted and caroused on the sandless
Pebbles, affecting our day of piracy,
What prophecy of eaten plates could landless
Wanderers fulfil by the ancient sea?

More centrally, "The Mediterranean" pays homage to Baudelaire in its tone, imagery, and subject; it suggests a milder rewriting of "Voyage to Cythera," replacing the ominous hanged man with a less dramatic acknowledgment of the speaker's complicity and simultaneous betrayal of the past:

What country shall we conquer, what fair land
Unman our conquest and locate our blood?
We've cracked the hemispheres with careless hand!
Now, from the Gates of Hercules we flood

Westward, westward till the barbarous brine
Whelms us to the tired land where tasseling corn,
Fat beans, grapes sweeter than muscadine
Rot on the vine: in that land were we born.

The poem is Baudelairean in inspiration rather than in calculated allusion, but the echo of the French poet's aggressive verbs and images of decay ("We've cracked the hemispheres with careless hand," "Fat beans, grapes . . . / Rot on the vine") points to mutual social concerns and aesthetic empathy rather than to imitation.

19

Tate thought highly enough of "The Mediterranean" to place it first in his *Poems 1922–1947,* and it remains one of his most discussed poems, but no one has pointed out its strong structural, rhetorical, and thematic similarity to "Voyage to Cythera." Most critics dwell on the poem's classical allusions instead of its aesthetic sources. The poem may well have helped shape Lowell's approach to translation, which is a matter of free rewriting instead of conventional translation. Tate's poem is not really an "imitation" in the eighteenth-century sense; it is an original poem strongly shaped by his knowledge and love of Baudelaire, but it is similar enough to suggest that "Voyage to Cythera" was on his mind. He did claim, at least in one instance, to have rewritten a Baudelaire poem. In his late essay "Translation or Imitation?" he argued that "Death of Little Boys" evolved from a translation of Rimbaud's "Le chercheuses de poux." [8]

More than anything else, the conjunction of aesthetic and historical senses embodied in "The Mediterranean," the "Ode," and many of Tate's other poems was the central lesson that he offered the young Robert Lowell. Lowell learned much about the formal aspects of verse from Frost, Eliot, and Ransom, but the historical sense, as well as much of the structural understanding that went into "The Quaker Graveyard in Nantucket," "For the Union Dead," and "Waking Early Sunday Morning," derives from Tate.

From the start, Lowell's poetry manifested a lifelong struggle for faith and the aesthetic to express it. His interest in religion preceded his trip to the South, but it surely was reinforced by Tate's conversation and work. Tate was no evangelist, however. He had little of the mystic in him; his approach to issues of faith was rational and considered rather than ecstatic, but, like Eliot, he ascribed to religion a central role in any viable culture. The relationship between religion and culture occupied him in the 1930s more than the personal issue of faith as personal experience, but in the 1940s, his poetry would show him to be moving closer to his eventual embrace of Roman Catholicism.

When Lowell first met him, Tate's religious concerns were bound up with his interest in history and culture and with his role as a critic of regional culture and values. One source of his dissatisfaction with the contemporary South was its lack of faith. In "Religion and the Old South," he complains that the religious life of the old South failed to provide a healthy ongoing tradition because southerners "had a religious life, but it was not enough organized with a right mythology. In fact, their rational life was not powerfully united to the religious experience, as it was in medieval society. . . ."[9] This linking of religion and the intellect characterizes Tate's approach. If at times he sounds skeptical, he never doubts the efficacy of faith but is daunted by the difficulty of finding and using it. He reflects New England Protestantism in this more than Lowell ever did. From Tate, as well as from T. S. Eliot, Lowell learned the importance of religion as both a personal and a societal experience. Without this insight, the poems of *Land of Unlikeness* and *Lord Weary's Castle* could not have been written.

Tate, who taught high school Latin and English for a year after graduating from Vanderbilt, was thoroughly educated in the classics; Lowell would follow his example at Kenyon and learn from the same teacher. John Crowe Ransom was an important common element, and Tate and Lowell have described him in terms that, although differing, suggest that he was a father figure for both. As a student, Tate found Ransom cold and distant. That distance offended him, as though he had expected the warmth that his own father apparently could not offer: "I hope the reader will understand it when I say that I didn't like him while I was his student. That was more than fifty years ago. I thought him cold, calculating, and highly competitive. I can say this because I, too, was calculating and competitive, and I was arrogant enough as his student, and even later, until about 1930, to think I was a rival!"[10]

Rivalries in poetry often resemble father-son rivalries, as Harold Bloom has demonstrated and as Tate's statement shows. We naturally compete most fervently with those closest to us or those we think we resemble, but Tate's memoir, a product of maturity, is surprisingly objective toward both Ransom and himself. Even in its praise, it is cool and distant, as if their relationship had defined itself forever in that early perception of rivalry.

Lowell's early essay "John Ransom's Conversation" is also coolly objective, suggesting that both Lowell and Tate had learned from Ransom a dispassionate manner of looking at one's mentors, indirectly reconsidering important aspects of one's own life. Lowell, in discussing Ransom's teaching, hints at such dispassion:

> No other American English teacher has had as many talented students. In the last thirty years Allen Tate, Andrew Lytle, R. P. Warren, Cleanth Brooks, Randall Jarrell, and Peter Taylor have studied under him. Among them are several of the country's best teachers; several of its best writers. That many, or any, writers should come from the Thracian Athens of Vanderbilt University and the *declension* of Tennessee, was surprising; but, perhaps, their being with Ransom was an irrelevant accident. And yet, I think the teacher may have made the difference—a hard one to put one's finger on. It was not the classes, but the conversations that mattered. We used to endlessly memorize and repeat and mimic Ransom sentences. We learned something from that. Somehow one left him with something inside us moving toward articulation, logic, directness and complexity—one's intuitions were more adroit and tougher after one had contemplated the stamina and wit that his writings had required of him. So much for imitation. Imitation of Ransom was not like that of another great teacher, Yvor Winters. Fortunately, it was not possible to become a replica. One took what one could, and went on, God willing, as one's self.[11]

Years later Lowell would write a much warmer prose eulogy for Ransom; the difference between it and the earlier essay is part of the story of Lowell's development. The fact that Tate's memoir is contemporaneous with the later Lowell essay may suggest how Lowell developed away from the high modernist objective stance, with which he was never wholly comfortable, while Tate retained it. This essential difference would shape their friendship to a great extent, and as time went on, it would be responsible for many of the stresses and strains between them.

The Tate-Lowell relationship has sometimes been described as father and son (even Caroline Gordon sometimes saw it that way), but in a sense, they were almost schoolmates, with Tate the more advanced older student. When Lowell met him, Tate was not only a far more experienced writer but had traveled widely and enjoyed a wide exposure to the literary world; he had lived with Hart Crane in New York City and Tory Valley, had been to Paris, and had sat at the feet of Gertrude Stein.

22

Tate and Lowell in the Thirties

After graduating from Vanderbilt in 1924, Tate had taught for a year before going to live in New York where he tried to break into the literary world with mixed, but eventually undeniable, success. In 1925, he married Caroline Gordon, who was already pregnant with their only child, Nancy. In New York, the Tates met Malcolm Cowley, Dorothy Day, John Hall Wheelock, Kenneth Burke, and other literary and intellectual figures, many of whom would become their lifelong friends. The Tates lived for a time in the country with Hart Crane but inevitably (though not irreparably) quarreled with him. When they returned to New York in the fall of 1926, Gordon became Ford Madox Ford's secretary, and this turned out to be providential. Not only would Ford prove to be a loyal friend who introduced the Tates to many literary people on both sides of the Atlantic, but he also helped Gordon publish her first novel.

Tate's own literary career, as social and literary critic and as poet, developed rapidly in the late 1920s. In order to publish his own poetry in book form, Tate agreed to first write a biography of Stonewall Jackson. The research for this and the subsequent Jefferson Davis biography immersed him in southern history and directed his thinking toward the Jeffersonian agrarianism that he would envision for the contemporary South. In the fall of 1927, *Fugitives: An Anthology* appeared, a book that Tate had managed to persuade Harcourt, Brace to publish. The notice in the *Nashville Banner* of 2 February 1928, quoting jacket blurbs, summarized the reception the poets presumably expected:

> "Fugitives," the publishers state in the jacket description, "is a collection which represents the very best of a small but important group which, to quote the tribute of Mr. Untermeyer's 'Modern American Poetry,' 'did much to disprove Mencken's contention that the South was a vast Sahara of the beaux arts.'" W. S. Braithwaite says that the work of these poets has "more spirit and verve than can be found in any other group-expression in the country." John Gould Fletcher, in a recent article in the *Saturday Review*, reviewed the career of the Imagist group and pointed to *The Fugitive* group as representing the main impulse in America in the development of a "school of intellectual poetry" which has replaced the experiments in free verse of the elder school.

The anthology was widely reviewed and helped promote the reputations of the poets most heavily represented. Tate was not at first singled out as a poet of particular importance although his "Ode to the Confederate Dead," still his best-known poem, was included.

The year 1928 saw the publication of Tate's biography of Stonewall Jackson, his first trip to Europe, financed by a Guggenheim Fellowship, and the appearance of his first major collection of poems. In England, the Tates met T. S. Eliot and Herbert Read, and they visited Robert Penn Warren who was studying at Oxford. In Paris, living in Ford's apartment, Tate resumed work on his Jefferson Davis biography and met F. Scott Fitzgerald, John Peale Bishop, and Ernest Hemingway. *Mr. Pope and Other Poems* appeared that fall. The title poem, one of his most anthologized, exemplifies the qualities most critics have found in his mature work:

When Alexander Pope strolled in the city
Strict was the glint of pearl and gold sedans.
Ladies leaned out more out of fear than pity
For Pope's tight back was rather a goat's than man's.

Often one thinks the urn should have more bones
Than skeletons provide for speedy dust,
The urn gets hollow, cobwebs brittle as stones
Weave to the funeral shell a frivolous rust.

And he who dribbled couplets like a snake
Coiled to a lithe precision in the sun
Is missing. The jar is empty; you may break
It only to find that Mr. Pope is gone.

What requisitions of a verity
Prompted the wit and rage between his teeth
One cannot say. Around a crooked tree
A moral climbs whose name should be a wreath.

"Mr. Pope" exposes about as little of the poet's presence as is possible in a lyric poem. Yet it is hardly unique in that regard; in tone it suggests some of Robinson's poems of the first decade of the century as well as Eliot's quatrain poems of the 1920 volume. Its distance from its subject does not conceal but depersonalizes its

deep irony. The substitution of "I" for "one" in lines five and fifteen would expose the clenched voice of the poet's own "wit and
rage," but Tate, following Eliot's example as he understood it,
bases his aesthetic on distancing himself from certain of the feelings in his poems in order to expose the fundamental emotional
and intellectual issues underlying momentary or passing sensa-
tions. Tate refuses to depict the emotional state engendered in
Pope by the fearful response of genteel ladies confronted by his
deformed figure. Instead, he invokes a more general and conventional metaphor of mortality—the urn—to place Pope in the great
tradition and remind us that his deformity was merely accidental,
not essential. Pope's person does not reenter this poem, nor does
his motivation survive bodily dissolution. Only his voice, the "wit
and rage between his teeth," survives the breaking of the vessel.
No trace of his incidental feelings lingers. Lowell would, at times,
attempt to imitate this cool stance in his *Land of Unlikeness* poems,
but overwrought with both the speaker's emotions and his societally directed outrage, they fail to attain a distance that, in some
instances, would have improved them by making a less painfully
wrenched diction possible.

In a poetic era dominated by the first-person lyric voice, we
might too quickly dismiss the utility of less immediate voices.
Even by the 1950s, before the full onslaught of frankly autobiographical verse, some critics found Tate too repressed and too monotonous. One critic, writing in 1960, described Tate's poetry as
"Notably intellectual, compressed to the point of ellipsis and even
of obscurity, referential, bold in imagery, and often desperate in
tone." [12] This accurately describes some of Tate's poems, but it
overlooks his tonal range. Without looking ahead to Tate's openly
autobiographical poetry of the 1950s, we see that the 1920s and
1930s poems have a range of feeling and tone akin to Eliot's, but
without his incomparable virtuosity. The ironic bitterness of "Mr.
Pope," the different, though perhaps equally ironic, grief of "Ode
to the Confederate Dead," the satiric religiosity of "The Subway,"
and the philosophical and religious meditation of "Causerie" (a
poem of enormous importance to Lowell's work of the 1940s) represent a tonal range greater than that generally credited to Tate.

25

Some of his poems "leave us longing for the warm pulse of human blood and the feel of flesh,"[13] but the same has been said of Eliot's *Four Quartets*. Poetry is not always intended to be sensuous, much less sensual, yet the texture of the great "Ode to the Confederate Dead," like that of *Lycidas* and "Ode to the West Wind," its forebears, is sensuous in the way that only language at its most powerful can be:

> What shall we say of the bones, unclean,
> Whose verdurous anonymity will grow?
> The ragged arms, the ragged heads and eyes
> Lost in these acres of the insane green?
> The gray lean spiders come, they come and go;
> In a tangle of willows without light
> The singular screech-owl's tight
> Invisible lyric seeds the mind
> With the furious murmur of their chivalry.

The varied end rhyme scheme, repetitions, and internal rhymes lend momentum and inevitability, and the oxymorons ("verdurous anonymity," "furious murmur") give these lines the force of the irrational and undeniable rightness of language. Tate, at his best, displays a technical ability that is not merely virtuosity but the genuine poet's instinct for language that is true because of its sound not its content. The voice of this poem is uniquely Tate's, and in that most important sense, it is personal. As Lowell said of Tate, "His poems, even the slightest of them, are terribly personal. Out of splutter and shambling comes a killing eloquence."[14] Tate's poems are personal not because they are about himself but because no one else could have written them; in reaction against what he came to call "mass language," he has, to some degree, freed his language from merely conventional reference.[15] For this same kind of individuality, Tate admired Hart Crane. If Crane was the more eloquent poet, it was because he was even more fearless in freeing his language from easy literalness. In this way, Bradbury's worry about Tate's "ellipsis" and "obscurity" should be taken as praise since, for a poet with Tate's fine ear, the temptation, one to which he should occasionally surrender, is to write a poem of purely sonic effect and let referentiality take care of itself.

Lowell, acknowledging a link between Crane and Tate, argued that Tate was a better model for him:

> There's a relationship between Crane and Tate and for some reason Tate was much easier for me. I could see how Tate was done, though Tate has a rhythm that I've never been able to imitate. He's much more irregular than I am, and I don't know where the rhythm comes from, but I admire it very much. Crane said somewhere that he could write five or six good lines but Tate could write twelve that would hang together, and you'd see how the twelve were built. Tate was somehow more of a model: he had a lot of wildness and he had a lot of construction. And of course I knew him and I never knew Crane.[16]

Tate's rhythms are, as Lowell says, slightly mysterious, but better poets all have highly individual senses of rhythm, and Tate is no exception. Probably what Lowell learned from him in this regard was to vary his rhythms from the strict pentameter and, like John Donne, ignore the metrical regularity that exists only in textbooks.

So, by the time Tate returned from his first European stay at the end of 1929, he was a fully developed poet and was about to enter his most fruitful decade as a critic. After a brief stay in New York, during which he negotiated the contract for what would become *I'll Take my Stand* (which appeared that October), he bought a house overlooking the Cumberland River, three miles from Clarksville, Tennessee. Because Allen's brother Ben had put up a $10,000 loan to buy the house, the Tates named it Benfolly. For the next few years, Benfolly would be the center of Agrarian activity, with Ransom, Lytle, and others as regular visitors.

In 1932, Caroline received a Guggenheim, and the Tates returned to Europe. Again, much of their time was spent with Ford Madox Ford, living in his apartment in Paris or in his villa in Toulon. During that idyllic summer, Tate wrote his first short story and "The Mediterranean," and by now, he had begun to write his important criticism. When Lowell arrived at Benfolly in 1937, Tate was well established as an important essayist. In the critical writing of the 1930s, we can find dicta that, although Lowell would later react against them, were important in shaping the younger poet's attitudes in his early maturity.

Tate's 1938 essay, "Tension in Poetry," is not exactly an ars poetica, but it represents his expectations for poetry at the time Lowell first met him. Tate attacks the idea—or rather the presumption—that poetry is "communication." He argues that this presumption leads to the use of what he calls "mass language" in poetry,[17] a language of easy reference, easy leaps from object to object, and finally to sentimentality, the unforgivable sin. Instead of relying on this fallacious use of language, effective poetry, Tate argues, makes its meaning through tension, which he defines as the relationship between a poem's development of its imagery and induction of feeling, or between its language taken metaphorically and that same language taken denotatively. The best poem is effective in both a literal and a metaphorical reading. This kind of tension is analogous to the musical tension that characterizes the strongest English-language poetry, the tension between the artificial rhythm of syllable-stress meter and the more natural rhythm of the speaking voice.

Though the New Criticism in 1938 was too new to have a name (Ransom would inadvertently give it one in 1941), Tate's essay practically defines it. As a critic, he values unity and "tension," respects honest obscurity (which he argues arises from resistance to "mass language," an argument that would later become commonplace), and abhors sentimentality and the inaccurate use of metaphor. His poetry demonstrates these values and adds a preference for irony, perhaps as a way of assuring that no note of sentiment—even an honest one, if such is possible—intrude into a tonally consistent poem like the "Ode."

Even in his later years, Lowell shared many of Tate's aesthetic and poetic values, but in the 1930s, he was still unformed, sure only of his commitment to an art he only imperfectly understood. Tate's ease of critical expression must have awed the younger poet. "Tension in Poetry" remains impressive because of Tate's ability to describe what would otherwise seem indescribable, a mysterious something he so surely names as a clear source of the power of the best poetry, a power that Lowell, in 1937, sensed but could not yet command.

28

Tate and Lowell in the Thirties

Although Tate, according to T. S. Eliot, was one of the best poets working in America by the 1930s, Lowell came to him largely by chance. Merrill Moore, a Boston psychiatrist and author of thousands of witty but undisciplined sonnets, had advised Lowell's parents to get their son out of Boston, let him indulge himself among poets and students of poets, escape the tedium and conformity of Harvard and—most tempting for Lowell's father—get him away from his cousin Anne Dick, whom Lowell was determined to marry. She had been the subject of a near fatal quarrel between father and son. Lowell senior had informed Anne's parents that she had been seeing Lowell in his room at Harvard. Anne's parents were unperturbed by the report; they trusted their daughter and were undisturbed by her relationship with young Lowell. When Anne passed along to Lowell the note his father had written to hers, a serious quarrel followed, in which Lowell knocked his father down. Lowell brooded over the incident for the rest of his life and recounted it in several versions, the first being in "Rebellion" in his second book:

> There was rebellion, father, when the mock
> French windows slammed and you hove backward, rammed
> Into your heirlooms, screens, a glass-cased clock,
> The highboy quaking to its toes. You damned
> My arm that cast your house upon your head
> And broke the chimney flintlock on your skull.

The poem continues as a paean to Lowell's guilt, which he portrays as archetypal, Cain-like, of biblical proportions. He did not exaggerate; the incident haunted him until his death. In various poems, published and unpublished, he reconsiders the dramatic incident and reshapes his own guilt, trying to come to grips in aesthetic terms with a grief that no one of his sensitivity could expunge. In his last book, published only a month before he died, he returns once more to the troubling subject of his father, regretting, as so many of us do, the role-playing that distances adolescent children from their parents:

> I futilely wished
> to meet you at my age;
> the date never came off.

29

The Years of Our Friendship

It would take two lifetimes
to pick the crust
and uncover the face
under our two menacing,
iconoclastic masks.

After the violent confrontation, Lowell's father was enraged, and his mother was convinced that her son had lost his mind. Her first impulse was to persuade Merrill Moore to have Lowell confined to an institution, but Moore handled the situation with tact and consideration for both parents and the supposedly crazed son. He asked Lowell to apologize to his father, which he did, but the incident had poisoned the atmosphere of the Lowell home, and something more than an uneasy truce was required. Moore, who was aware of Lowell's literary ambitions and privy to his early poems, arranged for him to meet Ford Madox Ford, who was staying at Harvard. Moore arranged a party at the Lowell home, and Lowell's friends, Frank Parker and Blair Clark, assembled an appropriate gathering of local literary people, but the party failed miserably, as such carefully orchestrated events usually do. It did, however, serve its purpose: Ford decided that Lowell was "the most intelligent person he'd met in Boston," and he agreed to support Lowell's literary apprenticeship with academically respectable poets who were safely distant from Boston.[18] Moore, who had been one of the Fugitives, planned to bring Lowell south in the spring of 1937, introduce him to John Crowe Ransom, and, if all went well, enroll him in the fall at Vanderbilt, where he could study with Ransom, letting distance and time heal the difficulties between parent and son.

When Lowell traveled south to meet the Fugitives, he was already a thoroughly committed poet who had read a fair amount and written several notebooks full of verse, but he had yet to find his voice. His early unpublished notebooks reveal his groping through the thick layers of platitude so common to the poetry of beginners. At St. Mark's in 1935, he had published his first poems in *Vindex*, the school magazine. His early work showed little promise, yet his notebooks record a poignant and dedicated effort to make himself into a poet. By examining the early attempts, we can understand how much and in what ways he improved after he had met Tate and had studied with Ransom. In tracing his development from the 1930s through the notebooks of the early 1940s, especially the material he wrote during the winter of 1942–43 at Monteagle with the Tates, we can understand how hard he had to work to develop his deeply latent talent and how much Allen Tate meant to him as example, model, catalyst, and friend.

In the summer of 1935, fresh from St. Mark's and about to enter Harvard, Lowell was writing such poems as "At Dawn When God Arose," a delicate attempt to combine world-weariness and religious ecstasy that is reminiscent of some of Lionel Johnson's verse:

AT DAWN WHEN GOD AROSE

I trembled all the while,
And day was at her close
Before I saw his smile:
Ah woe, my youth was gone
Before I saw the guile!
The vigils at the grave,
The shaking from its brim,
Life is a dreary song.—
Yes, I looked on him:
The words that I would save!
          August 1935 [19]

This is far from the portrayal of religious ecstasy he would achieve in "At the Indian Killer's Grave," with its strong closing image of Mary's "soul a bridal chamber fresh with flowers / And her whole body an ecstatic womb, / As through the trellis peers the sudden Bridegroom." The fin de siècle tone of "At Dawn When God Arose," the emphatic rhymes, and the unconscious adolescent homoeroticism (hardly unusual in being directed at God) suggest other poems written by earnest but less talented young men. Lowell differs in showing more interest in technical matters than in subject, tone, or word choice. Rhythm and rhyme constitute the purpose of the poem, so the lack of a clear relationship between the rhyme scheme and the development of the poem's argument is not as important to the poet as the problem of

31

getting the rhymes to work. He would write dozens of poems like this. If improvement is not always consistent or even obvious, ten years later, when he was revising the best of the *Land of Unlikeness* poems and writing the new poems of *Lord Weary's Castle,* these exercises in rhyme and rhythm served him well.

For the adolescent poet, suitable subject matter is as elusive as syntactical precision, fluency, and technical virtuosity. Lowell's early poems—right through *The Mills of the Kavanaughs,* in fact—seem obsessed with their own virtuosity, largely because he would not, until the 1950s, admit to himself that he, like so many poets, was his own real subject. That does not mean that all of his poems were autobiographical, but even in the early notebooks, poems that touch on Lowell's actual experience, however reimagined, tend to be noticeably stronger than the more abstract poems that dwell on issues of great and abiding interest.

Like T. S. Eliot (and perhaps this similarity is one of the sources of his attraction for Lowell), the youthful Lowell was fascinated with religion as ritual and as the source of powerful mysteries. He has left both a prose and a verse account of one of his earliest attempts to fathom the theological approach to the human condition. The prose account is more detailed, if less dramatic. The Lowells' Irish Catholic nurse had lost her rosary, and when it was found, the silver figure of the crucified Jesus was missing and the chain had been chewed: "Later mother saw me pushing a whole handful of paper strips down the register. 'You are setting the furnace on fire,' she said. I smiled and smiled, to her intense displeasure. 'Yes, I know,' I said, 'That's where Jesus is.'" [20]

This unconventional approach to religion would characterize Lowell for the rest of his life. The adolescent poems are typical, however, of those that any young person in search of an elusive faith might write. His interest in religious poetry may have peaked in the mid-1940s while he was a practising Catholic and writing essays on Eliot and Hopkins, but he never lost his concern with faith.

To make poetry demands more than a fascination with the infinite; in fact, one might argue that the best poetry (Tate's, for instance) displays a healthy skepticism toward anything unavailable

directly to the senses. Lowell, in the mid-1930s, had trouble keeping his eyes on the world around him. Instead, he wrote about
elegant but remote things such as "Venice" (though this poem
may have been suggested because Lowell had just graduated from
St. Mark's School):

> The mighty lion of St. Mark
> Smiles blandly at the passersby
> That pass her in the day
> But in the night the Venetian kitten
> Spreads her wings, sails the seas
> And catches fishes in the dark.
>
> 4 / 35[21]

Or he modeled his poems after the work of the very great, like
this unlikely echo of Milton's "On the University Carrier" and
Housman's "To an Athlete Dying Young":

> AN ELEGY
>
> Let drop an athletic wreath
> On our head-monitor,
> Prefect of a corridor,
> Torpedoed to death
> In a tight, stampeding car;
> For once he outbloomed all
> And lit his boarding school,
> Competing at football.
> The three assaults they tried:
> Neither winter contagion
> Nor a hard cold region
> Killed him; quickly, he died
> Wrecked by a roadside,
> And we who walked when he
> Ran by, now drop his wreath
> As token on the broken chassis;
> —A mourning flower in brief.[22]

Elegy would play an important role in Lowell's poetic and become the dominant note in his last work, but this little poem fails
to catch the elegiac voice, fails even to mock it. His mature elegies

33

avoid attempting to mix the ironic and elegiac voices, and he substitutes a gentler humor that avoids mockery, as in his poem on
"Alfred Corning Clark," in which the portrayal is straightforward
and uncompromising, but gentle:

> You were alive. You are dead.
> You wore bow-ties and dark
> blue coats, and sucked
> wintergreen or cinnamon lifesavers
> to sweeten your breath.

The fact that "lifesavers" could not save Clark is too sly a wit-
ticism to give offense, but the awkward humor of "torpedoed to
death / In a tight, stampeding car" would surely disturb the head-
monitor's survivors by both its clumsiness and the mixing of inappropriate metaphors.

Lowell spent the summers of 1935 and 1936 on Nantucket writing in the company of Blair Clark and Frank Parker, both of
whom he mercilessly tyrannized. In the notebooks covering these
periods, we find the beginning of his fascination with the sea that
would later result in "The Quaker Graveyard in Nantucket." A
little of the imagery for that great elegy occurs in this poem from
one of those idyllic summers:

LANDSCAPE: THE NORTH COAST CLIFFS

> The six foot brawned and browned,
> A coast-guard stood grey domed and somber fogged,
> Swirled by gulls and carrion upon a cragged brink
> Waters curled about the cliffs
> Of Madaket and thru the caves.
> Stooping he drew a gallon bucket,
> A dulled bucket on a rotten cord,
> A hempen cord;
> The bucket contained, with bottom banged,
> A quart o' conquered brine
> Clinging to jutted rock the bucket swung
> Dented and dinted.
> Three rods down below the bucket
> Angelica, a puppet in a blue apron,

Swung her lunch in a reed basket
And clambered jagged malachite,
Spotted green-coloured rock.
Hubby an angler, climbed a knob,
And having casted, jaggled on crested surges,
A bright brittle plug with gilded hooks
Water curled about the cliffs
Of Madaket and thru the caves.[23]

The "conquered brine" and "crested surges" suggest the "heavy surf," "bilge and backwash," waves that "wallow in their wash," and "blue-lung'd combers" of the great elegy Lowell would write in the mid-1940s. Even though "Landscape" displays a difficulty with free verse and an uncertain and sometimes awkward word choice, such as "somber fogged" and the attempt to make "brawn" into a verb, it struggles toward the more powerful diction of the *Land of Unlikeness* poems, in which incongruities are forcibly yoked into conjuncture with great dramatic effect. Notably, this poem is devoid of abstractions and vagaries. It represents a marked advance over the poems of a year or two earlier.

Later, in "For Frank Parker 2" in *History*, Lowell parodies his early work with gentle humor, but in the 1930s, he was deadly serious about poetry and determined to succeed at it. In fact, he wanted all of his friends to dedicate themselves to the arts and to succeed. He acknowledges this sense of vocation in "To Frank Parker":

We looked in the face of the other
for what we were.
Once in the common record heat
of June in Massachusetts,
we sat by the school pool
talking out the soul-lit night
and listened to the annual
unsuffering voice of the tree frogs,
green, aimless and wakened:
"I want to write." "I want to paint."

Was it I wanted you to paint? . . .

(*Lowell's ellipsis*)

35

As he was forming this early dedication to the arts, Lowell entered Harvard, where, from the fall of 1935 through the winter of 1937, he read Eliot, Pound, and Williams, and his poems became more specific and more dramatic. A comparison of "At Dawn God Arose" with "Landscape" suggests how much he learned in a year, but he would describe the poems that he wrote in his first months as an undergraduate, under the spell of Drinkwater, Longfellow, and Swinburne, as "grand, ungrammatical, and [having] a timeless, hackneyed quality."[24] The notebooks illustrate his difficulty in finding a sure voice, an adequate vocabulary, and a strong point of view. None of the poems written during the 1936–37 school year, following his second summer in Nantucket, demonstrates any clear advance over "Landscape." The emotional drama of that Christmas season, when Lowell quarrreled with his father over Anne Dick, and Lowell's dissatisfaction with Harvard seemed to temporarily stifle his development, particularly in the early months of 1937, but during that summer, he would make substantial advances toward the poetry he was destined to write.

Harvard did help prepare Lowell, however. He undoubtedly would have read Eliot and Pound wherever he had gone to college, but Harvard exposed him to influences that he otherwise might not have felt until much later. The first was Robert Frost. Lowell described their encounter in an interview:

> He was actually the first important poet I met. He was lecturing at Harvard and I was, I think, a freshman. I was writing a tremendous poem in blank verse on the First Crusade, and I thought he'd like to see that. So I went round to see him and he was very nice. He read about half a line, then he got out the Oxford Book of English Verse and he showed me a poem by Collins, "How Sleep the brave by all their country's wishes blest." He said something like: "This is not very deep, but it's concise." Then he read me the opening of Keats's "Hyperion," which wasn't in the Oxford Book, I think, couldn't have been, and which I thought was all marvellous—a real tonic thing. He hit the line, "No stir of air was there . . ." and he said, "Now it comes to life," and he was right. "The naiad pressed the cold reed to her lips"—something like that. It was the best reading I had ever heard: about 12 lines he'd read, and he showed me two lines which made all the other lines come to life. I'd never encountered anyone like that.[25]

Tate and Lowell in the Thirties

Lowell's poems of 1935 and 1936, however, show no discernible influence of Frost, but they do display many of the ill-digested mannerisms of Keats's later imitators. Perhaps of more immediate importance, he met James Laughlin, already an ardent follower of William Carlos Williams. Lowell described Laughlin's importance in bringing Williams to his attention:

> Our only strong and avant-garde man was James Laughlin. He was much taller and older than we were. He knew Henry Miller, and exotic young American poetesses in Paris, spent summers at Rapallo with Ezra Pound, and was getting out the first number of his experimental annual, *New Directions*. He knew the great, and he himself wrote deliberately flat descriptive and anecdotal poems. We were sarcastic about them, but they made us feel secretly that we didn't know what was up in poetry. They used no punctuation or capitals, and their only rule was that each line should be eleven or fifteen typewriter spaces long. The author explained that this metric was "as rational as any other" and was based on the practice of W. C. Williams, a poet and pediatrician in Rutherford, New Jersey. About this time, Laughlin published a review somewhere, perhaps even in *The Harvard Advocate*, of Williams's last small volume. In it, he pushed the metric of typewriter spaces, and quoted from a poem, "The Catholic Bells," to show us Williams's "mature style at fifty"! This was a memorable phrase, and one that made maturity seem possible, but a long way off. I more or less memorized "The Catholic Bells," and spent months trying to console myself by detecting immaturities in whatever Williams had written before he was fifty.[26]

In the same essay, Lowell explains that he had been reading "introductory books on the enjoyment of poetry, and was knocked over by the examples in the free-verse section."[27] His early pseudo-Miltonic efforts ended when he read Williams. With an amazing metaphor, he describes the encounter between the bombastic young poet and the presiding genius of the pared-down American idiom: "It was as though some homemade ship, part Spanish galleon, part paddle-wheels, kitchen pots, and elastic bands and worked by hand, had anchored to a filling station."[28]

Williams was twice to have a vital impact on Lowell's development. In the first instance, Williams's poetry shocked the boy-poet out of his false grandeur and love of abstraction; the second time was in the 1950s when Williams encouraged Lowell to reshape his metrics and idiom into the free-verse poems of *Life Studies*. Lowell was by no means initially converted into a free-verse poet. The most important effect of Williams was to particularize Lowell's verse. It would be many years before he seriously considered even temporarily abandoning iambics. Even in the *Life Studies* poems, the ghost of a discernible meter lingers. Not until he was writing some of the poems included in *For the Union Dead* would Lowell completely divorce himself from that controlling voice.

The experiments with free verse in the poems of 1936–37 surely helped Lowell, at least momentarily, to escape the simple intoxication of iambics and to focus more on the language and subject matter of his poems. Further, these poems established Lowell's commitment to an aesthetic that would include specificity of place and setting. Focused and particularized poems such as "North Coast Cliffs" are better than the earlier vaguely religious poems because they are simply more interesting. It remained for Lowell to bring his fascination with traditional metrics and rhyme to bear on subject matter of personal import. Reading the poetry of Tate and Ransom, as well as working with Tate and discussing contemporary poetry with him—especially that of Crane and Eliot—would help Lowell consolidate his growing skills.

Benfolly, Monteagle, and Beyond

Lowell's early interest in Williams, to whom he would turn again in the 1950s, suggests a direction for his development other than toward the tradition-oriented modernism represented by Tate. The late 1930s and early 1940s were a time of experiment, social awareness, and cross-fertilization in American art. Most powerfully, the documentary photographers of the Farm Security Administration, including Walker Evans, Dorothea Lange, Arthur Rothstein, and Russell Lee, offered a new standard of social realism with which literature would have to compete or incorporate. The early attempts to link literature and photography simply combined both media in one book, as in Erskine Caldwell and Margaret Bourke-White's *You Have Seen Their Faces,* Archibald MacLeish's *Land of the Free,* and Walker Evans and Carleton Beals's *The Crime of Cuba.* The finest effort was James Agee and Walker Evans's *Let Us Now Praise Famous Men* (1940), a masterpiece that redefined the boundaries of literature and forged a new relationship between visual and verbal art. These efforts reinforced the preference of modern literature for visual imagery and suggested how far a

39

documentary aesthetic might go in forging new relationships between art and its subject matter.

The documentary aesthetic of the late depression, though prophesied in poetry by the work of Whitman, had no immediate effect on Tate and Lowell, but they could hardly have been unaware of *Life* magazine and its staff of brilliant photographers; of the new social-realism painters like Ben Shahn, James Michael Newhall, and Philip Evergood; and of the native school of music and dance led by Aaron Copland and Martha Graham. This artistic ferment produced relatively few works of lasting value, but the energy it gave off was great, and some of the work—most notably the photography—has retained its power through the intervening years. Lowell, as a young unformed poet, could not have remained untouched by this activity, but his aesthetic had not yet opened itself to experience other than what was sanctioned by his predecessors. Through the 1940s, he would adhere to a symbolist and modernist poetic. Later, though, when he began the *Life Studies* poems, a documentary aesthetic began to assert itself. By the time he wrote the sonnets of *Notebook*, he had finally found a voice that could incorporate any kind of immediate experience in a mode that has been called journalistic or diaristic but may owe something to the documentary art of his early maturity. When he refers to his late aesthetic as "a snapshot, / lurid, rapid, garish, grouped, / heightened from life, / yet paralyzed by fact," he defines its limitations, yet throughout his career, he struggled to make room for the verbal equivalents of visual facts such as those that engaged painters like Edward Hopper and photographers like Berenice Abbott and Russell Lee.

In 1937, though, Lowell needed a more personal kind of help. When he received that help from Tate, he adopted much of the elder poet's working poetic and some of his views of literature and society. These views were generally congenial to Lowell, but if, instead of placing himself in the hands of Tate at such a vulnerable time, he had continued groping about on his own, he might have discovered more quickly—perhaps through further consideration of Williams—his desire for a poetry of greater immediacy and documentary content. On the other hand, without Tate's support,

40

he might well have given up or never found any sort of viable poetic voice. He surely would not have written the powerfully formal symbolist poems of *Lord Weary's Castle* without the example and encouragement of Tate, who was for him a direct link with Eliot and Crane.

That spring, when Lowell—in his own words—"crashed the civilization of the South," Tate had recently begun his first and only novel, *The Fathers*, and Gordon was finishing *The Garden of Adonis*. It was characteristic that, despite their commitment to their writing, despite their poverty and the impending visit from Ford Madox Ford, Janice Biala, and her sister, the Tates took in Lowell, who later described himself as "like a torn cat" at this time in his life.[1] Perhaps the oddity of his arrival intrigued them. Gordon described his appearance (in a letter to Sally Wood) as "the strangest visitation we ever had" and goes on to describe standing in the driveway admiring two blossoming lemon lilies when a car stopped at the gate and a young man got out, paused by the mailbox, and "answered a call from nature."[2] She claimed that she and Allen had wanted to call out "Defense d'uriner" but had restrained themselves. The Tates, despite their immediate interest in Lowell, were dismayed at his unannounced appearance. It was surprising that they did not send him home although it is difficult to find an instance in which they turned away even the most unpromising visitor. Gordon, in the same letter, wondered about Lowell's pilgrimage:

> He is a young man named Lowell from Massachusetts who heard Ford lecture in Boston and as he wasn't getting on well at Harvard decided to come South to learn how to write. We kept him overnight and sent him on to Nashville to learn further about writing. I think Ford really rescued him from a bad situation. His family decided he was crazy because he wants to be a poet and had him in a psychopathic sanitarium. He does have a queer eye on him but is very well behaved and affable, but imagine a Lowell (yes, the poor boy's mother is a Cabot)—imagine one coming all the way from Boston to sit at Southern feet.

Lowell's mother was a Winslow, not a Cabot, and Gordon had not yet learned of Merrill Moore's role in Lowell's sudden appearance. It was odd that a Harvard student should decide that the South was the place to learn about poetry, yet, considering the high regard in which Tate and Ransom were then held by critics, it is perhaps not so surprising after all. Harvard had no important poet and little interest in contemporary literature. Lowell was willing to go anywhere for the company of real writers, so he had traveled south with Moore, then gone on alone to the Tates' home, unannounced and unexpected. Why Moore or Ford had not warned them of Lowell's visit is a minor mystery, but Ford may not have expected Lowell actually to show up, and Moore probably thought him sufficiently capable of explaining himself.

Lowell had not read Tate before this trip, but his first exposure was favorable. As he wrote to Anne Dick, "Reading over the 'Fugitive' poets on the train I decided Allen Tate is very topnotch, a painstaking technician and an ardent advocate of Ezra Pound."[3] The young Lowell badly needed the help and example of Tate's technical example, but his need to be around working writers, to learn about work habits and self-discipline, and to talk with someone who cared about poetry as much as he did were probably as great as his need for an experienced professional poet to work over his verse with him.

Tate's wide reading impressed Lowell as much as his poetry: "All the English classics, and some of the Greek and Latins, were at Tate's elbow. He maneuvered through them, cooly blasting, rehabilitating, now and then reciting key lines in an austere, vibrant voice. Turning to the moderns, he slaughtered whole Chicago droves of slipshod Untermeyer anthology experimentalists. He felt that all the culture and tradition of the East, the South, and Europe stood behind Eliot, Emily Dickinson, Yeats, and Rimbaud. I found myself despising the rootless appetites of middle-class meliorism."[4]

This was the sort of talk that Lowell already had learned to relish, and he was hungry for more. He returned to Nashville the following day to arrange for his enrollment at Vanderbilt that fall. Like Tate, Lowell would study with Ransom, whom he had also read and appreciated on the train. On 10 May, Ford and Janice

Biala arrived at Benfolly, and Nancy Tate brought her friend Elizabeth Jones to visit. The house was crowded, and then Lowell returned and asked to stay. The Tates could not refuse him directly, so they pointed out that the house was so full that the only way he could stay would be to pitch a tent on the lawn. Lowell took their comment literally and bought an olive-green umbrella tent at Sears and Roebuck. He later said, "The Tates were too polite to tell me that what they had said was just a figure of speech," but the Tates were probably more amused than annoyed. The presence of genuine writers and the sensuous immediacy of tent life inspired a poem that is more visual and evocative than most of Lowell's previous work:

AN AFTERNOON IN AN UMBRELLA TENT AT BENFOLLY

A shaggy orange dog, large as a sheep,
With spongy calloused paws and ponderous
Unshaven claws, pawed on my canvas walls
Blowsy and sagging transluscent green and seamed;
Breathing to bits a drowsy afternoon
Of muggy fitful sleep. I thought the bulgy scratching
Was but the slipping body of a cat,
And thumped my walls to shove it sprawling on the ground.
A mongrel stalked before my tent flap
Sniffing the air, investigating grass;
Aloofly gaped as though his casual breath
As cobwebs would collapse my house of gauze.[5]

Despite some awkward diction ("Breathing to bits," "Aloofly gaped") this poem is more clearly linked to experience than most of his previous work; it appears that he had finally begun to free himself from books and begun to live through his poems. The lack of melodrama and the humorous subject represent a real break with his early rhetoric. It also marks the introduction of a recurrent motif. The ironic metaphor of the intrusion of the animal (as the primitive self or as an alien intruder) into the pastoral garden recurs later in "Fourth of July in Maine" as mother and daughter guinea pigs, in *For Lizzie and Harriet* in a pair of gently humorous

43

turtle poems, and in *Day by Day* in the ferocious revenge poem "Turtle" and in "Shifting Colors" as the vaguely empathetic, anti-apocalyptic figure of an "ageless big white horse."

Later he would describe the poetry of this 1937 summer, written under Tate's eye, as "grimly romantic . . . organized, hard and classical as a cabinet."[6] Lowell also later said that during this summer he "became converted to formalism and changed [his] style from frail free verse, all in three months,"[7] but his notebooks indicate that he had continued to write more formal, metered verse than free verse. For the first time, he had begun to combine the best aspects of the two kinds of verse he had been writing. His free-verse poems were more concrete and specific in their imagery but lacked any apparent sense of rhythm. The poems in rough iambics lacked strong imagery, but at least they read like verse. The poems of the summer of 1937 are strongly visual and have a rudimentary sound of genuine verse.

Soon after Lowell returned with his tent, he wrote to his mother to reassure her that he was not wasting his time, and he enthusiastically renewed the commitment to his art that he had first made two summers previously on Nantucket: "I am of course back at the Tates, camping in my tent, reading and working. I feel convinced that I have never worked so hard or reaped such favorable results before. This interim between Harvard and the writers schools has convinced me more than ever that my vocation is writing. . . ."[8]

Despite Lowell's cheer and confidence, all was not well at Benfolly at first. Lowell's presence, so unexpected and so insistent, worried Tate. On 19 May, he wrote to Andrew Lytle, "The Lowell boy turned up twice, and we like him but feel that he is potentially a nuisance. His family decided that anybody who wanted to be a writer was insane; so they tried to have him judged crazy and committed to an asylum. Merrill [Moore] evidently put on his bedside manner and got their consent for him to come to Tennessee, which doubtless in the Lowell mind is not unlike a madhouse."[9]

Ford was more openly annoyed and refused to speak to Lowell for a time. "Maybe he was frightened I might gather a little store of humorous anecdotes about him and pass them on to posterity," Lowell later speculated.[10] Eventually, Ford softened and began to converse with Lowell, whom he addressed as "Young man." By July, when the Tates, Ford, Biala, and Lowell went together to a writer's conference at Olivet, Michigan, they were on good terms. Meanwhile, Lowell had written this rueful poem:

A MONTH OF MEALS WITH FORD MADOX FORD

I crouched at board next to the grumpy man
And scarcely dared look upon his span
Of sleepful, swollen flesh, rolling in line
Naively as a cow in the noon-time;
And sweated one long month afraid
Since he as child had met the bard Swinburne,
And had immortalized himself in one
Clear-written book, deathless in style and tone:
My fingers quaked to lift the salad cheese,
Sensing untutored effort would displease.
When furtively for change I'd fall to peeking,
His china eyes would glare, he wasn't speaking;
To earnest callow questions only grunt,
He could not understand what I could want!
While words drooled out of me as benison,
Harsh as the largest rotten pear on (a) stone
His huge inflated hand dropped on a spoon.
Ruddy with gout and boneless as his jowl
A plump left foot, wrapped in a turkish towel
Slept underneath his chair, limply a prey
To puppies tumbling avidly for play;
Yet he immortalized himself in one
Clear-written book, deathless in style and tone.[11]

Although the syntax is even more awkward than in the tent poem, much of the language, as in the lines on Ford's gout, is concrete and frank, and the resulting portrait effectively catches his pomposity and the poet's self-effacement. Lowell's later poem on Ford in *Life Studies* is more subtle in its cadence, avoids self-effacement, and imitates the rhythm of Ford's own heavily allusive speech ("'What is art to me and thee? / Will a blacksmith teach a midwife to bear?'"). Both poems mingle admiration and irreverence, but Lowell greatly admired Ford and later recalled "For me Ford was part of a great line of immortals that I hadn't read, D. H. Lawrence to Wells, etc." [12] That admiration did not blind him to Ford's eccentricities and improbable appearance. In the same interview, Lowell suggested in graphic terms why Ford might have taken a temporary dislike to the young poet: "I don't think he much liked the idea of a young man seeing him lounging around unshaven, with a fat bulging stomach and all his buttons undone, like he did at the Tates'." [13]

Ford and Lowell became so firmly reconciled that the elder novelist condescended to dictate parts of the book he was then writing to the young poet, his encyclopedic *March of Literature*. After the Olivet writers' conference, the group broke up. The Tates and Katherine Anne Porter toured through Washington and Virginia before returning to Benfolly; Ford, Biala, and Lowell moved on to another writers' conference in Boulder, Colorado. This conference would be especially important to Lowell; there he met Jean Stafford, whom he would marry three years later.

The summer of 1937, most notable for the concentrated work of all the writers at Benfolly and the demanding round of conferences, also caught Tate and Lowell up in a round of academic politicking. In the spring, Kenyon College had offered Ransom a position at an attractive salary, and Tate believed Vanderbilt was having trouble deciding whether it was worth trying to match the offer. In May, he wrote an open letter, published in the Nashville *Tennessean*, to the chancellor of Vanderbilt urging him to recognize Ransom's "distinction" and make every effort to keep him on the faculty. To press his point, he refers to Lowell's pilgrimage to the South: "The Lowell family of Boston and Harvard University has just sent one of its sons to Nashville to study poetry with Mr. Ransom—I do not say Vanderbilt, because young Mr. Lowell will follow Mr. Ransom to Ohio." [14]

Tate, who respected family background, was not immune to the weight of Lowell's surname. The chancellor was unimpressed—in fact, Tate's letter, which may have been taken as a public insult, as Tate intended it, probably confirmed Vanderbilt's determination to do nothing further to keep Ransom, whose willingness to leave seemed unrelated to the salary issue anyway. Apparently it was more a matter of dissatisfaction with the college's curriculum and Ransom's course and committee load. Vanderbilt's principle interest, like that of any other conservative educational institution, was not in poetry but in training businessmen, lawyers, and other solid citizens. Ransom believed that the more experimental Kenyon College would offer opportunities for both teaching and writing that were not available at a more conventional college. That September, Ransom packed his books and went to Kenyon, taking Lowell and Peter Taylor, as students, and Randall Jarrell, who had nearly completed his M.A. requirements at Vanderbilt and would become an instructor of English at Kenyon.

Early in 1938, the Tates began teaching at the University of North Carolina's women's college in Greensboro, where they would remain until September of 1939 when Allen began his three-year stint at Princeton. During these years, Lowell completed his undergraduate education at Kenyon, where he majored in classics and struggled with his poetry. His work in this period shows substantial progress; the effort of the summer of 1937 was not wasted. The best poems from this period are the two Ransom selected for the first issue of the *Kenyon Review*. One of them, entitled "The Cities' Summer Death," is an early version of what would become the first section of "In Memory of Arthur Winslow":

The summer hospital enframes
In its fashionable windows
Boats brow-beaten by varnished storms
And curbed-off grass where no cows browse.

Grandfather feathery as thought
Furls his flurried wrapper and floats
Off his adjustable bed
Wafted on somnolent swan-boats.

Cancer ossifies his features,
The starved skeleton shows its teeth,

47

The Years of Our Friendship

Flamingo crackling embroiders
Italian bones with shameless froth.

But the honking untainted swans
Float over the deathly stream
And the aghast oarsmen of Charon's
Ferry raise their skeleton rhythm.[15]

The rhythm is pedestrian compared to the more subtle metric of the version later entitled "Death by Cancer," which opens with a Miltonic extra half-stress and the subtlety of assonance instead of full rhyme:

This Easter, Arthur Winslow, less than dead,
Your people set you up in Phillips' House
To settle off your wrestling with the crab—

The metaphor of the swan-boat as Charon's ferry is coherent and effective and is carried over in more complex form into the new version, in which "the wide water and their voyager are one," fulfilling ten years later the implications of a metaphor invented in Lowell's undergraduate days. The third stanza of the early draft echoes Eliot's "Whispers of Immortality," but in its harsh, consonantal modifiers and heavy symbolism, the poem is an authentic precursor of Lowell's first mature poetic voice.

Not many of the poems of this period are individually successful. Looking back on the work of his Kenyon College years, Lowell later said, "Each poem was more difficult than the one before, and had more ambiguities. Ransom, editing the *Kenyon Review*, was impressed, but didn't want to publish them. He felt they were forbidding and clotted."[16] The Kenyon notebooks show less productivity than those from the earlier St. Mark's and Harvard periods, but although fewer and still crude and uncertain, the Kenyon poems are much stronger.

After graduation in 1940, Lowell married Jean Stafford at St. Marks-in-the-Bowery, with Allen Tate on hand to give the bride away. The courtship had not gone smoothly. Like so much in Lowell's life, this relationship, from the start, had seemed the product of will as much as of passion, a will that often concealed Lowell's motives even from himself. His attraction to Stafford was genuine but was fuelled by his parents' opposition. The drive to outrage them did not die until they did, and even then, his poems about them are a mixture of apology, self-justification, self-mortification, and defiance. The circumstances of his family life give this marriage the urgency and willfulness of fatalism. In 1938, he brought Stafford home to Boston for Christmas. The elder Lowells were icily polite. On Christmas Day, Lowell, driving drunk, smashed his parents' car into a wall at the end of a dead-end street in Cambridge. The crash broke Stafford's nose so badly it required a long series of operations to repair, an ordeal she later described in "The Interior Castle," her most vivid and excruciating short story. In addition, she suffered a fractured skull and jaw and came out of the hospital permanently, although only slightly, disfigured. In order to collect her medical expenses from the Lowells' insurance company, it was necessary for Stafford to sue them. Although this was mutually agreed upon, the lawsuit can only have furthered unpleasant relations.

Lowell's attachment to Stafford survived this trauma, his feeling of guilt, his father's anger, and his mother's continuing conviction that her son was mad, a conviction she presented to Carl Jung in Zurich during the summer of 1939. Jung's comment, according to Lowell in a late poem, was, "If your son is as you have described him, / he is an incurable schizophrenic." Most likely this was Charlotte Lowell's misreporting—Jung was hardly the man to make such an offhand diagnosis. Such a misreporting, if it occurred, is cruel, but Charlotte probably did not intend to hurt but only to assert some control over her wayward son. She may have thought to curb him by convincing him that he was mad and, therefore, necessarily dependent on his parents. Perhaps by presenting him with a diagnosis that proved his problems were not the result of parental error but of innate mental imbalance, she could convince him that she was on his side after all. At the very least, he might begin to question his own judgment and reconsider his attachment to Stafford. Even if Charlotte was not guilty of such misreporting, it is revealing that Lowell should remain convinced—and feel a need to convince his audience—that she was capable of such devious dealings with her son.

By comparison, the Tates must have seemed especially open, generous, and accepting. As Ann Waldron has pointed out, the Tates worked hard at self-improvement, worked hard at religion (after they had both been baptized as Catholics), worked hard at gardening and house repairs, and brought an unusual intensity to everything they did. Unlike the senior Lowells, they were unfailingly hospitable, passionate, thoroughly intellectual, and well informed. They moved about with a Bohemian abandon from New York to Benfolly, to London, Paris, Toulon, Memphis, Monteagle, Greensboro, and now Princeton. The senior Lowells, in staid upper-class New England style, had settled so immovably in Boston that they had come to seem as firmly rooted as their red-brick townhouse on Marlborough Street. The Tates' peripatetic life, their passions and rages, and the very intensity of their efforts would tear their marriage apart. Lowell, as well as they, was willing to pay a price for the kind of life he wanted.

Lowell graduated at the top of his class at Kenyon and decided to accept a fellowship at Louisiana State University, where he would study under the guidance of two of Tate's old friends, Cleanth Brooks and Robert Penn Warren. He would recall Baton Rouge without visible affection:

The torch-pipes wasting waste gas all night,
O Baton Rouge, your measureless student prospects,
rats as long as my forearm regrouping toward
the sewage cleansing on the open canals. . . .

In the same poem, he speaks affectionately, if slightly critically, of Warren (the poem is dedicated to him) and concludes by addressing him as "old master," acknowledging the literary acumen of another former Fugitive who, like Tate and Ransom, haunted Lowell's career.

Tate, meanwhile, was promoting the New Criticism at Princeton. His essay "Miss Emily and the Bibliographer" made a stir there since it challenged the historical philology and bibliography that had been the Princeton approach to literature since time immemorial. In fact, Tate's essay, read before the assembled faculty in the spring of 1940, not only called favorite old methodologies into question but ridiculed them. He unfavorably compares contemporary bibliographers to Faulkner's Miss Emily, who refused to acknowledge the death of her lover and kept his body in her bedroom years after his demise. The bibliographer denies that literature is a living thing and treats it as a relic. Tate aptly says, "It is better to pretend with Miss Emily that something dead is living than to pretend with the bibliographer that something living is dead."[17]

The Princeton faculty must have been outraged to hear the "academic mind" derided as insincere and self-deluding, but Tate argues persuasively and with an overriding moral purpose that crushes the pointless antiquarianism of the bibliographers. He believes that a denial of literary criticism as an intrinsic and central part of literary education is a denial of humanity's moral nature: "There is no doubt that the most powerful attraction offered us by the totalitarian political philosophies is the promise of irresponsible perfection in the future, to be gained at the slight cost of our present consent to extinguish our moral natures in a group mind. The moral nature affirms itself in judgment, and we cannot or will not judge. Because the scholars as much as other people today are involved in the naturalistic temper, they also refuse to judge."[18]

This is strong stuff, and shows Tate at his most powerful as a critic. No wonder the Princeton faculty wanted to get rid of him, and no wonder it took them three years to gather the courage to do so. Many contemporary institutions also would make short work of such a boat-rocker.

In this period of close association with Lowell, Tate's moral fervor found direct expression in his criticism, and his poetry parallels the younger poet's in an effort to sort out personal and societal religious concerns. Both faced the problem of finding an aesthetic to accommodate shifting attitudes toward faith and moral purpose. Tate, with his established voice, was successful first. "More Sonnets at Christmas" (1942) and "Seasons of the Soul" (1944), like the earlier "Sonnets at Christmas," dramatize the war between the Freudian drive toward salvation through the exploration of childhood guilt and the drive to salvation through the embrace of Christ and the consequent expiation of guilt. Through this drama, these poems chronicle Tate's groping for faith and certainty in the decade of the war. The first "Sonnets at Christmas" series (1934) is skeptical of the speaker's motives and uncertain of the possibility of any sort of salvation, but it attempts the discovery or the invention of faith:

> Yet I, stung lassitude, with ecstasy
> Unspent argue the season's difficult case
> So: Man, dull creature of enormous head,
> What would he look at in the coiling sky?

Intellect and the will to faith are at odds here, the "enormous head" committed to mapping the limits of human senses rather than to "ecstasy." It would leave the latter "unspent" rather than surrender its prerogatives of will, choice, and memory. This is the dilemma that Tate wrestled with for years. For him, Freud was as much a prophet as Jesus, and Freudian family drama (as he demonstrated in *The Fathers*) was a more aesthetically satisfying motif than the puritan drama of wrestling the self into submission and acceptance of something he was not sure he believed.

Lowell, who, in his early poems, is less inclined to self-examination than Tate was in the 1940s—or Lowell himself would be later on—ached for a transcendence he could not achieve through his metaphors of urban incongruities and violence. Although the poems of *Land of Unlikeness* and *Lord Weary's Castle* use religious iconography, they contain little of the objective correlative for ecstasy and transcendence found in the poetry of Herbert, Traherne, or even Hopkins. When Lowell sent John Crowe Ransom a group of poems destined for *Lord Weary's Castle*, Ransom congratulated him on "giving up the effort to communicate more than was communicable."[19] The dilemma of the poet who is wrestling with religious faith in a post-Freudian and (in many respects) post-Christian era is that transcendent ecstasy is not only incommunicable, or nearly so, but is at odds with the modernist aesthetic program that both Tate and Lowell had endorsed.

52

Unlike Lowell, Tate never attempted to communicate the un-communicable, but his very reluctance to attempt the transcen-dence of language inhibited his religious passions and, as the second series of "Sonnets at Christmas" shows, led him to insist on the need for a faith rooted in the social order rather than the isolate self:

Give me this day a faith not personal
As follows: The American people fully armed
With assurance policies, righteous and harmed,
Battle the world of which they're not at all.

The only possible melioration of this terrible irony would be a Christianity powerful enough to reshape the social order; private doubt and the poet's aesthetic preclude a personal faith. Tate's reli-gious vision is still linked to his vision of a traditional society, one in which the moral nature and the economic nature of humanity are linked in the "greatest of all human tasks," that of forming a homogenous traditional society.[20] Yet part of the complexity of "More Sonnets of Christmas" derives from Tate's confounding of personal and societal failures. His own vision at this time is one of a dead Christianity, unresponsive to either his personal or so-cietal needs:

Ten years are time enough to be dismayed
By mummy Christ, head crammed between his knees.

The violence of this image is that of the blasphemer who wants to shock himself into belief. Written in 1942, as Lowell was writ-ing the poems of *Land of Unlikeness*, this imagery resembles the desperation of Lowell's "Christ for Sale":

In Greenwich Village, Christ the Drunkard brews
Gall, or spiked bone-vat, siphons His bilged blood
Into weak brain-pans and unseasons wood. . . .

Lowell, too, confounds his outrage at a purposeless and now war-directed society with his personal drive for salvation, and the resulting poems, like Tate's, are unusually difficult and compelling. Tate, though, in "The Seasons of the Soul" (1944), begins to work toward a more personal religious vision and an aesthetic that will accommodate a more introspective groping toward faith. Vivienne Koch, writing in 1951 just before Tate became a Catholic, saw "Tate's mature view of the religious problem" in this poem.[21] She felt that he thought Christianity to be dead and argued that the lines "the drying God above / Hanged in his windy steeple" resolved with "brutal finality" the question of faith.[22] Yet, given his subsequent conversion, "Seasons of the Soul" seems more ambiguous even though it entertains Nietzschean ideas of the relationship of religion to culture. In attitudes of both irony and humility, the speaker descends into his own dark night and emerges at a moment when the tension between the ironic and the humble precipitates a momentary equilibrium. Here salvation seems, if not within reach, at least conceivable. Tate links irony and humility in a 1930 review of Eliot's *Ash Wednesday:*

> Humility is subjective, a quality of the moral character, an habitual attitude. Irony is the particular and objective instance of humility—that is, it is an event or situation which induces humility in the mind of a spectator; it is that arrangement of experience, either premeditated by art or accidentally appearing in the affairs of men, which permits to the spectator an insight superior to that of the actor, and shows him that the practical formula, the special ambition, of the actor is bound to fail. Humility is thus the self-respect proceeding from a sense of the folly of men in their desire to dominate a natural force or situation.[23]

In "The Seasons of the Soul," the speaker gradually comes to realize the folly of trying to dominate the drama of his own soul. The irony of the poem derives from our full realization and his half-awareness of the inadequacy of the poem's iconography to embody a drama of grace and salvation until the humble and humbling figure of the Mother of Silence appears in the last ("Spring") section.

The four sections of the poem, organized around a cyclical imagery that echoes Eliot's *Four Quartets,* represent the four seasons, the four ancient elements (air, earth, water, fire), and the four stages of the soul's drive to faith and salvation. This drive is neither satisfied in the poem nor is it entirely forestalled. Each of the an-

54

cient elements is inhospitable in a different way and deters the search for a redeemable self. Air, for example, the bright hot air of summer, "dries and draws . . . the flesh . . . Into the summer's jaws," and the cold winter sea engenders a shark to "nudge and tear / The livid wound of love." Love is the crucial stage that the soul needs to attain, but the elements and the seasons, everything that shapes our earthly life, conspire to focus our attention on the flesh and its varied sufferings. The "Mother of Silences," envisioned in the poem's final section, is a figure of salvation but an ambiguous one, too self-contained and too remote to readily share her comforts. Koch identifies her with St. Monica, "the Virgin, the Mystery, and through St. Augustine's unmentioned wound . . . the principle of Love." [24] Rather than embracing death and abandoning the hope of regeneration through love, as Koch asserts, the ending of the poem suggests that confession, renunciation, and the frank recognition of mortality are possible keys to salvation:

> Speak, that we may hear;
> Listen, while we confess
> That we conceal our fear;
> Regard us, while the eye
> Discerns by sight or guess
> Whether, as sheep foregather
> Upon their crooked knees,
> We have begun to die;
> Whether your kindness, mother,
> Is mother of silences.

Although the Mother of Silences does not respond, we might feel that she speaks through the speaker of the poem, that he provides his own modest and tentative approach to the faith that Tate in life—not in poetry—would eventually embrace.

Lowell, meanwhile, had already become an ardent, even fanatical Roman Catholic. In the fall of 1940, he had begun reading Catholic theology and philosophy at Baton Rouge and shortly thereafter, in the spring of 1941, was baptized as a Catholic and remarried Stafford under the auspices of the church. For him, unlike Tate, the rush to faith was precipitous. Although his earliest poems indicate an interest in religious faith, nothing he had written to this point contained the sort of complex, agonized soul-searching found in "More Sonnets at Christmas" and "Seasons of the Soul." Lowell had written very little since 1937 and nothing that represented a substantial advance toward a mature poetic voice. During his entire life, he would write his best work in sudden bursts of closely related poems. His most prolonged stretch would be from 1968 through early 1973 when he composed his unrhymed sonnets, but most of these prolific stretches were relatively brief and separated by a year or more of nonproductivity. This is one of the reasons that Lowell's poems from different periods are stylistically distinct. In the early 1940s, he was gathering his talent, however unconsciously, for his first mature production, the poems he would draft in 1942–43 and would revise into the strong poems of his first two collections. His newfound religious faith played an important role in this creativity, providing much of the iconography, the structure, and the argument of these poems, but it also would cause a terrible strain in his personal life, damaging his marriage and, perhaps, stressing his psyche to the point at which it eventually surrendered to the chemical imbalance that would trigger a serious manic episode in 1948. Not that Catholicism drove him mad; rather, his overly ardent embrace of a faith that possibly was not as deeply felt as he needed may have driven him into a dangerously aggressive stance.

After completing his studies at Baton Rouge, Lowell worked for a time in New York at Sheed and Ward, a Catholic publishing house. Stafford sent a section of *Boston Adventure* to Harcourt, Brace and received a positive response from Robert Giroux, who would later edit the work of both Lowell and Stafford and would become one of their closest friends. To cement the instant friendship and acknowledge the Lowell's symbolic literary parentage, Giroux brought the contract for Stafford's book out to Princeton for a ceremonial signing at the Tate's.

By early 1942, when the ceremonial contract signing occurred, Tate knew that his Princeton job would not be renewed. Although a position at Louisiana State University might have become available, he decided he had had enough of teaching for awhile and elected to spend the fall, winter, and spring at Monteagle with his writing. Lowell, though still obsessed with Catholicism, had tired of his work at Sheed and Ward, and when the Tates invited him and Stafford to winter with them, they gladly accepted. No one had much money, but Jean and Caroline had advances on their novels, Tate had savings, and Lowell had a small trust fund.

Lowell's notebooks record the astonishing outburst that followed. During his last two years of undergraduate work, his year at Baton Rouge, and his year in New York, he had written relatively little poetry. What he did write demonstrates a broadening of vocabulary, a growing sense of the power of imagery, but no individual sense of rhythm or of the structure of poetry, the peculiar way it makes arguments. The poems of this period are leaden and despairing. Their arguments are expository rather than worked out in imagery and metaphor and, consequently, sound preachy. The last stanza of "The Protestant Dead in Boston" (1941) illustrates Lowell's difficulties:

> Boston cemetery is the world—here in the heyday
> the spirit hawked elections, and the decemvirate
> Of Morals, Ten Commandments, fostered
> the perfection of a faction, regimented a mortal
> yard of provincial, enterprising, prolific
> Protestants. These dissenters, now the servants
> of the earth were fatally chosen and beatified:
> secured from temporal torrents, the ocean's
> masterless surges, the contagion of human
> contact, their lives were as single as their skeletons.
> Ah, diet and raw material for a creation's consumption,
> this was an unbaptised inattention to Epicurus,
> who, basket in hand, rambled through worlds
> and worlds, the basket his garner of perishable
> flowers.[25]

In "Park Street Cemetery," written only a year or two later and published in *Land of Unlikeness*, well-chosen imagery (suggested possibly by Tate's "Ode to the Confederate Dead") summarizes and, by implication, dismisses as unnecessary much of this polemic: "Dusty leaves and the frizzled lilac / Liven this elder's garden with baroque / And prodigal embellishments." Lowell's streak of didacticism clashed with the need to learn to place his trust in imagery; in this, too, he resembled Tate. The sixteen poems he would complete and the various others he would begin during the months at Monteagle are much stronger, more economical, more dramatic, less willed, less prosaic than the poems immediately preceding them. In their early versions, they are obscure and even private in reference, but they have momentum and a forcefulness derived from their complex patterns of symbols.

Lowell, in a letter to his mother that was written from Monteagle, seemed clear about his intentions:

> What I am saying will be much more obvious and constructive. All of them [the poems he had recently been writing] are cries for us to recover our ancient freedom and dignity, to be Christians and build a Christian society. I think of Blake's hymn:

> I shall not cease from mental fight
> Nor shall my sword sleep in my hand
> Till we will have built Jerusalem
> in England's green and pleasant land.[26]

"To Our Lady on the Eve of the Immaculate Conception: Dec. 8, 1942," an early version of the poem that appears in *Land of Unlikeness,* is typical of the poems that Lowell more or less completed this winter.

> Mother of God, whose burly love
> Rebuffed the sword, I must improve
>   On the big wars
> And make a holiday with Mars
> Your feast-day, while the pacifist's bluff,
> Courage or call it what you please,
>   Plays blind man's bluff
>   Through virtue's knees.

> Freedom and Eisenhower have won
> Significant laurels, where the Hun
>   And Roman kneel

To lick the dust from Mars' boot heel
Like foppish bloodhounds; yet you sleep
Out our distemper's evil day
    And hear no sheep
    Or hangdog bay!

Bring me tonight no axe to grind
Or hones of a utopian mind:
    Six thousand years
Cain's blood has drummed into my ears,
Shall I wring plums from Plato's bush
While Burma's and Bizerta's dead
    Must puff and push
    Blood into bread?

Oh, if soldiers mind you well
They shall find you are their belle
    And belly too:
Christ's bread and beauty come by you,
Celestial Hoyden, when Our Lord
Choked with Golgotha's bloody tide
    You took the sword
    From his torn side.

Over the seas and far away
They feast the fair and bloody day
    When mankind's Mother,
Jesus's Mother, like another
Nimrod danced on Satan's head;
The old snake lopes to his shelled hole,
    Man eats the dead
    From pole to pole.[27]

Although this draft suffers some of the faults of Lowell's earlier poems—particularly a difficulty in choosing appropriate verbs (the idea of a snake loping to its hole is unintentionally comic), a sometimes awkward and forced syntax, and overly obvious rhymes—it also displays more energy and passion than his previous work. Like many of the other poems that would eventually appear in *Land of Unlikeness*, this displays the mingling of Catholic iconography, historical allusion, and societally directed outrage that characterizes the book as a whole. *Lord Weary's Castle* is more meditative, the language generally less violent, but it is often an even denser mixture of the language of religion (both Catholic and Protestant) and the language of history, and it embodies a strong sense of place. *Land of Unlikeness*, though its poems are urban and explicitly set in Boston, Salem, and Concord, and despite opening with "The Park Street Cemetery" (the Old Granary Burial Ground in Boston), is not as firmly rooted in the particulars of landscape, and for this reason it is a slighter book, but the final versions of the poems Lowell wrote for it in 1942–43 are astonishingly mature compared to what he had produced only a year or two before. Further, by the end of his stay at Monteagle in June of 1943, he not only had notes and drafts of almost all of the *Land of Unlikeness* poems but had tentative drafts or notes for "The Quaker Graveyard in Nantucket" and many of the other poems in *Lord Weary's Castle* that were not revised from the earlier book.

Some of the poems that found their way into *Land of Unlikeness* are as strong as anything Tate had so far written. Like the senior poet's best poems, Lowell's now display a powerful historical sense. Stimulated by the war, his newfound religion, and Tate's example and presence, Lowell found a way to write what John Crowe Ransom would call genuine metaphysical poetry, yoking imagery and references from incongruous eras to make a meditative whole, as these lines from "Christmas Eve in the Time of War" demonstrate:

Tonight in Europe and America
All lights are out. Tonight the statesmen lurch
Into some shuttered houseboat, mosque or bar;
Blue lines of boys and girls are on the march:
The Child has come with water and with fire.
Stone Generals, do you tremble for your perch?
Tonight our ruler follows his own Star;
Pretorians shake the Magi's Star for gold.
How can I spare the Child a crust of mould,

His stocking is full of stones!

Lowell would drop these lines, except for the last two, when he rewrote the poem into "Christmas Eve Under Hooker's Statue" in

Lord Weary's Castle, and even those lines become more immediately personal ("I ask for bread, my father gives me mould"). In keeping with the new title, he deleted some of the overt references to the ongoing war that was almost concluded by the time of his revision. He retained the image of the blackout, but instead of "statesmen" and "Blue lines of boys and girls," he centers the opening stanza on the first-person speaker and his childhood memories:

> Tonight a blackout. Twenty years ago
> I hung my stocking on the tree, and hell's
> Serpent entwined the apple in the toe
> To sting the child with knowledge.

Lowell, by 1946, already displayed a preference for centering the first person in the vortex of history and personal memory. Like Auden (whom these lines may echo), he sometimes revised to delete merely contemporary references, but these lines effectively link childhood to the timeless mythology of Western civilization and place the consciousness that makes this link at the heart of the poem. Both the early and the later versions establish the war in an ongoing Christian world of revelation in which the elements embody visions of salvation and hell, and the stone generals installed on their pedestals seem the very embodiment of the dead poised for the Judgment, but the later version brings more life to the poem by identifying its empowering consciousness as dramatis persona rather than authorial bystander.

Tate also was productive this winter. He wrote or completed four of his strongest poems, "More Sonnets at Christmas," "Jubilo," "Ode To Our Young Pro-Consuls of the Air," and "Winter Mask: To the Memory of W. B. Yeats." In addition, he wrote an essay, "The Hovering Fly," and translated the *Pervigilium Veneris,* making this one of the most productive periods of his career. He had intended to write a novel, and Lowell had planned to write a biography of Jonathan Edwards. Both worked on their chosen projects, but their actual output was unanticipated and more bountiful than perhaps they expected. No wonder Lowell vividly remembered this winter as late as 1974 in a letter to Tate: "It's so much colder here [i.e., in England]. We only have fireplace heat, and it's as bad as the windy days during our Monteagle winter of 42 and 43. Nothing could be—I remember going to bed then, and read the three volume St. Simon. Our famous fire must have been a protest against the cold." [28]

Lowell never wrote his projected book on Jonathan Edwards, but at least three poems eventually grew out of his research— "Mr. Edwards and the Spider," "After the Surprising Conversions," and "Jonathan Edwards in Western Massachusetts." When he and Tate finally admitted that their major projects were not progressing, they decided to collaborate on an anthology. They both admired "rather formal, difficult poems," and as Lowell describes it, this interest seemed to inspire both of them to write poetry: "We were reading particularly the sixteenth and seventeenth centuries. In the evening we'd read aloud, and we started a card catalogue of what we'd make for the anthology. And then we started writing. It seems to me we took old models like Drayton's Ode—Tate wrote a poem called 'The Young Proconsuls of the Air' in that stanza." [29]

Of Tate's poems of 1942–43, "Ode To Our Young Pro-Consuls of the Air" is probably the best known and the one Lowell most admired. As Lowell says, Tate's "Ode" derives its stanzaic form from Drayton's "The Virginia Voyage." It also suggests Marvell's "Horatian Ode" in both form and subject matter, but where Marvell uses tetrameter and trimeter to give the poem a dignified movement that is appropriate to its subject, Tate, following Drayton, shortens his lines to trimeter and dimeter, which increase the air of comic urgency and threaten to (but do not) degenerate into doggerel:

Once more the country calls
From sleep, as from his doom,
  Each citizen to take
  His modest stake
Where the sky falls
With a Pacific boom.

The pun on "Pacific," the warning that the sky is falling, and the linking of patriotism and doom signal both the topic and the tone of the poem. Tate satirizes war, facile thoughtless patriotism, and even the poet himself:

> Marvelling day by day
> Upon the human kind
>   What might I have done
>   (A poet alone)
> To balk or slay
> These enemies of mind?

Lowell would echo these words years later in "Waking Early Sunday Morning," a poem that derives its stanzaic form from Marvell and its topic of exhaustion and helplessness in the face of militarism and violence from various sources, including Tate's "Ode." The "enemies of mind," here as in Lowell's poem, are not simply aliens or foreigners, "the puny Japanese" or the Germans, but are closer to home. Specifically they are those powerful and influential people who should be defenders of the autonomy and independence of poetry but who now argue that literature has to assume a role in this war and claim that literature can be shaped to serve a cause:

> It was defeat, or near it!
> Yet all that feeble time
>   Brave Brooks and lithe MacLeish
>   Had sworn to thresh
> Our flagging spirit
> With literature made prime!

The poet cannot "balk or slay" anyone, but perhaps he can find a language adequate to the problem of war. In the instance of the "Ode," that language is bestial:

> O animal excellence,
> Take pterodactyl flight
>   Fire-winged into the air
>   And find your lair
> With cunning sense
> On some Arabian bight

Or sleep your dreamless sleep
(Reptilian bomber!) by
   The Mediterranean. . . .

The response offered to war is the embrace of tradition, mythology, faith. Tate's poem offers the alternative of a tradition that is ancient, broad of view and scope, and pacifist, a view he expects the young proconsul to reject along with a culture that, like the swan, is dying anyway:

Take off, O gentle youth,
And coasting India
   Scale crusty Everest
   Whose mythic crest
Resists your truth;
And spying far away

Upon the Tibetan plain
A limping caravan,
   Dive, and exterminate
   The Lama, late
Survival of old pain.
Go kill the dying swan.

To kill what is already dying is the peculiar art of war. As Pound noted, World War I demolished a European culture that had been reduced to "two gross of broken statues, / . . . a few thousand battered books." World War II completed the task.

Lowell's "Satan's Confession," Tate notes in his introduction to *Land of Unlikeness,* also uses the stanza from Drayton's "The Virginian Voyage," but if Lowell had learned from Tate's borrowing of form, he was also impressed by his mentor's adept satire. At about this same time, Lowell wrote "The Bomber," which chastizes the bomber pilot for acting like a god, addressing him with an irony so heavy that it makes Tate's poem seem lighthearted:

Bomber like a god
You nosed about the clouds
And warred on the wormy sod;
And your thunderbolts fast as light
Blitzed a wake of shrouds.
O godly Bomber, and most

64

A god when cascading tons
Baptized the infidel Huns
For the Holy Ghost,
Did you know the name of flight
When you blasted the bloody sweat
And made the noonday night:
When God and Satan met
And Christ gave up the ghost?

While Tate's poem concerns itself with the destructive effects of war on culture, Lowell's is specifically religious; but it draws on more than the Roman Catholic idea of God. Lowell is willing to confound Zeus, the Old Testament god, and the Holy Ghost to give shape and resonance to his metaphor. This willingness to sacrifice orthodoxy for poetic effect characterizes most of the more or less religious poems of his first two books, but as he knew (he was studying Hopkins at the time), the aesthetic imperative often takes precedence over the religious in English poetry. This is a sort of poetry, though, that he later claimed he had not wanted to write, an *"engagé* poetry." Looking back in 1960, he considered himself an entirely different kind of poet: "The third group [after the imitators of nineteenth-century poetry and the *engagé* poets], which I more or less belonged to, I think it derives somewhat from Yeats and from Eliot, and in this country friends of mine, Allen Tate and John Crowe Ransom. . . . There were great arguments that poetry was a form of knowledge, at least as valid as scientific knowledge, and in certain ways more so, because it didn't abstract from experience. We claimed . . . the whole man would be represented in the poem."[30]

Lowell was not yet certain how to write poetry that represented the whole man, and poems like "Ode: To the Young Proconsuls of the Air" and "The Bomber" demonstrate how easily, during the war period, a certain didacticism slipped into the work of otherwise nonpolitical poets. In Lowell's case, this didacticism indicated latent interests that would find their full expression later in the public poems of *For the Union Dead* and *Near the Ocean.*

Lowell was attracted to war and had studied it extensively, fascinated by such figures as Napoleon and Alexander the Great, but his idea of war centered about individual dignity and heroism, not the bombing of civilians. He had dutifully registered for the draft in 1942 and had investigated the possibility of enlisting, but that was before the massive bombings of German cities had begun. In August 1943, he received his notice of induction. By that time, after composing most of the poems that would make up *Land of Unlikeness,* he had considered the realities of modern warfare and his religious commitment, and he had decided to declare himself a pacifist. On 7 September, he sent a letter to President Roosevelt and mailed a copy of a "Declaration of Responsibility" to the federal district attorney in New York. Though the letter may show signs of incipient megalomania (with its reference to "family traditions"), the declaration is, nonetheless, carefully composed, reasonable, and displays a highly rational historical awareness. One paragraph suggests how some of that historical awareness came through Tate: "Americans cannot plead ignorance of the lasting consequences of a war carried through to unconditional surrender—our Southern States, three quarters of a century after their terrible battering down and occupation, are still far from having recovered even their material prosperity."[31]

The problem with the "Declaration of Responsibility" is that it is not what a draft board required. It is not a declaration of personal principle that opposes violence or the taking of lives but an argument against the strategies by which the United States was carrying out a particular war. Although Lowell later described himself as a conscientious objector, his statement is not that of one who opposes violence for its own sake but of one who simply does not approve of the way this war—a necessary one, he concedes—is being handled. The federal district attorney in New York prosecuted Lowell for draft evasion. He was sentenced to a year and a day in the federal prison in Danbury and would actually serve five months (plus ten days in the West Street jail, described in "Memories of West Street and Lepke") before being paroled to work in a Bridgeport hospital. While on parole, Lowell kept busy with literary matters, writing poetry again and thinking about book reviews, as indicated in a letter written to Tate on 31 July 1944:

66

Thanks for the two books to review. Hopkins and Baudelaire are an interesting juxtaposition but I wonder if the two books *on* them will combine. The Ruggles is a very [easy?] uncritical biography. Bennet's will be something else. I know very little about Baudelaire. . . . I think the seven poems I am sending you are a new style, more lyrical and lucid. There may be echoes from Eliot. Two you have seen in earlier versions. Two others are pillaged from my long poem on England, which John Ransom described as "big and oppressive" and I have decided to scrap. I have also heavily revised my sonnets and written two more. . . .[32]

Although Lowell wrote no poetry while in Danbury, he was able to kill some time by correcting the proofs of his first book. Tate had helped him place his recent work with prominent journals and arranged for the Cummington Press to publish *Land of Unlikeness*. While Lowell was in prison or working at his grimy parole job, his poems appeared in the *Sewanee Review* and *Partisan Review*, journals that, without Tate's assistance, might have been unreceptive to the work of an unknown and difficult poet. The book appeared in the fall of 1944. By then, Lowell was writing again, revising poems he had begun at Monteagle and writing new ones that were less strained and violent than those in his first collection. Although he may have felt he had already outgrown *Land of Unlikeness*, he must have been gratified by the attention it received: more than a dozen reviews, most of them quite favorable or at least encouraging. This is a remarkable response to a small-press book by an unknown poet, but Tate's introduction lent it the imprimatur of an established poet and instructed reviewers on how to approach these difficult, sometimes unwieldy poems.

Tate begins by pointing out a trait common to Lowell's verse and his own, its formal patterning. He even mentions Lowell's use of the stanza from Drayton's "The Virginia Voyage," a stanza Tate had also borrowed. He then argues that Lowell's Catholicism and his strict forms are interrelated. Typically of the New Critics, Tate considers a poem successful only when its form and content seem to render each other inevitable. Even though Lowell's poems sometimes suffer from appearing forced or willed, Tate claims that the effect is a sign of strength, reinforced by the formal stanzas. He then identifies the controlling dualism of the book by pointing to the apparent gap between personal experience (in poems like "Death from Cancer") and social satire. Inner and outer experience, the experience of observation and the experience of personal emotions, have not come together yet in a single poem, but they nearly do so in "The Drunken Fisherman," which, even in its earlier version, is probably the strongest poem in *Land of Unlikeness*. Tate does not single out this poem, however. For him the poems of social satire, though perhaps not as effective at this point, are of equal interest. He is drawn to Lowell's implicit argument that Christian experience has disappeared from contemporary America and looks forward to more effective poetry of social commentary from Lowell. He is more concerned with the spiritual decay of the "slave-society" than with Lowell's personal angst (an unduly Romantic trait anyway), and sees the younger poet as healthier than the society surrounding him: "The spiritual decay is not universal, and in a young man like Lowell, whether we like his Catholicism or not, there is at least a memory of the spiritual dignity of man, now sacrificed to mere secularization and a craving for mechanical order."[33]

The implication is that Tate remains uncertain about Catholicism; it would be another seven years before he joined the church. He is certain, however, about the importance of a spiritual order as a basis for a healthy society and about the value of a poetry that embodies that order. Later, with *Life Studies* (though the title poem of *The Mills of the Kavanaughs* may well portend what was to come), Lowell would allow personal experience to shape his poetry in a way that was difficult for Tate to accept, but before that, in *Lord Weary's Castle*, Lowell fused the contrary voices of *Land of Unlikeness* in a poetry of experiential immediacy and social commentary, religious vision and personal emotion.

The good reception of Lowell's first book and the enormous success of his second book occurred in a context of personal strain and disruption. Both the Tates and the Lowells suffered (and created) marital problems that resulted in divorce—the Tates' only temporary, the Lowells' permanent and painful for both parties.

68

The Tates' difficulties came first. Allen's infidelities were notorious, and Gordon had grown understandably bitter over them. Her faithfulness to Allen, despite his own trespasses, was unchallengable and a wonder to their friends, but by 1944, their quarrels had become prolonged and unbearably painful. Tate had become the editor of the *Sewanee Review,* a position that brought them back to Tennessee, where the lack of work for Gordon increased the tension between them. Finally, by October of 1945, Gordon left Tate and Tennessee and went to Connecticut to stay with the Cowleys before moving back to Princeton to live alone. Aware of her plight, the Lowells invited her to stay in Maine with them for the winter.

The Lowells were living in Maine because Stafford's novel *Boston Adventure* had been published in November of 1944 and had become a considerable critical and financial success. The book eventually sold 350,000 hardcover copies (many of those to book clubs), a huge sale by any standard. Tate, with playful irony, wrote to Lowell in July of 1945, "Bob Daniel (who knows everything) says that Boston Adventure has sold over six hundred thousand copies. I hope people are now treating you more respectfully than they did before, seeing that you have so much money. . . ."[34] Lowell's reply takes the exaggerated story seriously and underscores his youthful dislike of bourgeois success: "Bob Daniel as usual is only half-right. 150,000 of Jean's 600,000 are an oversea's edition, for which she is supposed to get $400. Another 150,000 are a book guild. Actually, Harcourt Brace has only sold about 40,000 which is tremendous but nothing like Bob's 600,000. We are neither respectable nor rich."[35]

The Lowells, however, were rich enough to buy a house in Damariscotta Mills, Maine, to which they moved in September 1945. They had remained in close touch with the Tates during the summer of 1945 while they were living in Boothbay Harbor and their house was being renovated. Lowell described Boothbay Harbor to Tate as "a sort of Maine Monteagle; the nights are cool, the scenery is beautiful and the summer people, to the number of 15,000, are atrocious."[36] When Caroline left Allen, it must have seemed natural for the Lowells to invite her to Maine. She, as well

69

as Allen, was their friend, and in looking after her, they probably thought they were helping both parties rather than taking sides. In fact, the ensuing quarrel helped drive the Tates back together.

The Lowells met Gordon in New York and planned to take her back to Maine with them. As Lowell wrote to Tate, "We are out here for the day [in Princeton] and find Caroline the same person we have always known. She is going back with us to Maine and I think it will be much the best for her and we will be more than delighted to have her with us. The country there is heavenly and the woods are full of mushrooms." [37]

But Lowell came down with appendicitis, and Gordon had to go on to Damariscotta Mills alone. Although she had lived a winter in the New York countryside, she was not accustomed to dealing with the extremities of a Maine winter and found the house fraught with problems. She wrote to the Lowells that the pipes were in danger of freezing, the stove difficult to keep going, and the bathroom devoid of heat. Storms downed the power lines, and high tides swept the streets, but Gordon still managed to work on her novel and was reasonably content for a time.

The Lowells arrived at the end of November and relations with Gordon promptly collapsed. Apparently Stafford and Lowell felt that they could freely discuss Allen's love affairs, about which Gordon knew less than they. When Lowell left the two women alone in the house, they got into a quarrel and Gordon threw a glass of water at Stafford. In a frenzy, Gordon smashed dishes and glassware, broke a window, and frightened Stafford into running next door to call the sheriff. Gordon, in turn, called Tate, who was in New York. He suggested that she return to New York, which she did, and a temporary reconciliation ensued.

The Tates took sides with each other against the Lowells. Tate, according to Peter Taylor, complained to Stafford, "You don't call the sheriff on your friends." [38] Stafford defended herself in a dramatic letter to Tate in which she carefully leaves room for reconciliation:

Water did not, as Caroline has suggested in a letter to Cal [Lowell's nickname given to him at Saint Mark's], accidentally come in my direction and the fact that she does not remember what she did strengthens the belief I had that night that she was clean out of her mind.

She deliberately threw a full glass of water into my face and she accompanied the gesture with the words, "You've probably ruined the lives of two people by what you've done to me." I got up from the table and went to get paper towels to wipe off my face and my sweater and my hair. As I was doing this, she threw the glass that had contained the water and it crashed on the wall above my head and she then got up and said, "I'm going to break every goddamned thing in your goddamned house." She did not say "in *the* house." She said, "in *your* house." These are the facts.

If it is any pleasure to either of you, I remain entirely wretched. What I did was awful but it was not deliberately awful: I remember everything that happened and I did not imagine that Caroline threw a glass of water in my face nor could her act have possibly been construed as accidental.

There is no point in going into other details, but I did want to clear up this one misunderstanding. I now realize that if Caroline doesn't remember what she did, she was not responsible and in that case, probably was not throwing the water at me, the person, but at me, an object across the table from her—so, in those terms, I suppose the incident *could* be called accidental.[39]

The Tates and Lowells so quickly called a truce that, by January 4, Jean could write to Allen, "They're fishing for smelts in the bay now. Don't you want to come up and catch salmon and bass in the lake?"[40] Yet, on January 16, Tate again was chastizing Jean for what he called her "hostile remarks."[41] Not for several months would the Tates and Lowells settle back into easy friendship.

The reconciliation between Allen and Caroline did not last long, and on 8 January 1946, in a fifteen-minute court hearing, the Tates were divorced. On 8 April, after an earnest courtship through the mail, they were remarried, but their marriage would be even less comfortable than it once had been, and years later they would divorce again, this time for good.

After the incident with Gordon, the Lowells found the Maine winter too difficult and depressing, so in mid-January, they moved to Cambridge to stay with Delmore Schwartz and remained there until the end of March. Lowell had completed the manuscript of

Lord Weary's Castle, and Robert Giroux of Harcourt had agreed to bring it out in the fall, so this winter marked the completion of another stage of his career and development. At first, living with Schwartz worked out well, as Lowell recounted it later in "To Delmore Schwartz" in *Life Studies:*

> We drank and eyed
> the chicken-hearted shadows of the world.
> Underseas fellows, nobly mad,
> we talked away our friends. "Let Joyce and Freud,
> the Masters of Joy,
> be our guests here," you said. The room was filled
> with cigarette smoke circling the paranoid,
> inert gaze of Coleridge, back
> from Malta—his eyes lost in flesh, lips baked and black.
> Your tiger kitten, *Oranges,*
> cartwheeled for joy in a ball of snarls.

But this Bohemia did not last. Lowell's obsession with Jewry and his partially Jewish ancestry irritated Schwartz, who ridiculed Lowell's parents. Finally they fought with their fists.

At the end of March, Stafford went to Maine while Lowell visited Trappist monks, Peter Taylor, and other friends. The Lowells had grown uncomfortable with each other. Stafford's excessive drinking and preoccupation with her new home irritated Lowell, who seemed more interested in a life of wandering asceticism. When the Lowells were together, they fought more frequently and more woundingly. Stafford's fictionalized account of the summer of 1946, in her story "An Influx of Poets," lends dramatic coloring to their respective voices, but the fact that she remembered the quarrels so bitterly makes the story of some biographical interest. Lowell comes off as a sneering, sarcastic prig when the speaker in the story (a Stafford persona) reports his saying to her, "I learned to drink at home in the drawing room, so I know how. No fault of yours—just bad luck. You don't drink well, dear. Not well at all." [42] No one else who knew Lowell then (or later) has recorded this sort of behavior, however, and Stafford is almost as hard on her own persona, describing herself as obsessed with "nesting and neatening" and lacking in the "vitality" and "taste" to decorate a house properly.[43]

The plot of this story bears a darker truth. The summer, as Stafford describes it, was one of unrelenting company, and it ended in disaster. During that "awful summer," John Berryman and wife Eileen Simpson, Philip and Natalie Rahv, R. P. Blackmur, Robert Giroux, and others came for visits of varying length. Simpson's engaging memoir describes in detail the heavily literary atmosphere of their visit and suggests, in passing, the importance of Tate as mentor to both Lowell and Berryman:

> Throughout the weekend literary talk ran in counterpoint to autobiography. Not since Delmore had John found a contemporary who was as obsessed with poetry as he was, and who felt that next to the greatest joy of all—the "tortured joy" of writing poems—was the joy of discussing them. Cal, like Delmore and John, believed that in heaven, or paradise, or "the chambers of the end" (as John later called it), poets would spend eternity in one another's company, exclaiming, explicating, parsing, doing what Cal and John were doing now—talking about poetry. They began with their own generation: Schwartz, Jarrell, Dylan Thomas, Ted Roethke, Elizabeth Bishop, Karl Shapiro. Each had his favorites, and urged them on the other. Randall was Cal's; Delmore, John's. They worked backward to their mentors: Tate, Ransom, Van Doren, Blackmur, Hart Crane. Tate's influence on both of them was immense. John had been his student in a summer school course at Columbia and had had "the top of my head blown off" by Allen's brilliance and erudition. The summer after John returned from England he stayed with the Tates in Connecticut, showed Allen what he had been working on, and decided that there was no better reader, no one from whom he could learn more about composition.[44]

The dark side of the summer was plainly visible, though. The Lowells had no privacy in which to work out their differences and consequently were forced to nurse their grievances until they broke out in uncontrollable quarrels. Simpson was aware of Stafford's drinking problem and notes that "Cal's discreet attempts to control her drinking had led her to stow a glass of sherry behind the cookbooks in the kitchen and to keep a hidden supply so that the house would never be 'bone-dry.'"[45] Lowell, on the other hand, lived the life of a literary and religious fanatic. Simpson quotes Stafford as saying, "I fell in love with Caligula and am living with Calvin. He's become a fanatic. During Lent he starved himself. If he could get his hands on one, he'd being wearing a hair shirt." [46] The Lowells were struggling with differences that neither of them could or wanted to understand.

At the end of August, Gertrude Buckman, Delmore Schwartz's former wife, arrived, and Lowell eventually became embroiled in a serious affair with her. In September, the Lowells, thoroughly exhausted by each other, took the train to New York and split up. Stafford stayed with friends while Lowell rented a room by himself. Sadly, the marriage ended with Stafford in the Payne-Whitney clinic undergoing treatment for her drinking and her psychological deterioration. Despite her lengthy and dramatic letters pleading for reconciliation, Lowell turned his back on both her and the Catholic church and entered the next phase of his life alone.

Literary Peers

The failure of Lowell's marriage coincided with the rise of his literary reputation. In 1945 "The Quaker Graveyard in Nantucket" (still incomplete) appeared in *Partisan Review,* and in 1946 his poems appeared in such leading journals as *The Nation, Poetry,* and *The Virginia Quarterly Review,* as well as in *Sewanee Review* and *Kenyon Review,* where he had already published some of the poems of *Land of Unlikeness.* The new poems differ from those of 1944 in word-choice, syntax, and structure rather than in subject matter or tone. Lowell found a way to unite the disparate tendencies that Tate had noted in his introduction to *Land of Unlikeness.* The complex network of symbols in the newer book seems drawn from personal experience or observation rather than simply willed into existence. The poems are metrically more carefully controlled, and the rhetoric is less that of the savage would-be prophet than of the passionate witness. The opening stanza of "Christmas in Black Rock" typifies Lowell's new voice:

Christ God's red shadow hangs upon the wall
The dead leaf's echo on these hours
Whose burden spindles to no breath at all;
Hard at our heels the huntress moonlight towers

And the green needles bristle at the glass
Tiers of defense-plants where the treadmill night
Churns up Long Island Sound with piston-fist.
Tonight, my child, the lifeless leaves will mass,
Heaving and heaping, as the swivelled light
Burns on the bell-spar in the fruitless mist.

Specificity of place ("Long Island Sound"), contemporary imagery ("tiers of defense-plants"), the iconography of Christmas
("green needles" and the evocation of the Christ-child), and an
original vision ("red shadow," "treadmill night," "piston-fist,"
"swivelled light," "fruitless mist") combine in a passionate stanza
that is unified by consonance ("shadow," "echo"), alliteration
("hard," "heels," "huntress"), and internal rhyme ("lifeless,"
"fruitless"). Nearly every phrase has that mysterious originality
we expect of poetry at its best. Everything Lowell learned from
Tate, Crane, and Eliot has been subsumed by a more ample technique and a fresh and mature vision. He has learned how various
areas of knowledge or vision create their own languages of con-
notation and symbol: a language of religious iconography, a language of quotidian landscape, and a language of personal vision.
The poems of *Lord Weary's Castle* are so richly textured because
Lowell interweaves these languages without depriving them of
their discrete significance. This is poetry of complexity, of dignity
and inclusion, poetry that simultaneously expresses a personal
and a social vision. Tate's poems, strong as they often are, are relatively homogenous in their referent languages. Lowell had grown
away from his mentor in some respects, though he had yet to
match (and perhaps never did match) Tate's unique and delicate
prosody.

Tate and Lowell's other mentors were impressed, even aston-
ished. Lowell, in the poems of one strong book, had become their
peer. In a previously quoted letter, Ransom, accepting some of
these poems for the *Kenyon Review*, wrote, "I don't know who has
grown up in verse more than you, these last few years; mostly, I
think, by way of giving up the effort to communicate more than
was communicable, and by consulting the gentle reader's traditional range of intelligence rather than your own private article."[1]

Ransom himself had become a more transparent poet in his later verse and certainly had come to appreciate clarity, but the poems of *Lord Weary's Castle* "communicate" only to readers who share at least some of Lowell's range of reference. Without a basic grasp of Christian iconography (more and more restricted to better-educated readers, at least in our own time) and some awareness of history (why Napoleon's crossing of the Berezina is significant, for example), the reader will flounder in these poems. Even Eliot hoped for a popular success. As an admirer of music-hall performances, he believed in popular art in a way that Lowell's generation generally did not. Lowell's poems were widely admired by the same sort of audience that Tate and Ransom had cultivated—a well-educated group that had the knowledge and patience to wrestle with lines like

> How dry time screaks in its fat axle-grease,
> As spare November strikes us through the ice
> And the Leviathan breaks water in the rice
> Fields, at the poles, at the hot gates to Greece. . . .   ("The Crucifix")

It is fair to argue that Lowell invented an audience for himself, as all successful, well-publicized art eventually does. *Lord Weary's Castle* would not sell in the way *Boston Adventure* had, but it ran through four printings fairly quickly. For a hardcover volume of poetry, this is close to popular success. The book had a greater immediate impact than anything the Fugitives had written. Lowell had combined the density of argument of a Tate poem, the oblique shorthand of Hart Crane's metaphors, and the ethical, social, and religious imperative of Eliot in a poetry that was different from all of theirs. It is no wonder that it received immediate critical appreciation and the honors that commonly accompany such recognition.

Though still smarting from the quarrel earlier in the year, Tate could not ignore Lowell's achievement. Written in October 1946, the month of the book's publication, his comment, compared to the effusions he would later expend on *For the Union Dead* and *Notebook*, is restrained but ungrudging: "Both Caroline and I have been enjoying LORD WEARY'S CASTLE. The immense advance that you have made in the past three years is one of the most astonishing things in modern poetry."[2]

Tate, though rarely unwilling to promote friends, never reviewed this or any other Lowell book. Perhaps he felt that Lowell's poetry was too close to his own, a kind of poetic alter ego. Lowell's was not exactly the poetry Tate himself wished to have written, but when Tate's own poetic gift seemed to have largely dried up (except for the astonishing outburst in 1952), Lowell's had matured and achieved a success even greater than Tate's. This would be difficult for any older poet, and Tate may have felt inadequate to consider Lowell's sudden maturation objectively. Not only was Lowell the protégé, the apprentice poet, but his poetry at this stage seems to be a more intense and fully realized version of some of Tate's work from the 1920s, 1930s, and early 1940s. Most of Tate's reviews, even of friends, deal with work distinctly unlike his own, but even when Lowell's poetry grew in a direction different from Tate's, it may have been difficult for Tate to see with the clear eye of the reviewer that Tate was at his best. Lowell was simply too close to him in too many literary and personal ways. The later praise (and blame) would be more expansive and detailed, but Tate seemed completely comfortable in expressing himself privately and directly to Lowell.

Even as Lowell's poems grow more and more distinct from Tate's, the issue of direct influence lingers. Can a father review a son? Can the master review the apprentice? Lowell's great elegy "The Quaker Graveyard in Nantucket" must have caused Tate to wonder how much of his own elegy "Ode to the Confederate Dead" had been subsumed and superseded in Lowell's distinctly Miltonic poem. The answer, of course, is: very little. Not until 1961 would Lowell write a direct response to Tate's most famous poem when, for the Boston Arts Festival, he drafted "Colonel Shaw and the Massachusetts 54th," later known as "For the Union Dead." Certainly Lowell's "Quaker Graveyard" immediately suggests the graveyard setting of Tate's Ode (and Paul Valery's "Le Cimetiere marin"), but Lowell's graveyard occurs in the poem only briefly at the end of part II, and it is not clearly the location of the speaker, at least not for the entire poem. Tate's graveyard is the setting for a meditation deriving its movement and imagery from Shelley's "Ode to the West Wind," and the imagery of Lowell's poem derives from the opening chapter of Thoreau's *Cape Cod*, from *Moby Dick*, *Lycidas*, and (in a section suggesting Eliot's "Little Gidding") Watkin's *Catholic Art and Culture*. All of this is well documented, but sources are not poetry. What is essential in each poem is the emotional imperative that emerges from both borrowed and original imagery and the enshrinement of that imperative in the poem's meter and the larger rhythm of its structure.

The two poems are similar in tone and in their direct appeal to the emotions of the auditor or reader. Lowell's lines, addressed to the dead,

> All you recovered from Poseidon died
> With you, my cousin, and the harrowed brine
> Is fruitless on the blue beard of the god,
> Stretching beyond us to the castles in Spain,
> Nantucket's westward haven

echo Tate's, in which his speaker addresses his meditating self,

> Think of the autumns that have come and gone!—
> Ambitious November with the humors of the year,
> With a particular zeal for every slab,
> Staining the uncomfortable angels that rot
> On the slabs, a wing chipped here, an arm there:
> The brute curiosity of an angel's stare
> Turns you, like them, to stone,

not in imagery or rhythm, but in the grandeur of the emotional appeal. Both poems ask the real or fictitious self to accept that sweeping knowledge of eternal things that only the immediate or metaphysical presence of death can confer, a knowledge both speakers realize is nearly impossible to reconcile with a knowledge of life. Tate and Lowell learned to write in this manner from common sources—most obviously Milton—but although he acknowledged the importance of Milton, Lowell himself thought "Quaker Graveyard" owed something to Tate. In an interview with Cleanth Brooks and Robert Penn Warren, he said, "Personally, Allen Tate was the poet who was closest to me and I feel it's

79

["Quaker Graveyard"] like his poetry and yet unlike it, and I've never quite known how."[3] Yet after further musings, he became more explicit: "I wanted to write the way [Tate wrote] the opening of 'Aeneas at Washington' in parts of 'The Graveyard,' but I never could and I did something else. And I don't . . . no one has ever compared us in any detail. I always wondered how we resemble each other."[4] The opening lines of "Aeneas in Washington" strike an archaic note unlike anything in Lowell's poem:

> I myself saw furious with blood
> Neoptolemus, at his side the black Atridae,
> Hecuba and the hundred daughters, Priam
> Cut down, his filth drenching the holy fires.
> In that extremity I bore me well,
> A true gentleman, valorous in arms,
> Disinterested and honourable. Then fled:
> That was a time when civilization
> Run by the few fell to the many, and
> Crashed to the shout of men, the clang of arms. . . .

Tate's poem moves leisurely, despite its sanguinary topic, while Lowell's poem is energetic, entirely modern in its wrenched syntax. Nothing in "Quaker Graveyard" sounds much like Tate's calculated imitation of Latin blank verse, but Lowell almost certainly had this poem in mind when he wrote "Falling Asleep Over the Aeneid" in 1947.

Perhaps the most important thing Lowell learned from Tate, as well as from Eliot and Yeats, was that such writing remained possible, if difficult, in the twentieth century. The conclusion of Tate's "Ode" sounds like a passage on the rose garden in "Burnt Norton":

> Leave now
> The shut gate and the decomposing wall:
> The gentle serpent, green in the mulberry bush,
> Riots with his tongue through the hush—
> Sentinel of the grave who counts us all!

This, however, predates Eliot by almost ten years. Lowell's conclusion, reaching for an epic weight that Tate deliberately rejects, sounds like the Old Testament:

You could cut the brackish winds with a knife
Here in Nantucket, and cast up the time
When the Lord God formed man from the sea's slime
And breathed into his face the breath of life,
And blue-lung'd combers lumbered to the kill.
The Lord survives the rainbow of His will.

By the end of this poem, Lowell had grown independent of Tate—and also of Eliot, Crane, Ransom, Williams, Frost, and all his other early influences, yet he acknowledged all or most of them along the way. His next step would be the reinvention of the narrative poem, a less successful venture than his transformation of the Fugitive lyric, partly because he could not yet give up the texture and allusiveness of his newly discovered voice. Tate, on the other hand, would write no poetry for several years, but when he did, he would also rediscover the narrative in a voice that seems in many respects the most powerful invention of his career.

By the beginning of 1947, the Tates were more or less firmly united again, with Allen working at Holt and Caroline teaching at Columbia. Lowell satirized Tate's job in a squib penciled on the back of a worksheet for "At the Altar":

Allen Tate
Sits in state
Dining dolts
For Henry Holt's:
Doing nothing,
Blowing, puffing,
Cramming, stuffing
Blabbing, bluffing[5]

Lowell had no need of such a bourgeois position. He was footloose in New York, successful but mentally deteriorating—slowly at first and then, in 1949, with sudden and frightening results. In April, he won the Pulitzer Prize, an honor neither Tate nor Ransom achieved (though their comrade Robert Penn Warren won it twice—once for poetry and once for fiction). Other awards followed, including a Guggenheim and the American Academy prize. In June, the Library of Congress offered him the post of Poetry Consultant, a position that Tate recently had held. Tate apparently was involved in the process of filling the post because, from Boston on 4 June 1947, Lowell telegraphed him in New York, "Would you give the library my official acceptance thanks for everything / Cal."[6]

Tate, in his letter on *Lord Weary's Castle,* had asked Lowell for an essay on John Crowe Ransom for a sixtieth birthday issue of the *Sewanee Review.* He had set a deadline of 1 April 1947, but on 17 October, 1947 and again on 8 November, he wrote Lowell to remind him to send the piece along. Lowell's tardiness became characteristic and, with some complications, eventually led to a serious quarrel between him and Tate. Though he finished the essay, which was "John Crowe Ransom's Conversation," Tate did not forget his dilatoriness.

But Lowell had much on his mind. His emotionally draining correspondence with Stafford prolonged the agony for both of them and even challenged his freedom to write frankly. After publishing "Her Dead Brother" (in *The Nation,* 22 February, 1947), he received this harrowing letter:

> Dear Cal,
>
> "Her Dead Brother" appearing in the Nation a week before the publication of my book with its theme of latent incest, at a time when you have left me and I am in the hospital seems to me an act of so deep dishonor that it passes beyond dishonor and approaches madness. And I am trembling in the presence of your hate.
>
> It could not have been by accident although I would give years of my life to have you tell me convincingly that it was: all the harm is done and cannot now be undone in the eyes of the world which will judge me in these awful terms, but if you did not mean this further injury, for God's sake, tell me, Cal, because this wound is deeper, I think, than all the others together.[7]

Given this paranoid challenge to his role as a poet, which should have been a refuge for him at this difficult time, it is no wonder that Lowell grew increasingly calloused toward Stafford and that his mental state grew murkier. In addition, the pressures of fame and honors lay upon him, and he was faced with a new job in Washington in the fall. He was writing little and felt pressed to follow up *Lord Weary's Castle* with something equally memorable. Poems like "Her Dead Brother," "David to Bathsheba in the Public Garden," both published in *The Nation* just after the appearance of *Lord Weary's Castle,* and "The Fat Man in the Mirror" (*Poetry,* August 1947) represented no advance from "The Quaker Graveyard in Nantucket." No poet wants to produce his or her best work at the beginning of a career and decline beyond that high point. Lowell now turned to narrative poetry because he was unable to improve upon his lyric.

Tate, at the same time, began to think of narrative poetry. He had not tried it before, but he had demonstrated a powerful narrative talent in *The Fathers* that he had not yet fully exploited in verse; and he was slowly reconciling himself to the idea of writing poetry that was more personal, even autobiographical, than anything he had attempted previously. In "A Reading of Keats" (1946), he hints at the necessity of sometimes employing personal experience in poetry as the appropriate way to deal with passion and sensation: "Is it saying too much to suppose that Keats's acceptance of the pictorial method is to a large extent connected with his unwillingness to deal with passion dramatically? (There is sensuous detail, but no sensation as direct experience, such as we find in Baudelaire)."[8]

"Sensation as direct experience" requires a more openly personal use of metaphor and imagery, a willingness to subsume the intellect and appeal to the knowledge of the grosser senses. For both Tate and Lowell, the personal narrative or dramatic monologue would provide a vehicle for the expression of sensate and emotional lives that their earlier poems could not present. It would be a few years before those poems would be written, and when Lowell's finally came to fruition, they horrified Tate by going far beyond what he had encountered, even in Baudelaire.

When Lowell assumed his duties at the Library of Congress, he moved into the Cosmos Club, which Tate had helped him join. On 4 November he wrote to Tate to thank him: "I've finally been admitted to the Cosmos Club—after mistaking one of the members for a waiter in dramatic recognition scene. Thanks for writing them. The only authors that I've heard of are President Chalmers of Kenyon and you. I think most of them are Marshall Petain's uncles."[9]

Lowell goes on to criticize Tate's new poem "The Eye," which is no more homiletic and minatory than Lowell's poetry in *Land of Unlikeness* but more so than what he now wanted to write. "What I admire most in *The Eye* is its rhythm and freshness, but I think you are right in your judgment of it. There's something rather symbol-cluttered and redundant about it—something mixed and curt about the style. Perhaps this is too strong—you must name this the beginning of a new start."

Lowell's strictures are apt, but they apply as well to the poems he had been writing only four or five years before. "The Eye" is a self-conscious performance full of allusions to Blake, Wordsworth, Baudelaire, and others and is rigidly structured around the rhetoric of the homily:

The ill man becomes the child,
The evil man becomes the lover;
The natural man with evil roiled
Pulls down the sphereless sky for cover.

The redundancy is structural, the symbols seem less important than the rhetoric, but the poem ends with an impressive Baudelairean chill:

Shut shutter of the mineral man
Who takes the fatherless dark to bed,
The acid sky to the brain-pan;
And calls the crows to peck his head.

"The Eye" was not a new beginning but a farewell to an old style. It revealed many of that style's weaknesses—its tendency toward direct statement, its difficulty with keeping metaphor in focus, its structural uncertainty—but it is a poem that Lowell would remember years later when he wrote "Eye and Tooth." Tate's concern with the relationship between visionary capacity and the frailty of physical sight would become an important issue for Lowell.

Lowell was busy at the Library of Congress arranging recordings of poets. He recorded Williams and Elizabeth Bishop, among others, and brought Tate to Washington in January of 1948 for a session. That winter Lowell met Carley Dawson and became engaged to her for about six months although he remained involved to some extent with Gertrude Buckman. In April, he and Stafford were formally divorced, and in May, he broke off the Buckman affair. Tate had left Holt, and he and Gordon had resumed their teaching careers, he at New York University and she at Columbia. Their perspective on Lowell's affairs was one of bewilderment at his increasingly strange behavior. It would be a year before that behavior manifested clear signs of illness, but the events of the summer gave some hint of what was to come. Lowell brought Mrs. Dawson to Maine to visit Elizabeth Bishop, who had borrowed the Dawson house in Stonington. Apparently becoming aware of her insufficiencies in comparison with the brilliance of Bishop, Lowell simply turned away from Dawson, who, realizing the affair was over, departed, leaving her house in their hands. Lowell, who had only recently met Bishop after writing a wonderfully insightful review of her first book *North and South*, unilaterally decided he would marry her. Bishop's rejection must have been tactful since they remained close friends for the remainder of Lowell's life.

That fall Lowell went to Yaddo, an artist's retreat in Saratoga, New York, for a memorable stay. It was during these next few months that he initiated a cruel and paranoid attack on Agnes Smedley, a writer on Far Eastern politics, and Elizabeth Ames, the director of Yaddo, both of whom he accused of being Soviet spies. It was also during this stay that he became involved with Elizabeth Hardwick, whom he would marry in July 1949.

Before the ugliness of the Smedley uproar, Lowell and Tate exchanged letters on less serious topics and even managed to meet in November for a fishing trip. Tate had been concerned about Lowell; for a month or so, his friends had lost sight of him, and it was rumored that he was drinking heavily and behaving oddly. But the worry seemed unnecessary for the moment. Lowell had attended an event at Bard College at which Elizabeth Bishop was also present, and wrote a brief, comical note to Tate: "Many odd things happened at Bard—low points: drinking GLUG (a gallon of boiling burgandy, a pint of whiskey and every kind of rind, berry, nut, and spice in the world) on a hot night in a steamy crowded room—the A.A. has nothing on GLUG; and an afternoon when all the poets read informally for mutual nomination—But it wasn't always coming."[10]

Shortly after this, Lowell and Tate met at the Bennington, Vermont, bus terminal for a fishing trip. Lowell, who took fishing seriously, was for the moment more concerned with his equipment than with poetry: "I have everything (Frank Parker's father's fly-rod with one broken tip, so you'd better [bring?] your's for a reserve) except the proper flies and a fly-line. In these small towns they seem to think trout are caught on cod-lines or bass-casting lines, so please bring yours."[11]

Yet the pressures continued. Lowell had found the Library of Congress job more taxing than he had expected. In December he wrote to Caroline Gordon that he was glad to be through with it: "I liked Washington, but what a delight to be done with it; and back to work. With what I've saved from the library and Yaddo and my Guggenheim I can easily last two years before I have to think of teaching."[12]

The demands he made on himself were unceasing and his production slow although he had written several good poems since *Lord Weary's Castle* ("Falling Asleep Over the Aeneid" and "Mother Marie Therese" appeared in the *Kenyon Review* in 1948). After these successes, he entered a long, less-productive period during which his few new poems ("Thanksgiving's Over," "The Mills of the Kavanaughs") were less effective than the best of those preceding them.

The controversy over the award of the Bollingen Prize to Pound for *The Pisan Cantos* had begun even before the prize was awarded in February of 1949. Lowell and Tate were both members of the Bollingen committee, and some of its members engaged in the public debate that followed the award. Tate, in particular, vociferously and eloquently defended the committee and the poetry. With John Berryman, he assembled a petition with over seventy signatures of well-known literary figures in support of the award.

Lowell had little to say, probably because 1949 was a difficult year for him, with an emotional breakdown, remarriage, and (Tate reported in a letter to Marcella Winslow) a struggle to write a long poem temporarily beyond his abilities.[13]

In February 1949, the month of the Bollingen Prize, the *New York Times* published an article that seemed to involve Agnes Smedley in a spy ring. Though the army disavowed the allegation, the FBI never got the message, and two agents visited Yaddo to inquire about Smedley. Their visit also raised questions about Elizabeth Ames. Lowell, along with three other visiting writers, attacked her in writing and demanded that the directors of the Yaddo corporation fire her. The unpleasantness of this episode cannot easily be dismissed. Lowell bore himself like the most rabid and mindless of anti-Communists, but the atmosphere of the times was tense and fearful. Other writers shared Lowell's suspicions, and the Yaddo board was divided on the issue of dismissing Ames. If she had been a Communist, would that have affected her ability to manage Yaddo? Lowell had no trouble in overlooking Pound's ugly political and racial views in order to vote him the Bollingen Prize, but he could not, at this time, extend a similar benevolence toward a purported Communist. In later years, his flexibility and generosity would render this sort of behavior unthinkable, but, unknown to him, he was entering his first serious manic episode, and his judgment and reasoning power, though superficially intact and persuasive, were probably not entirely under control.

Lowell was disappointed that the board in the end left Elizabeth Ames at her post. Back in New York in March, he made a show of returning to the Catholic church, but that effort was short lived. His concern for otherworldly matters was not as pressing as it had been in the early and mid 1940s. In the same letter to Gordon (December 1948) quoted above, he told her, in response to a question about his spiritual well-being, "I don't know how my soul is—pretty uncombed, I guess." [14] Gordon would worry for years about Lowell's spiritual well-being, but in the spring of 1949, he gave her and Tate reason to worry about his mental well-being as well.

Lowell's behavior that March and April would deeply affect his friendship with Tate, who was as uneasy with the idea of mental illness as with the public display of deep feeling. Tate himself suffered some disturbed periods and, according to Gordon, had been behaving atypically at about the same time. Confronted with the drama of psychological difficulty, Tate preferred to ignore or deny it or to overreact when he decided to face it. He would rarely discuss or mention in correspondence Lowell's recurring illness without dramatizing it, but he was also prone to ascribing the oddities of Lowell's behavior as mere perversity or crankiness. Lowell's first serious psychotic episode directly involved the Tates, and it requires careful examination. Wild legends have sprung from this event, and it is now difficult to sift fact from embellishment, but, by even the most sedate account, it was a frightening and unpleasant series of incidents, painful for everyone involved.

On 1 March, his birthday, Lowell sent Tate a peculiar telegram:

EARLE HOTEL 103 WAVERLEY PLACE PLEASE COME [15]

Under this in Tate's hand: "This was sent immediately after he left Yaddo. I was to come to fight evil." The Tates were in Chicago, where Allen was teaching at the University of Chicago. Gordon invited Lowell to visit them, and on 29 March he arrived, preceded by the flourish of another odd telegram:

ARRIVING BY PLANE 435 THIS AFTERNOON WITHOUT OLD ROBERT AND LIZZIE LOVE

UNCLE LIG [16]

A note in Tate's hand reads, "He was violent and in custody five days after this." The Tates were alarmed at his mental state when he arrived, and Tate wrote to Hardwick with a candor that would prove to be exceptional in his experience with such problems: "Fundamentally he [Lowell] makes a good deal of sense, but his mental condition is very nearly psychotic. We shall be able to get through the next ten days, till he goes to Kenyon: what worries me is his immediate future." [17]

Lowell frightened Tate and Gordon by repeatedly touching and kissing both of them, begging Allen to repent of his love affairs, and finally giving Gordon a list of Allen's various lovers, repeating the error Stafford and Lowell had committed three years earlier. It seemed that Tate would have no secrets as long as Lowell was around.

As Gordon and Tate had been angry with Stafford, so they were angry with Lowell. According to one version, probably exaggerated, Lowell, at this point, picked up Tate, dangled him out the window, and recited "Ode to the Confederate Dead" to him. Lowell was large and strong enough to do this, but more likely is the version in which he simply picked up Tate and squeezed him. Shortly thereafter the Tates took Lowell to a restaurant where he completely lost control and made a scene. Back at the Tates', he shouted obscenities from the window until the police arrived. After some struggle, they handcuffed him and took him to a psychiatrist. The following day, Lowell boarded a train to Bloomington to visit Peter Taylor.

After Lowell had left, Tate wrote to Elizabeth Hardwick to warn her further about his behavior. He argued that Lowell was actually dangerous, that "there are definite homicidal implications in his world, particularly toward women and children." [18] Tate may have misunderstood his state; certainly his later episodes were not obviously dangerous though sometimes he physically resisted restraint. Tate's conclusion implies a certainty that not even the psychiatrists of the time could profess, a certainty that he ascribes to Hardwick as well: "You know what is wrong with him as well as I do." The suggestion is that Lowell's problems are sexual, since Tate describes him as shouting to the police, "Cut off my testicles," but this might have been defiance of the police rather than a plea for relief from sexual conflicts.

Tate possibly felt some jealousy. He too had been attracted to Hardwick and may have considered Lowell to be trespassing, or, just as likely, he may have been genuinely concerned for her safety. Regardless of his motives, Hardwick was at least well appraised of the situation. When she married Lowell at the end of that summer, she had a reasonably clear idea of the potential for problems in the future. Tate's tendency to dramatize and exaggerate was not lost on her, though. Later she would sometimes respond with asperity to his letters about Lowell's mental states, but by then she knew better than anyone else the real complexities of Lowell's illness and their implications for those around him.

Lowell arrived in Bloomington on 4 April. Peter Taylor has given us the fullest account of that visit: "Allen Tate had called me from Chicago and said, 'Cal is not himself at all,' and that he and Caroline had just put him on a train! Well, of course I was furious— Allen had no business putting him on a train. But I also knew that Allen had a great dramatic sense, and I thought he must be exaggerating. I didn't think it was true when he said that Cal was beside himself,—I don't think *this was* true—that he tried to molest a child at the railroad station." [19]

As Taylor speculates, this child-molesting story is almost certainly false. It does not correspond to any other account of Lowell's sometimes odd actions and suggests that Tate was still angry enough to be malicious or to exaggerate to Lowell's detriment. Like the story of being dangled from the window (which may not have originated with Tate), this may have resulted from misinterpretation of a manic hug or embrace. Taylor's own experience with Lowell, as he describes it, is more plausible:

> As soon as Cal stepped off the train I could see he was out of his head. He wasn't the Lowell I knew. He was dirty and dishevelled [Lowell had been notably dirty and dishevelled in his undergraduate years, but not later]. So I took him to the faculty club and put him up there instead of taking him home. We had a new baby, and I told him the baby was not well. But while we were having dinner in this place, he began to sniff and say, "Do you smell that?" I said no, and he said, "I know what it is, it's brimstone. He's over there behind the fern." I took him to his room, and went to my house, but a few minutes later I was called by the people at the club. They said he had come out of his room and run through the kitchen terrorizing the cooks, and then run out into the streets. [20]

Taylor describes how Lowell went to a movie house, stole a roll of tickets, finally knocked on a policeman's door, and ended up in jail. The next morning, Taylor visited Lowell, and they prayed together ("Let's get down here and pray together to get out of this place," said Lowell) in adjoining cells. Because of a change of guard, Taylor found himself locked in for four hours. On 6 April, Lowell's mother, accompanied by Merrill Moore, flew in and took charge. She brought Lowell back to Boston and placed him in Baldpate, an elegant sanitarium in Georgetown, Massachusetts, where he remained until July.

Tate was right when he told Lytle that Lowell was "potentially a nuisance." After this episode, their relations would remain cordial, even affectionate, but the streak of hostility that probably inheres in all human relations would expose itself with some frequency, usually in Tate's letters to other friends, even to Elizabeth Hardwick on one or two occasions. The maliciousness of Tate's claiming that Lowell had tried to "molest a child" may have been completely unconscious. His fear of Lowell's mental state led him to believe him capable of murder (as he claims in the letter to Hardwick), so child molestation would hardly seem out of the question, but Tate's willingness to fear the worst is hardly what we expect from friends. Fear and repugnance for mental illness may explain Tate's reaction, but as parents often judge their children's behavior more harshly than the behavior of others, so Tate may have judged his protégé with an otherwise uncharacteristic harshness. According to Ann Waldron, Tate and Gordon agreed that part of Lowell's problem was that success had come too quickly,[21] but this suggests that their own slow achievement of success colored their judgment. As has already been intimated, Tate may have felt some sexual jealousy over Lowell's relationship with Elizabeth Hardwick. Most likely a complexity of motives underlay Tate's reaction to Lowell's illness, and this complexity would mark (and sometimes mar) their relationship from now on.

Immediately after being discharged from Baldpate, Lowell married Elizabeth Hardwick. This marriage would last more than twenty years and give him the support and center to his life that would help him survive numerous future attacks of mania. The marriage began with another attack, though a mild one, and Hardwick must have felt rather suddenly the weight of the burden she would have to bear. Lowell entered the Payne-Whitney Clinic in September. Shortly after visiting him there, Tate wrote a letter of brotherly advice: "I think you ought to practice a little couerism. Tell yourself every morning, five times, that you are one of the best poets, and that your friends feel about you precisely as they always have; that is, devotedly. You should never think as well of yourself as other people do; but you ought to think better of yourself than you do now. And you will."[22]

Apparently Tate thought that Lowell's ego was at a low ebb, and no doubt it was—Lowell must have been discouraged by the nearly year-long period of mental upset. Years later Tate would chastize him for his egoism, but in 1949, despite the enormous success of his poetry, Lowell must have appeared and felt distressed.

By December, though, he felt better enough to consider looking for a teaching post and wrote to Tate for aid. Lowell mentioned that Iowa had an opening but "others have applied," and he was "despondent of their refusal."[23] Whether this shows a lack of confidence or is a coy way of getting assistance, it worked. Tate used his influence to secure the job for him, as Lowell acknowledged in a letter written on 29 December: "Many thanks for all the trouble you've taken for me. Last night Paul telephoned to offer me the job, and I quickly accepted. We plan to leave for Iowa in about two weeks."[24]

Lowell and Tate, in the next decade, would not be as close as they had been in the 1940s. Their meetings would be infrequent, and they would write to each other less often than might be expected from their early intimacy. Yet they would continue to consider each other important in their lives, and their letters were often of significance, particularly regarding their important work of the decade, Tate's "Buried Lake" sequence and Lowell's *Life Studies*.

The McCarthyism of the late 1940s and early 1950s voiced a gnawing desperation in American society. Uncertain of our place in an increasingly complex world, threatened by an ideology as often misunderstood by its adherents as its opponents, Americans grew even more suspicious of difference and eccentricity, and the arts either became blandly ritualistic or withdrew into an underground that made the separation of culture from society a virtue. The characteristic verse of the early 1950s was Richard Wilbur's elegant, insightful, but remote and somehow unchallenging formal constructs. These elaborate lyric stanzas were self-consciously traditional and obsessed with craft rather than with problems of faith, politics, the nature of reality, or anything else of brooding significance. Wilbur has long since moved beyond his early work to a less formal but darker, more demanding exploration of the social psyche, but at the time, he was the perfect artist—elegant and accomplished but tame.

Lowell, whose mad embrace of McCarthy-like red-baiting was a momentary passion, only hinted at his own feeling about the early 1950s in his poem on Eisenhower's inauguration, but when he had successfully opened his aesthetic to more immediate forms of experience, he characterized the period as "the tranquillized Fifties," an image that brilliantly links his own mental state, dosed with Miltown, to the state of the republic that had found Ike "the mausoleum in her heart."

The decade began with the Lowells planning a European trip on a Guggenheim fellowship; the Tates were living in Princeton in a new house and commuting to New York to teach. Lowell's first teaching position lasted only a semester, thanks to the Guggenheim Foundation, but he apparently found his work pleasant enough and Iowa City amusing, as he recounted in a 15 March 1950 letter to Tate:

> All has turned out very well. We are living in a large light room and kitchen, furnished with borrowings, pick-ups, and two packing trunks—our own, and large as garages. The Macauleys are a block down the street, and the Wests a few blocks to the south in a frail brick Wormwood house with urns on the lawn. . . . Every afternoon a pack of very harmless and sorry-looking stray dogs settles on our pathway. This is one of the marks of Iowa City; the others are high-brow movies, the new criticism, a quarter of an inch of ice, and the Benasek murder trial, which Elizabeth is moving heaven and earth to enter as an accredited reporter.[25]

Lowell seemed to find both Iowa City and his students congenial if unchallenging, and he noted that his own teaching followed the path of least resistance: "Tame and friendly are the right words to describe almost everything—especially my own teaching. I find it surprisingly easy to talk and argue through my classes, but there are no fireworks, nothing of the icy lucidity of the professional." He also notes that the reputation of the Tates looms large: "Did you know that you and Caroline are Olympians here—much quoted, imitated, and appealed to? Familiar and awesome, Gods of the household."

For Lowell, too, Tate would remain a household god. As his career progressed, his acknowledgment of Tate as father-poet would disappear, yet his poems would continue to respond to Tate's in sometimes obvious and, more often, subtle ways. Lowell was actively writing poetry in 1950, but he would gradually come to feel that he had gone as far as he could with his old voice. Probably Randall Jarrell's frank 1951 review of *The Mills of the Kavanaughs* confirmed Lowell's sense that his poetry was self-limiting by its heavy allusiveness, its rhythmic intensity, its compressed and sometimes artificial syntax. Although the best poems of *Lord Weary's Castle* and *The Mills of the Kavanaughs* were stronger than most of Tate's work, they suffered from a similarly constricted and willed quality of language and syntax.

Lowell's sense of poetic argument, though, was stronger than Tate's, and consequently he had more faith in imagery. Tate occasionally weakened his poems by reverting to direct statement or abstraction—an error he surely did not pick up from Baudelaire. This is one of the problems that John Stewart refers to when he argues that the value of Tate's poetry "comes more from the knowledge of the human condition which it provides than from its artistic excellence." [26] One of Stewart's critical touchstones, that of seamless unity, is an arbitrary New Critical value that we might now question (though it is a value that Tate helped promote), but some of his other strictures still ring true. Because Tate does not always trust the image to convey the required feeling, he sometimes tries to wrestle it into a metaphor that, in its straining, fails to convey a seamless logic of association. Stewart quotes the section of "The Mediterranean" in which Tate "describes the breeze propelling a sailboat as being 'fierce as a body loved'" as an example. This also is an example of Tate's failure to trust his more natural speaking voice and the ordinary image and is a sign of his obsession with detail rather than the overall effect of the poem. Tate was not impressed with Stewart's critical acumen, and in a letter to Davidson, he calls Stewart's book a "very bad book."[27] In his response, Davidson complains at some length about Stewart and Princeton University Press and their mutual "carelessness about facts."[28] Tate gracefully accepted criticism similar to Stewart's from his poet friends (including Lowell), but he would not from mere academics.

Lowell and Tate had both become dissatisfied with their poetic voices—Tate after writing "The Eye" and Lowell after wrestling with the ultimately unsatisfying title poem of *The Mills of the Kavanaughs*. Later Lowell would suggest that the distinction he came to make was between symbolism and imagery,[29] a distinction referred to earlier as that between a symbolist and a documentary aesthetic. For him symbolism came to seem a weight of willed and obscure allusion, and imagery (echoing the long-standing poetic of William Carlos Williams) appeared to be the appropriate mode of the more natural voice of the free verse he would begin writing in the mid-1950s. Even the best writing in *The Mills of the Kavanaughs* seems a bit strained when compared to the easier syntax and the clearer, more pictorial, and more objectively presented imagery of *Life Studies:*

> Christ enticed
> Her heart that fluttered, while she whipped her hounds
> Into the quicksands of her manor grounds
> A lordly child, her habit fleur-de-lys'd
> There she dismounted, sick; with little heed,
> Surrendered.   ("Mother Marie Therese")

Randall Jarrell said, in 1951, that "'Mother Marie Therese' is the best poem Mr. Lowell has ever written," calling it "the most human and tender, the least specialized, of all Mr. Lowell's poems."[30] But its diction gives the impression of being forced, its imagery unevocative, compared to the best writing in *Life Studies:*

> I borrowed Grandfather's cane
> carved with the names and altitudes

of Norwegian mountains he had scaled—
more a weapon than a crutch.
I lanced it in the fauve ooze for newts.
In a tobacco tin after capture, the umber yellow mature newts
lost their leopard spots,
lay grounded as numb
as scrolls of candied grapefruit peel.
I saw myself as a young newt,
neurasthenic, scarlet
and wild in the wild coffee-colored water.   ("Dunbarton")

This imagery derives not from reading, from the traditional symbolism of the church, or from history but from direct observation and confrontation with memory and imagination. "Dunbarton" is the less showy but far more mature and sophisticated of the two. It does away with all of the obvious artifice of the earlier poem, all of the historical pomp and elaborate but constraining syntax; it substitutes a more direct and open vision in which the younger persona of the poet attains a dimension of actuality that was unobtainable through Lowell's earlier method. "Dunbarton" is also far more sophisticated in its imagery. The lines quoted above appeal to the sight, our sense of touch, and brilliantly link the mysterious otherness of nature (the newts) to the homey and familiar (candied grapefruit peel), then identify the child with that otherness rather than with a familiar domesticity. The argument here is between domesticity and otherness. The inherent wildness of the child (later to be willed into the domain of the unconscious) achieves a sensuous presence through Lowell's power to see things as they are and render that actuality in original metaphors. This shift from the symbolism of *Lord Weary's Castle*—with its Virgin Mary, its crucifixes, its rainbows, its dead Puritans, its saviors, and its Herods—to the images of newts, dirt piles, ponds, skunks, magnolias, and home furnishings decisively alters the tone of Lowell's poetry from strained grandeur to domestic musing. Lowell always had a more domestic subject matter available to him, but until the mid-1950s, he chose to deal with it in consciously formal terms. "In Memory of Arthur Winslow" and "My Last Afternoon with Uncle Devereaux Winslow" represent different, if perhaps equally successful, approaches to the problem of the family elegy, the first accepting the conventions of the formal elegy, the latter largely (though not entirely) ignoring them.

This breakthrough did not come quickly, nor did Lowell make it without the example of other poets. Tate's "The Buried Lake" and "The Swimmers" particularly impressed him, and the poetry of Williams, Bishop, and W. D. Snodgrass were important influences on his eventual abandonment of his earlier poetic and the invention of a new one. Lowell, in the early 1950s, was mired in his old style. Although he wrote a few fine poems (most notably "Beyond the Alps") between *The Mills of the Kavanaughs* and the *Life Studies* sequence, he floundered for several years. He spent the first two of those years in Europe—in Genoa, Florence, Paris, Greece, Turkey, Amsterdam, Heidelberg, Rome, and finally Venice. While he was there, *The Mills of the Kavanaughs* was published, his mother came to visit, and he suffered another breakdown, this one while lecturing at the Salzburg Seminars in August 1952.

Tate, meanwhile, had been appointed as a delegate to the Congress for Cultural Freedom in Paris in 1952. He had a pleasant reunion with Lowell in May and another in the fall when he visited Venice on a trip for UNESCO. It was after this last occasion that Tate wrote a rueful letter explaining that he had lost a gift from Lowell: "I'm terribly sorry I lost the Venetian glass. But Caroline is touched and grateful nonetheless."[31]

On this same day, 24 October, Tate wrote again with a new poem, a semiautobiographical poem of greater forthrightness and power than anything he had written previously. This was one of three new poems in terza rima that he would write in 1952 and 1953. The trilogy is the summit of his poetic achivement, but "The Swimmers," the second of these, was of the greatest aesthetic interest to Lowell. The trilogy, as a whole, still relies on the trappings of Christian symbolism, Christian allusion, and the conventions of the epic journey into the self which Tate had acquired from Virgil and Dante. Tate recasts these conventions into a highly original, three-part, post-Freudian study of memory and the individual, exemplifying the history of the race. In "The Swimmers," however, he abandons much of the inhibiting poetic baggage—the complex syntax, the portentous abstractions, the religious symbols—he had carried about with him since the 1920s. He had already composed "The Maimed Man," the first part of the trilogy, which Lowell would later echo in "The Severed Head" in *For the Union Dead*—a poem that Tate would single out for special praise. Tate had sent "The Maimed Man" to Donald Davidson, who immediately identified Virgil and Dante as its precursors. The first poem he sent to Lowell was "The Buried Lake," the third part in the final arrangement of the trilogy. The modesty of his letter barely conceals his justified pride in his achievement: "I started this poem two weeks ago . . . and wrote it in six days; the past week I've tinkered with it until it now seems to me what I want. I've never before written so many lines (126) in so short a time. Several good people tell me it is my best poem. Why shouldn't it be? St. Lucy is its patron." [32]

Lowell responded critically though favorably, but he would later assert an understandable preference for "The Swimmers" over "The Buried Lake." His letter of 5 November 1952, written from Rome, contains the fullest consideration he gives of any of Tate's poems and is worth careful examination. He begins by noting that Tate has found a new way to use his own life in his poetry, one that (in this poem, at least) is not exactly autobiographical but uses more fully his reserves of personal experiences and knowledge: "I think you've struck the wells of personal experience in your Buried Lake. I mean by personal, my feeling the push and tone of the poem are somehow the full you (more than ever before) not that this or that or any of the details are autobiographical." [33]

Next he considers the importance of the poem's formal shape as a means to self-revelation: "What your terza rima means to me, I think, is the terrific formal wrestling to speak out: 'imitate me if you have the presumption, Reader; what this has cost me is in the open.'"

Lowell indicates that he is not entirely satisfied with the results. The diction of "The Buried Lake" does not achieve the clarity of "The Swimmers," and Lowell argues that the poem "slides at times into muddiness." Tate has more or less denigrated the Romantics throughout his career, but Lowell knows that the essential comparison is to Shelley, though he avoids bringing up "The Triumph of Life," the best terza rima in English, and approaches the problem more obliquely: "In Shelley's West Wind, say, you feel how like breath the form is—with you, here and there, how like choking. You're more like Wyatt in the form than Dante."

The negative comparison to Dante is telling since the poem, in its final arrangement, embraces earthly and divine love as a single experience and bears a remote but distinct analogy to the *Paradiso*. Lowell is right—Tate's terza rima has nothing of Dante's ease, or even of Shelley's. English offers few rhyming words while Italian offers so many that a complex rhyme scheme for Dante was not a great challenge. The example of Shelley, though, shows that smooth terza rima is possible in English, if difficult.

Further, Lowell discovers some of the problems that Stewart would remark: "Also, I find a few repetitions of the Seasons, and Allenisms, i.e., tough wrenched words instead of the *mot juste*." Certainly this last difficulty is one that Lowell had come to recognize in his own work. The poems he had written up through *The Mills of the Kavanaughs* often force words into strained, cacophonous arrangements that create an effect of considerable power but occasionally seem merely willed. In pointing to this defect in Tate, he pointed to one of their major negative similarities. Surely this reinforced his growing sense that he needed to reconsider his own style. The direction he would eventually take is foreshadowed by his comment that the "young poets are going back to free verse," but he admires Tate's resolve to continue working with formal problems: "It cheers me up to see you using meter to smash into new ground."

Perhaps realizing that his strictures were not fully balanced by expression of the admiration he felt for Tate's new poem, Lowell wrote again on 28 November: "Your Buried Lake improves and softens with time and re-reading. It's surely the warmest, least armored, and most personal of your poems. I'm reminded most of the autumn section of the seasons, only you are now much simpler and can put in so much more. Nothing's harder than getting the unpretentious variety of letters or conversation into a poem. I've been turning out a lot lately, none of it good yet. It's either pedestrian, pompous or queer. But what I'm groping after really seems worth mastering."[34]

Lowell is praising qualities he would like to see in himself, but we might question whether Tate really had achieved so distinct a breakthrough. Lowell would achieve it only after first attempting a prose autobiography, part of which he revised into verse. Here he credits Tate with at least attempting the kind of poetry made famous by *Life Studies* and later made controversial, even notorious, by *The Dolphin*, but Tate does not go nearly so far in a new direction.

Tate's trilogy, as a whole, does "smash into new ground" in several ways. Unlike Williams's poetry, it does not break into new formal territory, and unlike Snodgrass's work, it does not deal with intimate family difficulties and feelings, but it does offer a fresh manner of examining the relationship between individual experience and the traditional body of knowledge and culture to which both Tate and Lowell felt committed. "The Swimmers" is autobiographical in the same sense that Lowell's *Life Studies* sequence would be, but each of these poems breaks new ground in bringing together Christian mythology, the Christian-epic conventions inherited from Dante, and a Freudian awareness of the self as something separate from, yet enclosed within, a hostile and difficult world. During Tate's lifetime, critics like John Stewart hesitated to comment on these poems on the grounds that the sequence was incomplete. Tate had planned seven parts, as he told Davidson in March of 1952, but he may well have ended the sequence when he considered that it was already complete. Regardless of his original intent, the trilogy is comprehensible as a unit. It is a very small-scale *Divine Comedy*, in which Christian motifs and autobiography mirror each other in a highly compressed but comprehensive argument among the individual ego, Christian idealism, the necessity of the loss of innocence and the assumption of guilt, and the universal healing power of love.

The headless figure of "The Maimed Man," as Robert Dupree argues, is "the symbol of the passive remnant of a once flourishing people."[35] It is a figure projected by the speaker's psyche, generated by his willingness to see the whole of Christian and pagan mythology brought to bear on the cultural present. As such, it is not merely the maimed representative of the antebellum South but of all civilization worthy of the name. This figure recurs in specifically southern terms as the hanged, mutilated black man of "The Swimmers," where it occasions the loss of innocence and the assumption of both individual and communal guilt on the part of the speaker, here a mere child. Once fully materialized and integrated within the speaker's psyche (as the embodiment of guilt, for Tate a necessary, natural emotion), the figure need not reappear in "The Buried Lake." This poem struggles to regain a vision in which guilt is not expunged for the speaker but is incorporated into a fallen, though still beautiful, natural world.

The identity of the various figures in the trilogy has caused critics some anguish, but granting them various roles resolves the apparent complexity of function. Like the lady in *Ash Wednesday*, they change as the speaker changes, and since their function is symbolic, they can maintain multiple identities. St. Lucy, for example, in "The Buried Lake," is the patron saint of music, the muse of poetry, the representative of the Virgin Mary, and the icon of human love. But the speaker himself is multiple in nature. In "The Maimed Man," he assumes a representative role; in "The Swimmers," he plays a specifically autobiographical role; and in "The Buried Lake," he resumes the stance of representative persona.

Both the representative suffering individual and the autobiographically specific self attain a psychological and aesthetic depth that is new to Tate's work, and this revamping of the speaker's role sets an example for Lowell. The representative sufferer easily shifts roles from epic voice to human witness:

Then, timeless Muse, reverse my time; unfreeze
  All that I was in your congenial heat;
  Tune me in recollection to appease

The hour when, as I sauntered down our street,
  I saw a young man there, headless, whose hand
  Hung limp; it dangled at his hidden feet. . . .

This confrontation with what becomes a form of alter ego recurs in Lowell's work, most notably in "The Severed Head." As R. K.

Meiners argues, "This confrontation with the alter ego has been obsessive with both men."[36] Lowell had learned from Tate how to dramatize that alter ego and how to give voice to a persona that can incorporate it into his consciousness. Meiners is correct in arguing that the superficial resemblances between the poems of Tate and Lowell mean little; it is the dealing with a dramatic confrontation with disparate aspects of the self that links the two poets here. This example did not necessarily make it possible for Lowell to write "The Severed Head," "Skunk Hour," and other poems in which the speaker feels that the constriction of his world is focusing him upon some distorted or maimed aspect of himself, but it did encourage him by the example of self-confrontation that Lowell praises in the opening of his 5 November letter.

The child persona of "The Swimmers" is more dramatically presented than the child persona of "My Last Afternoon with Uncle Devereaux Winslow" or "Dunbarton," but both function primarily as witness, secondarily in their willingness or need to assume the burden of what they have seen. "The Swimmers" uses an evocative summer setting to contrast with the cruelty of the unfolding drama, one in which the child has no direct part. "My Last Afternoon with Uncle Devereaux Winslow" does the same. Both narrators are passive, unable to fully comprehend what they witness, yet instinctly alert to its significance. Each child-narrator is more sensuously aware of the earth than of the dramatic horror unfolding before him:

> I knew I must
> Not stay till twilight in that silent road;
> Sliding my bare feet into the warm crust,
>
> I hopped the stonecrop like a panting toad
> Mouth open, following the heaving cloud
> That floated to the court-house square its load
>
> Of limber corpse. . . .   ("The Swimmers")

> Our farmer was cementing a root-house under the hill.
> One of my hands was cool on a pile
> of black earth, the other warm
> on a pile of lime.
>   ("My Last Afternoon with Uncle Devereaux Winslow")

In neither case is the child indifferent to the death that, in Tate's poem, has actually occurred or, in Lowell's, is forthcoming. Rather, as a child, he is limited in his options, forced by his immaturity into the role of bystander. Tate's child confronts the possibility of assuming a communal guilt and realizes the difficulty of admitting to the perceived crime:

> Alone in the public clearing
> This private thing was owned by all the town,
> though never claimed by us within my hearing.

Lowell's child-persona expresses his meager understanding of death in appropriate and sensuous imagery derived from a world already familiar to him:

> My hands were warm, then cool, on the piles
> of earth and lime,
> a black pile and a white pile. . . .   *(Lowell's ellipsis)*
> Come winter,
> Uncle Devereaux would blend to the one color.

Characteristically, Lowell's poem is more concrete and sensuous and creates the more convincing atmosphere, the stricter evocation of the child's point of view.

We might wonder, along with Meiners, what these resemblances and differences prove. Lowell is not merely imitating Tate. He became a poet under the mentorship of Tate, and his attachment to the elder poet is not merely personal; it is the relationship that Harold Bloom has so well described between the strong precursor poet and the ephebe who sets himself the task of rewriting—not merely imitating—the precursor's work. The relationship is more complicated, though, because after *Lord Weary's Castle*, Lowell is the stronger poet. When Tate comes to realize this, and realizes that, by the late 1950s, his own poetic career is complete, he rebels against the reversal of roles. Confronted with Lowell's most revisionary poetry—that of *Life Studies*—he simply declares the younger poet mad again. Still later though, perhaps realizing the importance of his own role in Lowell's success, Tate will reconcile himself to becoming the elder statesman and will show more critical flexibility in dealing with Lowell's further shifts of style.

103

Mastery and Madness

In that same 28 November letter praising "The Buried Lake," Lowell muses over his future with the growing confidence of an accomplished poet who is now assured of employment and can even bargain for terms: "The Kenyon business is the fault of my vagueness, or rather of my putting off deciding. It has been tempting to think of remaining in Europe almost forever, though I've never thought I would in earnest. In fact, I've by now almost accepted an offer from Paul Engle of Shapiro's job—commuting between Iowa and Chicago has been too much for him. It's $2000 for one course, supposedly two hours a week; I want to get it lifted [to] $2,500 or $3,000 for two courses. In that case I'll take it."[1]

The "Kenyon business" refers to the summer school that Ransom had begun some years before. In 1953 it would move to Bloomington, where Lowell would teach despite the tardiness in responding to Ransom's offer. The Iowa job came through on Lowell's terms, and by January 1953, he had returned from Europe and settled in Iowa City again.

Tate visited the Lowells in March. In a letter following their meeting, Lowell, after thanking Tate for his good fellowship, reinforces his praise of the terza rima poems:

104

I've been reading over the Swimmers a lot (Title unclear in itself, but not in the group) and now think it or the Buried Lake are the best poems you've written. The whole works ought to carry anyone's head off. Have you ever thought of doing a terza rima version of the Tournament of the Fathers? and perhaps something along the lines of your first lost chapter to the Monteagle novel. Then maybe something about Crane and New York, Ford and Provence. You have enough symbolism and abstraction to carry any amount of autobiography. Anyway I think you've got the bag you want to put all your apples in. The simple straight honesty of the swimmers takes art beyond itself.[2]

Lowell may not have been entirely serious about the terza rima version of the tournament in *The Fathers*, but he seemed to feel that, like himself, Tate needed to write autobiography and required encouragement in that direction. A few years later, Lowell would receive this same encouragement from Elizabeth Bishop, but he would write genuinely autobiographical poetry only after he had dropped his own tendency toward "symbolism and abstraction." In the early 1950s, he had not yet seen how necessary that step was, how difficult writing autobiography would be with those writers' tools he had praised Tate for possessing. He still thought of Tate's poetic development in terms he would like to have applied to himself. His own poem about Ford Madox Ford, for example, one of a series of reminiscences of writers he had known or admired, would appear in April 1954. It was unsuccessful although it was a more forthright, less symbolic, less abstract poem than most of what he had written to this point. It was still a step or two from the breakthrough into the colloquial imagism of the *Life Studies* group of autobiographical poems.

This same letter touches on the painful subject of Catholicism. Tate had finally joined the church in December 1950, and he and Gordon were eager for Lowell to resume his own religious life. Lowell's comments on this matter were not encouraging: "To tell the truth, I'm getting a lot of Catholic invitations, to join their panel of authors, etc. and find answering embarrassing. I'm not a Catholic, and find more and more that the only act of faith that I personally can make is that *I don't know what I don't know*. You, of course, accept this too; but for me, it's necessary that I stop there, for beyond it, there's only confusion and impossibility. This formula gives me personally a way of life that's sufficiently consistent, a spine no doubt that holds my head up—but I don't want to go on and be a bore."

Lowell would put religion even more decisively at arms' length in a letter responding to Tate's proposal for a Catholic writers' conference to be held in Newburgh, New York: "I'd like to come next summer, and maybe have a sort of discussion class in poetry. I'd like to make the proposal that art and religion *per se* have nothing to do with each other, but that in this imperfect world they are always colliding—they are always exploiting, avoiding and abusing each other, and that this is as it should be."[3]

Well aware of how extreme a position he would be taking, he directed this proposal to a conference that would involve the *Catholic Worker* staff and other Catholic intellectuals. Tate was emphatically Roman Catholic in the early 1950s, and Lowell's proposal to insist on the distance between art and religion could not have sat well with him. When Lowell had been a fervent Catholic, Tate had been neutral on the subject. Now Lowell proposed such neutrality for himself. The apprentice and the master had exchanged places once again. Lowell was only following Tate's argument in his 1951 essay "To Whom is the Poet Responsible?" which is concerned primarily with questions of political responsibility: "He [the poet] is responsible to his conscience, in the French sense of the word: the joint action of knowledge and judgment."[4] For Lowell, knowledge of eternal things now seemed an honest absence of knowledge, and conscience would not allow him to pretend otherwise.

Lowell knew that Catholicism was a pressing issue for Tate at this time, but he could no longer share Tate and Gordon's seriousness. His letter even mockingly begins "Dear Allen / Father Tate," referring to Tate's professed religious stance rather than to his relationship with Lowell. The entire tone of the letter is playful, and like the one of 15 March, it ends on a note of friendship and harmony. The ending of the earlier letter is explicit in its profession of continued friendship: "We seem to have come awfully close in an odd way . . . I was about to say that friendships are kept alive by the integrity that stands up to differences, but fare-well to sententiousness."

Tate certainly shared this commitment to friendship. In theory, he probably agreed with Lowell's point about "differences," but his reply to the 15 April letter about the writers' conference re-buffed Lowell for making light of matters he once took more seri-ously. Like any recent convert, Tate was slightly brittle about his dogmas and his response was humorless: "You've got to stop sa-luting me as Father Tate. I am not qualified to be anything like that. My situation seems to get rougher all the time, and the lines drawn; but where it will end nobody knows but God, who has His reasons for not taking me into His confidence. I patiently await the moment of revelation."[5]

In response, Lowell dismissed his own playfulness and respect-fully acknowledged Tate's newfound faith, but he made it clear that human, not spiritual, qualities were what he most valued in his mentor: "*Father Tate* was a joke. God is holding you, and you are standing up almost better than a man can. It seems to me that in the last two years or so, something human has grown in you without your really knowing it, all you could ask for has, though it's not what you would ask for, gives no pledges, or cushions. I liked what Arthur [Mizener] and Delmore [Schwartz] said in their reviews. The poems show the same things only with far more blood and body. But I was talking personally."[6]

Lowell's retreat from Catholicism also caused some friction in his relationship with Caroline Gordon, and he regretted that dis-tancing. Gordon was more committed to Catholicism than Tate, at least as obsessed with it as Lowell had been in his fiery early days of conversion. Her concern for Lowell's soul was genuine, and she was apparently hurt by what she saw as his apostasy. He recog-nized and rued the coolness that had grown between them and addressed it in this same letter: "I have been thinking about Caro-line a lot lately. I think we look at each other for the moment from behind fences, which is natural and right. One has to will and take positions, and once those positions have been assumed, there's no communion or even communication or talking without fences. But some day we will look at mushrooms or pictures together and talk ourselves blue, and all will be the same." In November of 1955, Lowell quietly rejoined the Episcopal church of his family and childhood.

Lowell was no longer as dependent on Tate's influence in job-seeking as formerly, but the older poet continued to help out with recommendations when required. Lowell made the rounds of writers' conferences, and in April 1953, the University of Cincinnati offered him their Chair of Poetry for January to June of 1954. Tate, equally in demand for visiting professorships, writers' conferences, and lectures, had accepted a permanent position in 1951 at the University of Minnesota, where he would remain until he retired. His peripatetic life, even with his home base established, would continue to be hectic and remain so throughout the 1950s. He apparently complained a little about his demanding schedule, and Lowell, in the same letter of 29 April in which he discussed his relationship with Gordon, responded: "I know a bit at least in imagination how you feel. I go to a poetry conference at Grinnell tonight, next Wednesday to Illinois, then Indiana, then here for the fall, then Cincinnati."

This is the characteristic life of the successful American poet established in the academic world, and Lowell and Tate would suffer and enjoy it for most of their remaining years. At the end of a peaceful year spent mostly in Iowa, Lowell wrote again to inform Tate of his pleasantly ordinary domestic life:

> Great changes in our lives! Last spring I bought a 1937 Packard, after a Dutch friend on a fellowship streamed through here in his new Studebaker and took us to an Iowa State Park, and I felt we were the only people in the world cut off from American progress. Now after six months, believe it or not, not an accident, not a scar, only safe misfortunes, such as letting my battery run down. I drive haltingly, as I imagine your cousin the Rev. Myers of Sewanee must. After that we bought a house in Duxbury Mass. near Plymouth. It's a section heavy with Pilgrim history and monuments and immortalized by Longfellow, but charming, with a three mile beach, and forty miles from Boston. The house was built in 1740 and has a 1950 oil furnace. We are gaily paying our monthly mortgages and wishing we were there. You must visit us when you return, Heroes from Italy.[7]

The frequency of the 1953 correspondence did not continue, and letters between the Tates and Lowell became annual or semiannual events for the next few years. In February 1954, with the Lowells only recently settled in Cincinnati, they received the news that Charlotte Lowell had suffered a stroke while wintering in Italy. Lowell immediately flew to Rapallo and arrived on the night of his mother's death. From there he wrote to the Tates: "My mother died here on Sunday night an hour after I arrived after flying from Cincinnati to Boston-New York-London-Paris-Milan etc. I'll be here from Wed. night till Sunday when I will sail back with her on the Constitution from Genoa. I don't suppose there's any chance of seeing you. There's nothing practical for once that I need your help for." [8]

That Lowell would turn to the Tates at such a devastating moment (Lowell and his mother were very close though they could hardly bear each other's company—thus the Duxbury house, forty safe miles from Boston) shows how important they were to him, and yet the closing sentences suggests that Lowell did not quite know what they meant to him, how they fit into his life. Certainly he did not want to think of them as parental substitutes; he wanted nothing to interfere with his grief for his mother, and yet, at that moment, it was as parental figures that he needed them, not for anything "practical."

Tate, though, was well aware of Lowell's ambivalent feelings about his mother. He had experienced Charlotte Lowell mostly as caretaker of the mad or unreliable son, but he knew how mutually dependent mother and son were. Shortly after Charlotte Lowell's death, he wrote to Lowell about his understanding of the mother-son relationship in regard to his own situation: "I am mightily glad to hear from you. We were much depressed that you had to make that long voyage for such a sad purpose. I am glad it is over. What one feels about one's parents after they are dead is subtly different as time passes. I am sure that my own relation to my mother was quite as unhappy as your own; but after twenty-five years it is now something else; and I feel now that she is trying to get free of me, rather than the other way around." [9]

Unusual for Tate in their reference to deep personal feeling, his comments touched Lowell and revealed probably more than intended. His reply (15 March 1954) acknowledges Tate's insight and extends it to his own situation:

> What you say of Mother hits home. At the end, she really was trying to free herself from me. And in her last months she *had*, at least for the moment. I am surprised how many people loved her. You won't understand this. But when they met her without me or my Father, marvelous qualities came out. A boldness and humor—all her own. I saw this more and more last fall when I was with her. Together, except sometimes when we were alone, we sat like stones on each other's head—inhibiting and inhibited. But with a drink or two and me in the distance people were charmed.[10]

His father had died in 1950, and now, with the death of his mother, Lowell was free to write as he pleased of his childhood and his parents. The next year, 1955, he would begin a prose autobiography, one section of which he published as "91 Revere Street." He later rewrote other portions in verse which became "My Last Afternoon with Uncle Devereaux Winslow" and some of the other *Life Studies* poems. Lowell's mother had indeed been obsessed with her son, and he remained obsessed with her until near the end of his life when he would write "Unwanted," a great inchoate purge of a poem. Freedom for both mother and son meant separation, so Lowell could not live in Boston while she was alive. Now he sold the Duxbury house and moved to Commonwealth Avenue, then to Marlborough Street in Back Bay, the same street his parents had lived on in the later years of their marriage.

Following his praise of Tate's insight, Lowell asked for permission to "Say something about the Fathers" and then proceeded to criticize Tate's novel for an air of unreality, for characters lacking dimension: "One feels that the melodrama is conventional, like some Elizabethan tragedies—Tourneur, for instance. One has been there before, but your characters aren't there, never could be, the air withers them."

Why attack Tate's novel of the 1930s now? Lowell had no doubt read the book many times before. Discussing his mother with Tate had put him on the defensive and he needed somehow to assert himself. Writing was the one area in which he could feel himself Tate's equal, so perhaps, by criticizing *The Fathers,* he could dispel that eerie feeling of learning that his friends understood his relationship with his parents better than he did.

Whether or not this conjecture is accurate, Lowell's urge to criticize immediately faded, and in the same paragraph, he turned again to Tate's recent poems as a source of wonder and admiration. Perhaps, instead of the more psychological reason, Lowell's urge to criticize came from this further contemplation of "The Swimmers," suggesting to him again how well Tate could handle narrative in formally complex verse. His admiration of the poetry is genuine: "But your poetry is different. There you have a hand of iron. I think the lynching section of your new poem ['"The Swimmers"] is the best thing you've ever done, the best terza rima in English. Better than Shelley even, for you have more weight. you know now how to write from what you are instead of fancying. Would I did! I have about a third of a book now and may send the lot on to you one of these days. The first part of your novel, by the way, really has the atmosphere that I was trying to (and occasionally *do*) get in my Kavanaughs, which you have never read."

No more qualification of the praise, no more hesitancy in comparing Tate's terza rima to Shelley's. "The Swimmers" suggested to Lowell the kind of poetry he now most wanted to write, a poetry written out of himself instead of out of his "fancy"—this term probably used as Coleridge used it. Certainly the lynching scene (post-lynching, actually) is powerfully written, the sections linked together by end-rhymes but by strong alliteration and assonance. The end-rhymes, though stressed, flow naturally and unobtrusively. The scene is nightmarish, not in the conventional Southern Gothic manner, but in the more Sophoclean way that it deals with the dramatic aftermath of violence:

The melancholy sheriff slouched beneath
  A giant sycamore; shaking his head
  He plucked a sassafras twig and picked his teeth:

'We come too late.' He spoke to the tired dead
  Whose ragged shirt soaked up the viscous flow
  Of blood in which It lay discomfited.

111

A butting horse-fly gave one ear a blow
   And glanced off, as the sheriff kicked the rope
   Loose from the neck and hooked it with his toe

Away from the blood.—I looked back down the slope:
   The friends were gone that I had hoped to greet.—
   A single horseman came at a slow lope

And pulled up at the hanged man's horny feet;
   The sheriff noosed the feet, the other end
   The stranger tied to his pommel in a neat

Slip-knot. I saw the Negro's body bend
   And straighten, as a fish-line cast transverse
   Yields to the current that it must subtend.

This passage—the entire poem for that matter—displays none of Tate's characteristic flaws. More than "The Buried Lake," it clearly represents an amalgamation of experience, a product of the true Coleridgean imagination, not merely cerebral fancy. Lowell had certainly written verse of equal quality, but Tate's poem represented something Lowell had not yet done, a self-probing or plunge into memory that would both free him of family ghosts and offer a broader, more flexible poetic.

The "third of a book" that Lowell had written probably included a number of poems that he later rejected for inclusion in *Life Studies*. It certainly included the poems he had sent Tate after the publication of *Mills of the Kavanaughs,* including "Epitaph of a Fallen Poet" (an early version of "Words for Hart Crane"), "Santayana's Farewell to his Nurses" (which he would expand into "For George Santayana"), "On Stuyvesant Square During a Blizzard" (later "Inauguration Day: 1953"), "From Rome to Paris" (an early six-stanza version of "Beyond the Alps"), and "A Mad Negro Soldier Confined at Munich" (on this typescript, Tate inexplicably wrote "Author unknown").[11] Also among these poems of the early 1950s is a curious item, previously unpublished, that is typed with a different ribbon on the same page as "On Stuyvesant Square," and it probably is in response to "The Buried Lake":

Mastery and Madness

Orley, oily, greasy Tate,
Slugging out three-bagger rimes,
While the batter at homeplate,

Watching how your digit climbs
Over short and center field,
Stoops to running down the times—

May Mercurial, winged-heeled
Verse of mine line-drive the blue
Formlessness my heart has sealed,

Faithlessly, with much ado,
My chalk, scratching on the slate,
Gives short shrift, then snaps in two,

Like Pope Alexander's state,
Gouged from Caesar, Master Tate.[12]

This odd mixture of seriousness and playfulness acknowledges Tate as the master poet, but the humorous declension from "Orley" to "greasy" is hardly complimentary. The slugger is no doubt Lowell. To outdo Tate, slugger of triples, Lowell clearly has to hit a home run and "line drive the blue / Formlessness," which may refer to the ineffable, to free verse, or to Lowell's new agnosticism. Lowell's current difficulties in writing poetry cause his chalk to snap in two, and the obscure ending, sacrificing clarity for the amusing reversal of Pope's name—linking Pope and the Master, who wrote a memorable poem about Pope—suggests that Tate, being a classicist, resembles the England of Pope's time. This England, once conquered by the Caesars but long since wrestled from their grasp, still paid homage (in the period known as the Augustan or the neoclassical age) to its classical past.

The poem about Tate illustrates little more than Lowell's admiration, alloyed with a slightly malicious envy for his mentor's recent achievements. The other poems demonstrate his continued allegiance to formal verse and to a learned rather than a more immediate and sensuous body of reference. They depend less on traditional symbols and attempt, within their controlled metric, to

113

reproduce some of the immediacy of conversation. Although the poems of *Lord Weary's Castle* have autobiographical elements, they are overlaid by conventional religious symbols that subordinate the experience of the speaker to its larger significance. In two discarded stanzas of "From Rome To Paris" (a few passages found their way into "For George Santayana"), Lowell presents a conversation with Santayana as a complex, significant encounter. Despite the conversational subject of Christ and the church, these stanzas center in the psychology of the dying man and the speaker's own religious doubts:

> Life is for children. At the hospital,
> Sister Angelica received my call
> Bluely, and put me in your shoes a mile
> From nowhere, Santayana. When you died,
> True to your boyish shyness of the Bride,
> No shock of recognition made her smile.
> While the rash Texan Thomist, sent to task
> Your old Franciscan wrapper's Mongol mask,
> Loiters, I see your child's red pencil pass,
> Bleeding deletions on the proofs you hold
> Under your throbbing magnifying glass,
> That worn arena where the whirling sand
> And broken hearted lions lick your hand,
> Refined as yellow as a lump of gold.
>
> "Spirit gives life," you say, "will letters kill
> The calm eccentric, if by heaven's will
> He found the Church too good to be believed?
> *He died,* the nuns will tell you, *as he lived.*
> That's how they rhyme and riddle what I wrote
> Of Christ, whose faith is too pragmatical
> To nurse illusion long. Believing Paul,
> Most miserable of men, had missed the boat
> By preaching truth was what his hand could reach,
> I gave the bottomless Evangel soul.
> Essence took heart and landscape from my speech.
> Dying, I fancied the Blue Sisters pressed
> Like geese-girls, hissing, Rome must give her best.
> Till Curtius in full armor filled the hole." [13]

114

The finished version of "Beyond the Alps," the first poem in *Life Studies*, takes as its theme the gap between the culture of the European past and a present in which even the Pope shaves with an electric razor. The Alps embody the gap that also separates Rome and Paris and their respective significance in European culture. Further, they embody the difficulty of conquering cultures and forging new art. Appropriately, the poem is written in a style halfway between the symbol-laden formally conventional poems of *Lord Weary's Castle* and the looser, more personal, more sensuous free-verse poems of *Life Studies*. The best poems in *Mills of the Kavanaughs* also depend less on the manipulation of symbols and more on an experiential voice, but as dramatic monologues with carefully objectified personae, they lack the immediacy of the more personal voice of "Beyond the Alps." The poems that Lowell would write a few years later went even farther beyond the Alps, farther than Tate at first was willing to follow.

A month or so after his 15 March letter, Lowell suffered another breakdown and consequently spent much of the spring and summer of 1954 in various hospitals. Tate returned to Minnesota from his travels in Italy and promptly embarked on another series of lectures and visiting professorships until the following summer when he returned to Europe. Lowell, meanwhile, settled down in Boston, first on Commonwealth Avenue and then, in late fall of 1955, on Marlborough Street. By February 1955, Hardwick reported him at work on a series of autobiographical prose pieces that, with revision, would become some of the important free-verse poems of *Life Studies*. On 15 October 1955, Hardwick wrote to Tate and informed him that Lowell was teaching at Boston University, "feeling quite himself and writing some delightful prose reminiscences of his youth, of old Grandfather Winslow houses, his father's resigning from the Navy, Uncle Devereaux dead at 30 or so. This work is quite unique, I think."[14] These pieces became "91 Revere Street," the only autobiographical prose published in Lowell's lifetime, and the poems "My Last Afternoon with Uncle Devereaux Winslow" and, possibly, "Grandparents" and "Dunbarton."

The next year was nearly devoid of communication between the

Lowells and the Tates. An uneventful year for Lowell (though he spent it working on his prose pieces), 1956 was difficult for the Tates. Shortly after buying still another house in Princeton, they separated again, this time for good. Gordon went to work at Columbia to support herself, and Tate went on a State Department trip to India before resuming his old life in Minneapolis. In January 1957, he won the Bollingen Prize, and that same month, Lowell's daughter Harriet was born. "Mother and child flourishing," Lowell telegraphed to Tate.[15]

In March, Lowell went on a West Coast reading tour. Encouraged by his recent prose composition, by his discussions and correspondence with William Carlos Williams, and by the general loosening of American verse since the 1940s, he was revising his poems as he read them, adding words, translating Latin phrases, adding syllables to tightly metred lines. This process enabled him to discover continuities between his prose writing and his poetry, and he began to rework some of his prose into verse—strictly metered and rhymed verse at first, then revised further into free verse that retained some of the rhymes. Prose was difficult for Lowell; verse seemed his more natural form of expression. Later he comments, "I found it got awfully tedious working out transitions and putting in things that didn't seem very important but were necessary to the prose continuity. Also, I found it hard to revise. Cutting it down into small bits, I could work on it much more carefully and make fast transitions."[16]

He then argues that the craft of poetry has become a matter of mechanical competence, that proficiency and inspiration have become divorced. Prose now seems a source of vitality "less cut off from life than poetry is." His most telling statement, "I couldn't get my experience into tight metrical forms," is rather like Williams's "No man can say what he means and rhyme."[17] Experience, not the tradition, is now the touchstone of Lowell's poetry and would remain so, more or less, for the rest of his career. He never abandoned the craft of poetry—in fact, he argued, in reference to Snodgrass's *Heart's Needle* poems, that the more personal and direct the poem the more important the role of craft in keeping the poetry from becoming lugubrious. Craft had become commonplace—what the 1950s required was inspiration. In the end, Lowell argues in the same interview, craft is somewhat beside the point: "I'm sure that writing isn't a craft; that is, something for which you learn the skills and go on turning out. It must come from some deep impulse, deep inspiration."[18]

Lowell's letters to Tate in the early 50s reveal this shift in his poetic from literary tradition to experience. Although Lowell thought he saw Tate to be moving in the same direction, the older poet was unprepared for the poems he received that November. During the summer of 1957, Lowell worked on a group of eleven poems, a number of them being revisions of work already in hand, such as "Beyond the Alps" and "Epitaph of a Fallen Poet"; others, like "Skunk Hour," were written as free verse from the start; and still others were worked out of his autobiographical prose pieces. He confided in William Carlos Williams, who could be counted on for empathy and support: "I've been writing poems like a house on fire, i.e. for me that means five in six weeks, fifty versions of each. I've been experimenting with mixing loose and free meters with strict in order to get more accuracy, naturalness and multiplicity of the prose, yet, I also want the state and surge of the old verse, the carpentry of definite meter that tells me when to stop rambling."[19]

These new poems owe little to Williams, except as an example of a more documentary aesthetic than Lowell was ready to embrace. The example is important and indicates the direction Lowell was taking, but the more important figures at this time were Tate and Elizabeth Bishop. Both offered examples of carefully controlled, yet seeming casual, verse in which the rhythm seemed intrinsic to the personal speaking voice. Tate remained the polished formal poet, but Bishop offered something freer, though not as free (not as uncontrolled, as perhaps Lowell sometimes thought) as Williams. Bishop had become particularly important to Lowell as a poetic model, and in 1957, he regarded her as "sort of a bridge between Tate's formalism and Williams's informal art."[20] Lowell was not yet prepared to commit himself to a Williams-style free verse. He had tried that in his undergraduate years, and it had not served him nearly as well as Tate's formalism. He was not prepared to abandon Tate's strict idea of craft, but he wanted a poetry that seemed more personal, more immediate, more flexible without going slack. Bishop offered one such example, but as he commented to Williams, "There's no ideal form that does for any two of us, I think."[21]

This was also true with subject matter. For Lowell, autobiography meant the drama of his childhood, poems about his relatives, poems about his parents and his relationship with them. Bishop expressed envy of his background, which gave his family an intrinsic interest that few others' families could arouse. She worried that if she tried to write such autobiographical or family poetry, about her "uncle Artie, say," no one would be interested. Her family was not famous like the Lowells and Winslows. Although this sounds disingenuous, since she had already published two successful stories in the early 1950s—"Gwendolyn" and "In the Village"—which are fascinating fragments of thinly disguised autobiography, Bishop may have meant that the prominence of Lowell's ancestry gave him an aesthetic assurance that became an intrinsic and important aspect of his poetic. In this regard, class and aesthetic issues mingle. Any good writer can excite an interest in any character, but a subject who is already famous gives the literary work an additional impetus, and an author with a famous name has himself as a character worth exploiting. Bishop's admiration for Lowell's new poems was wholehearted; she knew how hard he had worked to make literature out of the facts and impressions of his family's past and his childhood. Her long dust-jacket statement for the American edition of Lowell's book makes clear her understanding of his aesthetic: "As a child, I used to look at my grandfather's Bible under a powerful reading-glass. The letters assembled beneath the lens were suddenly like a Lowell poem, as big as life and as alive, and rainbow-edged. It seemed to illuminate as it magnified; it could also be used as a burning-glass."[22]

Bishop is describing how Lowell changed his material by rendering it life-size and brightly illuminated, the dross surrounding each incident, each indelible sense-impression, burnt away as if by a powerful glass. This is apparently how autobiographical poetry fictionalizes: by selecting and highlighting, as well as by artful arrangement and calculated tone. Lowell, in a later interview, described how he had fictionalized his apparently diaristic poems:

"They're not always factually true. There's a good deal of tinkering with fact. You leave out a lot, and emphasize this and not that. Your actual experience is a complete flux. I've invented facts and changed things, and the whole balance of the poem was something invented."[23] Still, he wanted these poems to render the illusion of nonfiction: "Yet there's this thing: if a poem is autobiographical— and this is true of any kind of autobiographical writing and of historical writing—you want the reader to say, This is true."

Lowell then worked on these autobiographical poems with much the same craft and consideration he had brought to his work in the past. A glance at any of the poems demonstrates how tightly controlled the rhythms are, how adroitly the sound of the lines reinforces the imagery. The third verse-paragraph of "Commander Lowell," with its careful end and internal rhymes, its open vowel rhymes ("dress sword with gold braid"), and its concise and accurate syntax, exemplifies the care with which he wrote these poems:

> "Anchors aweigh," Daddy boomed in his bathtub,
> "Anchors aweigh,"
> when Lever Brothers offered to pay
> him double what the Navy paid.
> I nagged for his dress sword with gold braid,
> and cringed because Mother, new
> caps on all her teeth, was born anew
> at forty. With seamanlike celerity,
> Father left the Navy,
> and deeded Mother his property.

Far from depending on previous knowledge of the Lowells and Winslows, these poems engage the reader through their sensuous appeal to the ear and also through the brilliance and clarity of their imagery in the mind's eye. What do we need to know about the Lowell family to appreciate the evocative opening of "Terminal Days at Beverly Farms"?

> At Beverly Farms, a portly, uncomfortable boulder
> bulked in the garden's center—
> an irregular Japanese touch.

119

A poet who can describe a boulder as "portly, uncomfortable" needs no famous-family background to sustain his readers' interest, but Lowell goes beyond local effect in adapting his autobiographical material to the demands of his aesthetic. As M. L. Rosenthal first noted, the completed *Life Studies* is a sequence in which interrelationships create a larger context that deepens the impact of the individual poems. Lowell's achievement, critics have generally agreed, is complex in that he broke new ground, not only in the individual poems, but in the group as a whole by further extending the modern concept of the poetic sequence. Although some reviewers would side with Tate in preferring the earlier poems for their powerful sense of metaphor (for instance, DeSales Standerwick writing in *Renascence*) and some would express other forms of doubt (the editor of the *Hudson Review* found the book "lazy and anecdotal") [24] most found Lowell's new work to be fascinating and original.

Far from being fascinated or impressed, Tate missed the aesthetic implications of Lowell's new poetic and saw it only as a manifestation of poor judgment and mental incompetence. On 3 December 1957, he wrote to Lowell and urged him to keep the family poems, which he found deeply flawed, to himself:

> I've been reading and rereading your poems. It is very difficult to decide just what I think about them. But I'm going to try to sort out my thoughts and give them to you quite candidly.
>
> To begin with, of the unpublished pieces, only one seems to me to be at all up to your old standard: "Skunk Hour," a very fine poem. I am not sure whether "Inauguration Day 1953" has been published. It is not one of your very best, but it is good, and you could publish it without compromise.
>
> But *all* the poems about your family, including the one about you and Elizabeth, are definitely bad. I do not think that you ought to publish them. You didn't ask me whether they ought to be published, but I put the matter from this point of view in order to underline my anxiety about them. I do not mean to say that in some of these there are not sharp and even brilliant passages, like the old Cal; it is simply that by and large, and in the total effect, the poems are composed of unassimilated details, terribly intimate and coldly noted, which might well have been transferred from the notes for your autobiography without change.

The free-verse, arbitrary and without rhythm, reflects this lack of imaginative focus. Your fine poems in the past present a formal ordering of highly intractable materials; but there is an imaginative thrust towards a symbolic order which these new poems seems to lack. The new ones sound to me like messages to yourself, or perhaps they are a heroic effort of the will to come to terms with the harsh incongruities of your childhood and of your later struggle with your parents, and you are letting these scattered items of experience have their full impact upon your sensibility.

Quite bluntly, these details, presented in *causerie* and at random, are of interest only to you. And I am disturbed that you may not see this yourself. They are, of course, of great interest to me because I am one of your oldest friends. But they have no public and literary interest.[25]

Tate's objections center on three important points. The first is his mistaken assumption that the standards for prose autobiography and for poetry are distinctly different, a distinction to which Lowell clearly did not accede. Quite the contrary, he relied on prose now as a source of the more flexible voice that would be, as he said in the interview quoted above, "less cut off from life." He had done exactly what Tate suggested he has done: he had transferred the "notes" for his prose autobiography into his verse "without change"—except to subject them to the compression and aesthetic reworking necessary to make them into poetry. Secondly, Tate could not hear Lowell's free verse. His ear for .meter was nearly perfect, as his own poems demonstrate, but, perhaps for that very reason, free verse to him often seemed lacking in rhythm although he appreciated, to a certain extent, the free verse of Pound's *Pisan Cantos*. Perhaps he simply could not believe that a poet as accomplished in formal meters as Lowell could abandon them. Why he did not detect the pronounced rhythmic scheme underlying Lowell's free, but fairly regularly stressed, verse is a mystery. Third, his inability to see how imagery and metaphor can make arguments by sheer juxtaposition, a process that Eliot described in 1921 in his famous essay on the metaphysical poets, rendered him unable to see that Lowell's details are, in fact, assimilated into "new wholes" (Eliot's phrase) that, if not always readily accessible to prose logic, are emotionally and sensuously clear.[26]

The first point Tate makes as an explicit argument. The second point depends on the reader's willingness to hear that such lines as

> There were no undesirables or girls in my set,
> when I was a boy at Mattapoisett—
> only Mother, still her Father's daughter.
> Her voice was still electric
> with a hysterical, unmarried panic,
> when she read to me from the Napoleon book

are, with their more or less regularly spaced and carefully controlled stresses, as effectively rhythmic (though not metrical) as Lowell's earlier poems. Rhythm and meter, as Tate surely knew, are not synonymous; meter is merely an arbitrary means of describing regular rhythms. Tate did not complain of a lack of regularity or the difficulty of describing this rhythm in metrical terms; he claimed that these poems, including "Commander Lowell," are "without rhythm," which is an absurd contention.

The third point refers to an issue of which Tate was not conscious, one that requires further exploration. The argument has already been made that Tate's poems occasionally suffer from the intrusion of abstract language where another poet might rely more heavily on metaphor. In "The Man of Letters in the Modern World," which was written in 1951, Tate argues against "mere sensation" as a route to secularization and worries that too great a reliance on sensation will lead to the kind of "specialization" that divorces "poetry from thought."[27] Yet sensation, or the approach to it through images of sense-appeal, is a form of thought, as the image of blowing leaves in "Ode to the Confederate Dead" illustrates. Tate did not devalue metaphor—quite the contrary; he devoted much critical ink to explaining its efficacy—but he wanted, perhaps too desperately, to reserve a place in the poem for that which is all too obviously "thought." The consequence, in his criticism, was that he found it difficult to see how fully image and metaphor, by mere juxtaposition without the intervention of abstract language, can encompass entire worlds of reference. The fact that his own poems, at their best, employ image and metaphor effectively does not matter. He wrote a superb essay on Dickinson, a profoundly oblique poet who is nearly devoid of the kind of "thought" that so often intrudes into Tate's own poetry, but he failed to see that Keats's "pictorial" method as he called it, is an active, expansive form of thinking. This led him into the absurdity of declaring that "'Ode to Autumn' is a very nearly perfect piece of style, but it has little to say."[28] Helen Vendler has aptly rejoined by arguing that the poem "says everything" and has demonstrated, in her 1983 study of Keats, how thoroughly and satisfactorily the "pictorial" method encompasses Keats's major concerns, how effectively it uses imagery to appeal to the senses and render a complex argument in a few perfectly chosen images. Apparently more sympathetic to Dickinson than to Keats, Tate sensibly assesses the place of "ideas" in her poetry in a manner that could have been extended to Keats as well: "Miss Dickinson and John Donne would have this in common: their sense of the natural world is not blunted by a too rigid system of ideas; yet the ideas, the abstractions, their education or their intellectual heritage, are not so weak as to let their immersion in nature, or their purely personal quality, get out of control."[29]

This is a reasonable positioning of sensation and thought in poetry insofar as they can be separated. The problem was that, for Tate, they were absolutely separate. What he missed is that, for Donne (as Eliot told us), Dickinson, Keats, and the Lowell of *Life Studies*, sensation *is* thought. The imagination, as described by Coleridge, transforms sensation and thought into a single entity by amalgamating sense-perceptions, ideas, emotions, and whatever other mental baggage into a unit that, if one is a poet, is best expressed as metaphor, symbol, or simply image. Tate knew this, as he knew that free verse has a rhythm; but this knowledge did not function consistently, and he would not or could not apply it to Lowell's new poems.

Why did Tate's most supple critical self resist these poems? Perhaps because, as already has been suggested, he had decided that Lowell was a fine formalist poet and should remain one, or possibly he resented Lowell's family background. Tate was also family-conscious and may have felt that Lowell had a decided and unfair advantage. But apparently there was a darker reason: he

123

thought Lowell had written these poems while mad or on the verge of madness, that their apparent shapelessness was not the product of a subtle sense of design but of the writer's inchoate mental state. The ending of his letter hinted at this when he said that he was "disturbed" that Lowell might not recognize the faults of the poems. Tate was correct in saying that writing these poems might have helped Lowell deal with unpleasant childhood memories, yet he apparently thought that to expose these memories was unhealthy or a sign of unbalance. His comment that Lowell was "letting these scattered items of experience have their full impact on [his] sensibility" suggests that he believed that the very act of writing the poems resulted from an obsession that may have driven Lowell into another breakdown. It may be that Tate, who was not prone to public or poetic displays of private emotions, equated such displays with irrationality. He argued, in a symposium in 1964, that poetry had become too personal, that "the retreat inward seems now to have become a rout"; but Lowell, at the same event, claimed that "experience should be brought in [to poetry] and perhaps, personal experience, to write about things that really concern your life, that go deep into it."[30] This apparent difference of aesthetic opinion could easily be exaggerated; both poets respected craft, and both wrote from personal experience much of the time. This time, however, Lowell's poems went further than anything that Tate had previously encountered or expected, and Tate's aesthetic could not bend to accommodate them. Perhaps Tate believed that only derangement could explain such an extreme self-exposure.

For whatever reason, Tate suspected that these poem signaled another bout of mental illness and conveyed this belief in a letter to Perry Miller. Hardwick was understandably indignant and, in no uncertain terms, made her feelings known to Tate. The problem was not merely the issue of Lowell's health, which was often precarious; it was the injustice of equating these fine poems with the symptoms of ill health. The injustice, in this sense, was startlingly impersonal, and all the more unjust for it. As it happened, Lowell did suffer another breakdown in December, but as Hardwick informed Tate, he had been well while writing the poems.

Hardwick's letter, though frank, was not intended to provoke a quarrel but only to allay Tate's fears that the poems were somehow linked to Lowell's dubious mental situation. In his reply of 18 December, Tate apologized for having written to Perry Miller, but he stood firm in both his opinion of the quality of the poems and his belief that they contained signs of Lowell's mental disturbance:

> Apart from the merit of the poems, there was something in all the new ones but one, which disturbed me; and I think not without reason, as the event has proved. (He was not overtly disturbed when he wrote his manifesto to President Roosevelt.) . . .
>
> I can only repeat that my firm opinion is unchanged. The consequences of publication would be very, very serious. No doctor's advice on this subject would be worth anything. And—to be perfectly candid—I don't think yours is. You are too deeply in love with Cal and are involved too deeply in his chronic illness to take any other position than the one which looks to his immediate welfare, so great is the strain. Anything you can do to ease him, short of letting him publish the poems, which would do great harm in the long run, is justifiable— even discrediting me, as I have said. It is not a question of a little poetic disagreement, as you put it; it concerns his eventual reputation as a poet and his immediate public persona.[31]

Exactly what sort of harm Tate feared for Lowell is unclear. Harm to his mental state or harm to his reputation as a poet? Tate seemed to confound the two possibilities, but most likely he was concerned with Lowell's poetic reputation since, in that area, neither a doctor's advice nor Hardwick's love could help. If Lowell's poetic reputation fell (his "persona," a term Lowell perhaps playfully would throw back at Tate), it is possible that his mental state would deteriorate even further. Tate's 1949 letter to Lowell when he was in the Payne-Whitney clinic suggested that he believed low self-esteem to be a factor in that first attack. In the years before the role of chemical imbalance in manic-depressive cycles had been discovered, all mental illness was considered immaterially psychological in origin. Tate's amateur analysis was as likely as any other and rational enough, considering some of the peculiar treatments Lowell had turned to in desperation over the years. If low self-esteem had caused the 1949 attack, a decline in Lowell's public reputation might indeed worsen his condition, or so Tate may have reasoned.

Lowell's reply on 24 January was calm and conciliatory, defending his poems: "Let's not have a fight about my poems. I like them, and people as different as my Washington Winslow relation, Elizabeth Bishop, Philip Rahv, and T. S. Eliot have liked them and thought they topped my work. But you don't have to, and I want us to stay as good friends as ever. I was going to say that you Southerners are always jamming Pickett's charge into a Stonewall. But forget it—I'm southern."[32]

That closing phrase may be Lowell's way of asserting his continued loyalty to the poetics of his mentor, or he may be conceding that his own eccentricities are as individual (or regional) and annoying as Tate's. He admitted that Tate's prediction of a breakdown was justified but shrugged off the attack as minor: "You *were* uncannily right about my getting sick again. I had a bout of about a month in the Boston Psychopathic and am now back—in fact I've [been] back teaching now for three weeks. Everything seems OK."

In the end, Lowell was willing to dismiss the whole matter and appeared more anxious than Tate to avoid a quarrel. He returned to the subject of Tate's "new" poems (now five or six years old), perhaps to demonstrate that his judgment was still sound enough to see the merit of his friend's work, or perhaps to point out that he was, at least, still willing to judge friends generously: "I am sorry you don't like my stuff because you are such a generous and good judge. I've been going to school to you for years and hope to life-long. Perhaps even Horace nods. At any rate I'm completely sold on *your* new poems and feel your terza rima lynching is probably your biggest (and most technically perfect) achievement. The rest of the poem too is full of dynamite. Anyhow, even if I have betrayed the persona you have of me, I hope you won't cut us when you come here in March."

It is possible that the comment about Horace offended Tate or that the reference to Lowell's persona, most likely made in jest, rankled. At any rate, Tate remained upset and unwilling to file the exchange under the category of merely aesthetic disagreements. For him, aesthetic disagreements were serious, but more importantly, he clung to the idea of an intrinsic connection between Lowell's poetry and his health. Tate's reply began somewhat disingenuously by shrugging off Lowell's attempt at reconciliation and pretending that there was no cause for a quarrel: "I am a little baffled by your letter; I had no intention of having a 'fight' with you or anybody else; I just don't feel angry."[33] The difference between them, he insisted, remained aesthetic, not personal, and he would not be teased into admitting that he has confused poems or poetic reputation with life or that his expectations were unrealistic:

> What I thought was quite simple, and it had nothing to do with thinking that you had 'betrayed the persona' I had of you. I simply thought that the poems contained intractable material, and that you were probably in a transition period from your early style to a new one. You have certainly reached the age when this is likely to happen. Nor did I think the poems *all* bad. It seemed to me that the personal poems were a little morbid, private, and unorganized; and I was not put off because they were not *like* your old work; rather because they lacked the concentration and power, lacking, as they seemed to lack, the highly formalistic organization of the old.

Although he would not back off from his negative stance, Tate also was ready to put the disagreement behind them: "Won't you just put down my dissenting opinion as the one negative vote, and let the opinions of the others count? We can't expect *all* our friends to like what we do *all* the time." He wryly noted that the conciliatory praise Lowell had extended was for poems written long ago: "I am much pleased by the kind things you say about my last poems. There is a good deal of time between me and them, and they are beginning to look like old poems."

Tate's complaint that Lowell's new poems seemed "a little morbid, private, and unorganized" presumably did not extend to "Skunk Hour," the one new poem he liked. Considering his failure to see the careful orchestration of such poems as "My Last Afternoon with Uncle Devereaux Winslow," and considering that "Skunk Hour" was truly the most "morbid" of the lot (with mental illness an explicit presence), it is not clear why he excepted this one poem from his general disapprobation. The morbidity and air

127

of violence are intense; Lowell later said that, while writing the poem, he "found the bleak personal violence [of the last four stanzas] repellent."[34] Ian Hamilton thought Tate approved of the poem because "it is in neat sestets and has an almost regular rhyme scheme,"[35] but to a formalist like Tate near-regularity could hardly be sufficient to earn approval. The sestets, which Lowell suggested he derived from Annette von Droste-Hulshoff's "Amletzten Tage des Jahres,"[36] are far from precise; the free verse renders the lines in such irregular fashion that some are only three syllables long and others are as long as sixteen syllables. Only intermittently does the verse approximate a kind of regularity. The principle of the sestets is that the first and last lines of each are noticeably shorter than the middle four lines, and a rhyming pattern of ABCBCA—some of the rhymes being slant- or off-rhymes—lends a further air of regularity and a sense of structure. In the penultimate stanza, the rhyme scheme is ABBCCA, and the last sestet is ABCACB. Among the rhyming words are such irregularities as "top" and "cup" (consonance) and "bleats" and "here" (assonance), and occasionally the end words find no rhyme at all. To readers who admire the poem, the irregular free verse reinforces the irregular but visible movement of the speaker's meditation, and the informal quality of the rhymes seems appropriate to a highly colloquial, though actually well-organized, poem.

Stylistically, "Skunk Hour" is a manifesto declaring Lowell's independence from a received aesthetic of impersonality. The poem opens with a cooly ironic and symbolic description of a village but turns on itself to become an agonized exploration of the speaker's mind. The poem displaces its own objectivity with a frank solipsism that returns the lyric voice to autobiography and substitutes the agony of self-realization for irony. It is the most Dantean poem Lowell had so far written. Its reference to his own mental illness, its Miltonic situation of hell in the human ego, and its rejection of the symbolic mode for a more naturalistic voice suggest a definite break with the tenets of modernism and make it arguably the first important postmodern American poem.

The voice is that of a man who notes illness, loss, and outlawry (of the minor sort) in everything around him. He links the break-down of community and tradition to his own illness, his lack of mental stability, his obsession with sex, and his loneliness. As Lowell commented, "Sterility howls through the scene, but I try to give a tone of tolerance, humor, and randomness to the sad prospect."[37] Into this metaphorical community of ill health, the unyielding purposefulness of nature enters in the form of "a mother skunk and her column of kittens." The skunks embody order, fearlessness, and a simple sense of presence that rebukes the partially disintegrated human community with its "hermit heiress" and "fairy / decorator" who would inappropriately "rather marry." Most importantly, the skunks bring their sense of order into the heart of the human community "under the chalk-dry and spar spire / of the Trinitarian Church." The "chalk-dry" aspirations of religious faith are nothing to these primordial beasts who, with their "moonstruck eyes' red fire," have a little of the devil in them. Too practical to worry over their souls, they "march on their soles up Main Street" and head directly to the speaker's garbage pail, finding their nourishment in the refuse of his life.

The argument of the poem, organized by the movement of the speaker's meditation, gives it a structure that is shapely, clear, and carefully organized. Every image reinforces every other image. The various figures of illness—the decorator, the heiress, the dead yachtsman who "seemed to leap from an L. L. / Bean catalogue"—suggest various aspects of the speaker's illness: his loneliness, his sexual uncertainty, his pretensions and mortality. The landscape, with its "red fox stain" covering "Blue Hill," its falling eyesore cottages, and its Golgotha of a hill where the carloads of lovers park, is as awry, disorderly, and symbolic as the inhabitants of the odd little community. No wonder that, in musing over the people and landscape of his village, the speaker comes to the conclusion that his "mind's not right" and that, like Milton's Satan, he himself is hell and is alone in it; the rest of the community is only a series of metaphors of his own state of existence. Only the skunks are independent of him. In their assertion of the natural order, the speaker at last finds something to take him out of himself, something that has a life independent of his, a life that embodies everything in nature—order, ruthlessness of purpose, disregard of inessentials, and a determination to survive.

Tate, in reading "Skunk Hour," may have felt that the poem's apparently affirmative conclusion indicated a healthy way of dealing with ill health, a determination on Lowell's part to face and conquer his mental difficulties rather than yield to them. Tate seemed to think that Lowell demonstrated this yielding in writing the family poems. Of course Tate would not have read the poem as strictly autobiographical. Lowell, in his later comments, pointed out that St. John of the Cross and Whitman (from whom the anecdote of spying on the lovers is derived) had gone into the shaping of the poem's persona. Tate would have realized that the voice of the poem contains literary elements and that those incorporated voices would not preclude the poem from speaking partially for Lowell himself.

The argument of "Skunk Hour" is almost entirely carried out through its imagery (though three brief direct statements—"The season's ill," "My mind's not right," "I myself am hell"—point the reader in the right direction), but the sestets do represent a structural regularity more immediately apprehendable than most of the other *Life Studies* poems. In contrast, a poem like "Terminal Days at Beverley Farms" must have struck Tate as lacking a viable organizing center and as dwelling to no purpose on morbid family facts—in this instance, the facts surrounding the death of Lowell's father. Certainly the poem lacks that strong sustaining presence of the speaker which so empowers "Skunk Hour." Its reliance on memory, rather than on the immediacy of the quotidian, requires that the poem organize itself around the subject of the elder Lowell's failing health, which, like the ill-health of the "Skunk Hour" speaker, takes its form from the objects and figures surrounding him—the "portly, uncomfortable boulder," comically matched by his head, "efficient and hairless"; the sky-blue tracks of the commuters' railroad, an ironic highway to heaven; the "little black *Chevie,* / garaged like a sacrificial steer"; and the curator of the Maritime Museum, whom Father refers to as "'the commander of the Swiss Navy,'" a figure as useless and superannuated as himself. Tate's reservations may have been prompted by the fact that the poem ends with no note of consolation, no redeeming metaphorical presence. The closure is the dying man's last words, "'I feel awful.'" To end on that note is dramatically satisfying and indicates an ironic recognition on the dying man's part that he should feel awful; everything surrounding him suggests how ineffective, uncomfortable and useless his life has been. This note of grisly humor may have escaped Tate, or he may have rejected it as inappropriate. Although capable of reading poetry even more subtly argued than Lowell's (his essay on Dickinson proves this), Tate extended little sympathy toward these family poems and an unsympathetic reading finds even the best of them to be inept.

In the family poems, Lowell has grown away from the precepts of Eliot, but Tate has retained his early allegiance. *Life Studies* decisively broke with the modernism of Eliot and returned to a Wordsworthian immediacy of experience. Although Tate found these poems too inward and, with his faith in the oneness of form and content, too slack and unrhythmic, other readers recognized that confronting private memory in the public form of the written word is a metaphor for the primary quotidian act of reconciling personal experience with the larger world.

Wordsworth demonstrated in *The Prelude*—a poem he thought not publishable on its own—the universality of the most intimate experiences, even those of an unusually gifted and self-aware mind. Eliot denied so forthright a role for the ego, yet his early poems, especially, allow that ego to speak through the flimsiest of disguises. Tate, more Eliot-like than Eliot, severely circumscribed private experience and limited the scope and vision of the first person voice in his early work; yet in "The Mediterranean" and certain other poems, Wordworthian "spots of time," experiences so personal as to be almost beyond language, creep in. After the mid-1950s, Lowell made self-confrontation the central act of his poetry and rejected many of the rationales for the decorum of impersonality, arguing against the conventional genres by claiming a privileged place for personal experience and memory. For example, in describing his poem "For the Union Dead," he noted, "I brought in early personal memories because I wanted to avoid the fixed, brazen tone of the set piece and official ode."[38] Tate might have objected to this characterization of the "official ode," especially if he suspected it applied to his own "Ode to the Confederate Dead" (which it surely does not), but Lowell was thinking with the spirit, at least, of the early Eliot and Pound, and the fresh results of *Life Studies* and *For the Union Dead* can be attributed to his willingness to question and reconsider received opinion.

The disagreement appears to have ended in a stalemate, and yet when the book finally appeared in the spring of 1959, Tate wrote to Lowell and said simply, "Your book is magnificent."[39] Most likely the larger structure created by Lowell's artful arrangement of the book and the final ordering of the family poems, as well as the elucidating presence of the elegantly written prose memoir "91 Revere Street" (assuming Tate had the American, not the British, edition) gave the book a sense of organization and sanity that quelled Tate's doubts. In the future, in dealing with *For the Union Dead* and *Notebook 1967–68*, Tate was more receptive to radical shifts in form and style, perhaps because Lowell had already marked what Tate would see as the extremes of his poetic and also because Tate remembered his failure originally to see the strength of the *Life Studies* poems.

Translation or Imitation?

The immediate aftermath of Tate's disapproval of Lowell's new poems was a continued uneasiness between the two. The winter of 1958 brought still another breakdown for Lowell, and at the end of January, he was back in McLean's. This stay resulted in some of the strongest poems in *Life Studies*, most notably "Waking in the Blue," in which the speaker's ironic view of his institutionalized self takes shape in an atmosphere of closure and failure that is inhabited by "victorious figures of bravado" who "ossified young." Lowell, though (or his persona), has not quite ossified, is for the moment still "cock of the walk." "After a hearty New England breakfast," he weighs "two hundred pounds," and takes some comfort in his solidity, but the ending of the poem suggests that he could go either way, that he is potentially one of the ossified and, although temporarily benign, still has the capacity to destroy himself:

We are all old-timers,
each of us holds a locked razor.

133

As Hamilton points out, this poem began, in part, as a love poem to Ann Adden, a young woman (one of many over the years) to whom Lowell, in his uncertain state, attached himself.[1] These young women not only angered Hardwick but, by their very presence, further confused Lowell and possibly may have delayed his recovery.

The complex story of Lowell's various breakdowns and love affairs is revealed in Hamilton's biography. What is to the point here is that Lowell was not the best example of emotional stability, and his remarks on the love lives of his friends at times were obtuse or inappropriate. In 1958 and 1959, Tate once again would suffer from Lowell's unwise commentary on his affairs. He and Gordon were getting divorced for the second and last time, and he had apparently already made plans to marry Isabella Gardner, another poet. Once again, Lowell involved himself in Tate's affairs, although he was not entirely uninvited. Tate was less than candid about his plans and on 8 November wrote to Lowell, "I couldn't plan to marry another woman; I can't afford it!"[2]

Lowell reported to Gordon in December that Tate was living with Gardner and planned to marry her after the divorce. Still worse, according to Gordon's biographer, "Lowell reported that Allen fancied himself as Lord Byron and that Isabella was his Countess Guiccioli. She was, Lowell said, 'bone stupid.'"[3] He also claimed that Tate had asked Natasha Spender to marry. Lowell's tendency to tell tales was already familiar to the Tates, so the consequences of this episode were not as dire as might be expected. Tate apparently used Lowell's "wild gossip"[4] as further excuse to avoid any reconciliation with Gordon and then claimed, in a letter to Andrew Lytle on 25 May 1959, that she was blocking the divorce partly because of Lowell's interference:

> Caroline is blocking the divorce. I waited to see whether she would give me any human reason, not merely the reason of the Church. Could she bring herself to say that she wanted us back again, instead of the theological line, I would have a very different view. But she is using the Church to "save" me. All this has been complicated by a new maniacal outburst of Cal Lowell's. He has had another violent breakdown, at the pitch of which he telephoned Caroline several times and

134

urged her to save me from a Boston divorcee. I like this woman, and will continue to do so, but I could no more plan to marry her than I could fly, though I am frank to say I'd like to. The lady is a cousin of Cal's and an old friend whom he trusted. I am the object of his hostility. The Lowell vulgarity reached its height when he told C. [Caroline] that the lady wasn't very rich—that I could look around and do better.[5]

The truth was that Caroline had countersued in order to improve her financial position. Although this further embittered the divorce, it did not prevent it. Further, though he claimed to have no plans to marry the "Boston divorcee," he did marry her, with Lytle as best man, a few days after the divorce decree. If Lowell was suffering from a breakdown when he phoned Gordon, it was unfair to accuse him of vulgarity when he plainly was not in full control. Tate was in a stressful situation himself and probably considered that admitting to anyone that he planned to marry Gardner might cause problems with the divorce settlement. Tate also wrote to Hardwick and blamed Lowell for complicating matters. Her reply began, "I am distressed . . . to learn that Cal's outrageous behavior is a really serious deterrent to Caroline and that it makes the whole thing more difficult." Tate underlined "serious deterrent" and wrote at the top of the letter "I am reassuring her about this."[6] Hardwick apparently was privy to Tate's plans to marry Gardner. In the same letter (dated 1 May 1959 but with "May" crossed out and "June" written above it), after expressing concern over Lowell's latest breakdown and the harm his derangement has done to her and others, she comments on the subject of Gardner, "I think you will have a good marriage and be a great joy and consolation to each other."

Tate's anger was undoubtedly genuine, but it was not deep and was tempered with concern for Lowell's well-being. In the same month in which he wrote his letter to Lytle, he had written to Lowell to finally praise *Life Studies* and had entered into correspondence regarding Lowell's candidacy for an international exchange program. Frederick Colwell, from the International Educational Exchange Service (officially a State Department function but funded in part by the CIA), wrote to Tate at the end of May to ask for a confidential recommendation of Lowell. Tate had already participated in the program by traveling to India in 1956, so his recommendation would be consequential both for his intimate knowledge of Lowell and his experience with the program. After some delay, Tate replied with a highly favorable recommendation but felt obliged, for once, to correct an "exaggerated" report of Lowell's mental problems: "I do not know whether you still plan to send Mr. Robert Lowell to South America. I understand that at least one of his references took a somewhat exaggerated view of a breakdown which Mr. Lowell had last spring. He is now in very good condition and plans a trip to Europe with his wife at the end of the summer. There is absolutely no doubt in my mind about his ability to carry through a program of reading and lectures in South America."[7]

If Tate harbored any grudge against Lowell for his involvement in the divorce proceedings, he was not the sort of man to satisfy himself with petty revenge. Instead, he defended Lowell against the exaggerated view that Tate himself had fostered at times. Regardless of his misdemeanors, Lowell was an honorable member of the republic of letters that Tate honored and defended against interference from the uncomprehending world outside. Further, he had long ago learned that Lowell's recovery from these breakdowns was quite complete; Lowell quickly resumed his normal functions, his writing, teaching, and lecturing abilities as strong as ever. Many psychiatrists had realized by the late 1950s that such breakdowns were chemical disorders rather than strictly psychological, and in a few more years, lithium would emerge as an apparent "cure," one that would work for Lowell for a time but would prove to be no permanent solution.

The autumn 1959 issue of the *Sewanee Review* contained a "Homage to Allen Tate," consisting of "Essays, Notes and Verse in Honor of his Sixtieth Birthday." Among these was Lowell's essay "Visiting the Tates," his own version of his 1937 summer visit to Benfolly. Lowell concludes this memoir with a brief but telling summation of his relationship with Tate and the importance and the quality of Tate's poetry. He recognizes the flaws of the poems ("splutter and shambling") but suggests that their beauty and force ("killing eloquence") emerge despite, and as a result of, these flaws. Most importantly, he grants Tate the distinction of originality and discovery through untiring attention to craft, demonstrating the seamless relationship between craft and inspiration:

> Like a torn cat, I was taken in when I needed help, and in a sense I have never left. Tate still seems as jaunty and magisterial as he did twenty years ago. His poems, all of them, even the slightest, are terribly personal. Out of splutter and shambling comes a killing eloquence. Perhaps, this is the resonance of desperation, or rather the formal resonance of desperation. I say "formal" because no one has so given us the impression that poetry must be burly, must be courteous, must be tinkered with and recast until one's eyes pop out of one's head. How often something smashes through the tortured joy of composition to strike the impossible bull's-eye! The pre-Armageddon twenties and thirties with all their peculiar fears and enthusiasms throb in Tate's poetry; imitated ad infinitum, it has never been reproduced by another hand.[8]

Couched in strikingly lucid prose, this one brief paragraph manages a compact critical assessment of both Tate's poetry and its value to Lowell as Tate's student. His argument that Tate is a "personal" poet does not refer to the kind of autobiographical writing found in *Life Studies,* or even in Tate's "Buried Lake" sequence, but to his aesthetic. "Splutter and shambling," although flaws, are surely highly individual—therefore personal—characteristics, and Tate's ability to force these dubious qualities into a "killing eloquence" is a measure of his self-discipline and highly individual ability to temper passion by formal means. This requires lengthy, patient revision. From Tate, Lowell learned to revise, and anyone who has examined Lowell's manuscript drafts knows that, for him, the poem only began to come alive after long, hard work. He rarely wrote brilliant or even complete first drafts; the majority of his poems, like Tate's, are pieced together from vague, unrhythmic, seemingly uninspired fragments after endless hours of work. As a result, the most unlikely early drafts and most apparently unrelated materials often metamorphosed into fine poems. The physical requirements of writing poetry in the manner of Lowell, Tate, Eliot, Ransom, and Bishop are exhausting, but the mental strain is even worse, and their faith in their ability to ultimately reclaim unpromising material is heroic. This faith depends on the belief that poetry is ultimately worth the effort, worth draining one's life dry through endless numbing hours of reworking drafts over word by word, rearranging, cutting, and reassembling until everything clicks into place. From Tate, Lowell learned the joy of striking the "impossible bull's eye," and this transformed him from a poetry-struck adolescent into a genuine committed poet.

Tate might have objected to being characterized as a poet of the past, of the "pre-Armageddon twenties and thirties," but he did not, nor did he seem offended at his former apprentice's offhand declaration of aesthetic independence. He admired the piece, at least on aesthetic grounds, and wrote to Lowell on 17 October to tell him so: "It's a very fine piece of prose, every word packed and precise, and every word, unless I am wholly bemused, very tender. If I am not bemused, I am at least dazzled. I could not have known that you thought so well of me, or that so many others did that I can put out of mind for the time being those who don't."[9]

Tate was not bemused; although it has its gently ironic moments, the memoir is suffused with a real fondness for Tate, and the respect for his poetry is genuine. Lowell's eloquence is that of deep feeling carefully expressed—not the machinations of the ironist, as one or two critics have proposed. He was not so Machiavellian, and Tate would never have been that easily taken in. Furthermore, in response to Tate's appreciative letter, Lowell related a recent incident that again reminded him of how important the elder poet has been to him. Lowell had given a reading at Tufts and answered questions afterward: "Among them I was asked what poets had served as my models, and I answered more than I could name might have, but that the only one that really got deeply and closely under my skin was Allen Tate. I don't suppose I would ever have written again, if it hadn't been for our year in the Old and New Wormswoods of Monteagle."[10]

In fact, Tate's poetry had begun to be more important than ever to Lowell; the poems he would write in the early 1960s would respond, in some ways, more directly to Tate's work than anything he had previously written. Stylistically distinct from Tate's and his own early work, a number of these new poems, in both theme and stance, echo Tate's poems of the 1920s and 1930s. Their fresh colloquial mode would be particularly appreciated by Tate. The early years of the new decade would also see the publication of *Imitations,* a book that Tate admired greatly. It is tempting to argue that some of the poems in *For the Union Dead* are related to particular Tate poems in somewhat the same way that the poems of *Imitations* are related to their European originals, a relationship Tate would later explore in his important essay "Translation or Imitation?" As Virgil had rewritten Homer, Lowell wrote in homage and to address his own place in the tradition, a tradition defined by his relationship to his predecessors as well as by the independent viability of his work. In his understanding of tradition, Lowell kept Eliot in mind and recognized that the making of a new literature is an act that takes place in thorough engagement with the old. For Lowell, Tate represented the tradition at its most forceful and eloquent, but tradition requires constant reinterpretation to remain alive. Lowell is as adept at revising and reinterpreting Tate's themes as he is at producing effective poems in English from models in various languages that, in some instances, he could read only with a beginner's ability or, like Russian, not read at all.

At the Boston Arts Festival in June 1960, Lowell read a new poem composed for the occasion. "Colonel Shaw and the Massachusetts 54th," originally and then later titled "For the Union Dead," responds to the apparent pessimism and the elegiac stance of Tate's "Ode to the Confederate Dead." The pessimism of Lowell's poem is more contemporary in that it derives from the contemplation of the destruction of landscape, the decay of childhood landmarks, the threat of nuclear annihilation, and the ugly manifestations of racism. Like Tate's speaker, Lowell's is helpless against the perversion of nature and the self-destructive forces of the modern world. Tate's graveyard stance is more psychological than political, but the themes of his poem are social and cultural. In addition to cultural shortcomings, he regrets the failure of individual memory,

139

the resultant anonymity of death, the cruelty of natural cycles and their inadequacy to illuminate human issues, and the aesthetic failure of a society turned inward toward the randomness of individuality, but the individual's inability to speak or act effectively shapes Lowell's poem also. Jerome Mazzaro has argued, "The tensions of [Lowell's] poem remain identical with those of Tate's poem except for Lowell's own voice and two new elements," which he describes as "a manufactured and impersonal nature" and a "backdrop of Heraclitean cyclicism."[11] He refers to Heraclitus's theories of knowledge as sense-perception and matter as eternal flux and cyclical destruction, concluding in a chaos of fire—in the instance of Lowell's poem, the fire of atomic warfare.

In the large context of Tate's work, his "Ode" is slightly anomalous since, although it directs its voice toward a fictional second person, it is essentially a meditation along the lines of what M. H. Abrams has called the Greater Romantic Lyric, a personal musing stimulated by a comparison of natural and human states. Although literary in origin, the "Ode" expresses a personal but accessible emotion, a nostalgia of the sort that Tate rarely admitted in into his poetry. The nostalgia is not for the myth of the antebellum South, which here is merely the occasion of failure and futile self-sacrifice, but for death itself as the universal paradox that links us to one another yet destroys the organ of understanding that would give that experience meaning. The only other forms of knowledge, the poem suggests, are awareness of sin and the indifference, impersonality, and persistence of nature. The memory of Confederate soldiers, Tate argued in "Narcissus as Narcissus," is victimized by the protagonist's narcissism and the decay of "active faith." In the unstructured world of the protagonist, the sacrifice of the soldiers is pointless. Even though the poem takes its note of nostalgia from Shelley, Tate obliquely corrects his anthropomorphosism by refusing the "fancy that the blowing leaves are charging soldiers."[12] Such correction implies, however, that metaphor and the human need for faith cannot fulfil themselves in a solipsistic world of individual, rather than collective or cultural, values.

Lowell's poem, which, in one letter to Tate, he referred to as his "most composed," is not so simple as to assume that, because Colonel Shaw fought on the "right" side of the war and led a black regiment, his sacrifice of himself and his soldiers is unambiguous. The historical Robert Shaw was complex in his racial views, committed to a cause yet unsure of the people whose cause he attempted to promote. Thomas Wentworth Higginson, in his autobiography (which Lowell probably had read), recounts an example of Shaw's uncertainty:

> The young hero, Colonel Shaw, when I rode out to meet him, on his arrival with his Northern colored regiment, seriously asked me whether I felt perfectly sure that the negroes would stand fire in line of battle, and suggested that, at the worst, it would at least be possible to drive them forward by having a line of white soldiers advance in their rear, so that they would be between two fires. He admitted that the mere matter of individual courage to have been already settled in their case, and only doubted whether they would do as well in line of battle as in skirmishing and on guard duty.[13]

Higginson saw the variety and complexity of the black soldiers while Shaw, who died with them, was uncertain, not of the rightness of his cause, but of the human nature of its object. As Higginson concluded, "He did not sufficiently consider that in this, as at all other points, they were simply men." That last leap of faith—that a black man is neither more nor less godlike but simply a man—was within the more introspective and experienced Higginson's grasp but not yet within Shaw's. One would wonder how he found the courage to die with men he had not yet accepted as completely human, but he had the saving conviction of righteousness to sustain him. It is this conviction that the contemporary world of Lowell's poem lacks. Like Tate, Lowell sees that moral ambiguity and the lack of persistent values have driven individuals into themselves. The speaker of his poem embodies that paradox of solipsistic moral longing in the midst of an economically and politically collective society that is unable to fulfill its commitment to what it believes is socially and ethically correct.

"Last March" the speaker stood behind a "barbed and galvanized / fence," safely separated from the destruction, just as Tate's protagonist at the graveyard is separated from the dead by being alive and contemporary, but his stance as observer does not absolve him from knowledge and the responsibility that goes with it. Knowledge begins in childhood, the poem reminds us. The "old South Boston Aquarium" at the moment of the poem "stands in a Sahara of snow," but the speaker remembers when he visited here as a child and wanted to "burst the bubbles / drifting from the noses of the cowed, compliant fish." This image undermines the apparently heroic figure of Colonel Shaw, "riding on his bubble" like Sintram, as Lowell wrote in an early draft, in Fouque's tale of knightly trial and endeavor. Instead of resisting fate, the colonel shares the timidity of the fish, "compliant" as he waits for the bubble to break. This rupture would be "blessed," an act or sign of divine intervention, but it will never come. Ironically, the colonel, along with the Mosler safe, is one of the few fixed points in the poem, one of the few unchanging and indestructible links between past and present. Like the Mosler safe, the colonel survived a great explosion, a war that, although it killed him, preserved him in bronze. His sculptural image now "is out of bounds" and can rejoice "in man's lovely / peculiar power to choose life and die." In his lifetime, he chose to affirm the value of lives other than his own by volunteering to lead a black regiment "to death." The irony of this choice lingers, embodied in "St. Gaudens' shaking Civil War relief," which depicts Shaw as a three-dimensioned figure riding while his nearly two-dimensional troops walk. Some of the irony of the poem derives from Lowell's presentation of the bronze Shaw as a living, present-tense person; but it is because he is dead and memorialized that he is "out of bounds," like the other Civil War statues scattered over "a thousand small town New England greens," statues that "grow slimmer and younger each year."

Lowell's poem implicitly asks and answers the crucial question of Tate's "Ode": "What shall we say who have knowledge / Carried to the heart?" The answer seems to be to remember, despite the way those "abstract Union soldiers . . . doze over muskets /

and muse through their sideburns," that monuments refer to complexities that survive their subjects; to realize that the contemporary world is self-devouring, and the last war and the wars to come will raise no monuments to the archetype of the hero; to understand that we are separated from the machinations of this world by galvanized fence and television; and to realize that separation cannot absolve us of complicity.

Like the bronze Colonel Shaw, we may wait forever "for the blessed break" in a world that destroys aquariums and builds parking garages for "giant finned cars" that "nose forward like fish," replacing the little aquarium fish of the child's memory with the gross machinery of the present tense. The speaker-observer, like the bronze Colonel Shaw, can only watch the world unfold about him. His modern helplessness contrasts with the Civil War hero's activist idealism, for the original Colonel Shaw could choose. Still part of a heroic age, he chose death for himself and for others. His reward or punishment was to be embodied in bronze, preserved for an age that no longer has any use for heroes, an age in which atomic war has rendered them obsolete. Black Americans no longer have to follow white patrician officers in the battle to end slavery, but the "drained faces" of their great-grandchildren appear on TV at a time when school integration crises have become newsworthy. The speaker of Lowell's poem cannot, as Tate's poem suggests, "set up the grave / in the house"; the grave has lost its dignity and now is the hole he observed "last March" that was being dug behind the fence:

> Behind their cage,
> yellow dinosaur steamshovels were grunting
> as they cropped up tons of mush and grass
> to gouge their underworld garage.

In a valueless age, the "underworld garage" will replace the old-fashioned underworld of Pluto and Satan; it is the "giant finned cars" that need accommodation, not the merely human animal.

Lowell answered Tate's charge to his protagonist to "Turn your eyes to the immoderate past," but instead of "the inscrutable infantry rising / Demons out of the earth," he finds the earth itself being devoured by the machinery of the modern world, the hero barely upright, propped like the statehouse by "a plank splint against the garage's earthquake." Statehouse and bronze relief, the symbolic artifacts, remain only by sufferance. Colonel Shaw's ironic decision "to choose life and die" has come down to the contemporary world as a set of crueler and more impersonal symbols—the atomic bomb, the yellow and archaically dinosaur-like steam shovels, the giant finned fish-cars. The city of Boston is rebuilding itself to accommodate its choice of impersonal modernity, a process Lowell had embodied years before in a poem in *Lord Weary's Castle* as the figure of the "green train" that "grinds along its buried tracks / And screeches" beneath the graveyard in which the Indian killer was buried. The cod, the traditional icon of Massachusetts (one that hangs in the House chamber in the statehouse), by losing "half its scales," suggests how far down the road to dissolution the state has gone during the speaker's lifetime.

This poem is an elegy for America, which like the bas-relief is barely propped up against the earthquake of history. In the figure of Colonel Shaw, the hopeless, naive, self-destructive idealism of the nation finds its focus. His death at one time rated a memorial, but the modern era—although it makes a nominal physical effort to uphold the past—places no faith in history or memory, and so erects plank splints instead of statues. The "Negro schoolchildren," however heroic their struggle for equality and education, earn no symbol of permanence. In contrast with their bronze ancestors, they fade in the flickering images of television, which the speaker must crouch to see. A crass advertisement ("Hiroshima boiling / over a Mosler safe"), the only reminder of the "last war," manages to mock Christianity by calling its product the "Rock of Ages," suggesting how complicit religion has been in the creation of a modern death-oriented culture. Having abandoned the nostalgia that led him to recall the aquarium, the speaker notes that the Colonel is present-tense and still rides on his immortal idealism, waiting for the world to free itself from history, fate, and materialism—the very negatives his embronzed state embodies. The aquarium, that primal place in which childhood met nature face to face, is gone in both fact and sentiment. The only fish in Boston are the "giant finned cars," which, despite their brute power, represent "a savage servility." The oxymoron accurately describes the debased, dehumanized state of the present.

"For the Union Dead" goes much further than Tate's poem in excoriating the present and finds even less comfort in the past. In the world of this poem, even the author's poetic past is relatively neglected. Lowell abandons the ghostly pentameter lurking behind most of the *Life Studies* free-verse poems in favor of loose quatrains that, in refusing all pretense of regularity, represent a new prosodic freedom. The poem remains characteristic in its textual and syntactical complexity. It employs a good deal of alliteration and consonance to mesh itself into a whole, and deliberately avoids the more Latinate sound of Tate's "Ode." When Lowell first published it in *The Atlantic* (1960), it was "For the Union Dead," but under the title "Colonel Shaw and the Massachusetts 54th," he attached it to the Vintage reprint of *Life Studies* (1961), making it the last poem in that book. After seeing it in print, Lowell realized the inadequacy of the more specific title, which was at least the fourth he had used; early drafts were titled "One Gallant Rush" and "Colonel Shaw and his Men." Returning to "For the Union Dead," an obvious riposte to Tate, he probably was more pleased with the euphony of the title than with the clarity with which it described his inspiration.

"For the Union Dead" isn't merely an imitation of Tate's "Ode," but for Lowell the issues of imitation and/or translation loomed large in 1960 and 1961. In the summer of 1960, he had accepted a request from Eric Bentley for a new translation of Racine's *Phèdre*. Describing his efforts in June 1960, he mentioned, almost as an afterthought, the new poem he had composed, referring to it by the title he would temporarily abandon then revive and disclaiming the obvious connection with Tate's poem: "I am two acts deep into it [Phèdre], and am amazed to realize I am about doubling my entire out-put of verse—hundreds of heroic couplets, rather a treadmill of declamation! All rather astonishing and engrossing. I've also done a Massachusetts Civil War poem, For the Union Dead,—not an ode though." [14]

Lowell told Tate that his new poem was not an "ode," and he omitted the implied word from the title, not so much because it would make the link to Tate too explicit, but because a free-verse poem did not embody the implied formality of the term. He may have worried that Tate would disapprove of the poem's loose quatrains; to give the poem the grandiose and highly conventional title of "ode" would raise the expectation of a formalism that the poem clearly lacked. He had no desire to incite again the wrath that Tate had directed at the eleven *Life Studies* poems.

On the other hand, translating *Phèdre* into heroic couplets would surely warm Tate's heart. Tate was an accomplished translator and had given considerable thought to the problems of translation. He could be expected to take an interest in Lowell's undertakings, in both the translation of *Phèdre* and the imitations of European lyric poetry that he had begun producing in quantity. Translation and imitation had long played important roles in Tate's work. Imitation, if defined as the inspiration of one poem by another, accounts for much romantic and modern poetry, as Harold Bloom's extensive work on poetic influence argues, but Tate, a more conscious critic than many other poets, pointed to the role of imitation in his own work. "Death of Little Boys," by his own description, derives from a translation of a Rimbaud poem. Like Lowell, he worked on translations when he was temporarily uninspired to create original poems. When Lowell stayed at Monteagle, Tate was working on a translation of the *Perviligium Veneris;* this may have stimulated "The Seasons of the Soul," the important poem that Tate would write the following year.

The relationship among original poetry, "imitation," or poetry directly inspired by previous poems, and translation is complex, with a long history that extends back to the time of oral poetry when poets were not so concerned with originality but built directly upon the work of their colleagues. In "Translation or Imitation," Tate argued, "It is a commonplace of English and American literary history that translations from foreign literatures have had a decisive influence upon the re-creation of style," and he cited Milton and Pound as examples of poets who discovered effects in foreign poetries that they brought into poetry in English.[15] His ex-

146

pectation was that a translation be a good English poem; otherwise, Tate argued, using the example of Lowell's version of a passage from Homer, "We mislead the reader without Greek into believing that Homer himself is mediocre."[16] In criticizing the Homer, Tate defined clearly what he expected of Lowell's imitations and why he, for the most part, admired them: "What is wrong with Lowell's fragment of Homer is something quite different [that is, different from the problem of not being literal]. It is not good Lowell." Tate summarizes by saying, "A translator ought to be a poet himself . . . he must be a master of his own language, whatever mastery he may have of the language from which he is translating."[17]

Tate's position, then, was that a translation must first be a good English poem, that it must be done by a poet not a scholar, and that it must convince the reader that the original is first and foremost a good poem. Further on, he compares a Kunitz translation and a Lowell translation of "Au Lecteur" and claims that Lowell's version is one of his best poems, better, or at least more intense, than Baudelaire's original. This worried Tate only slightly, but many of the reviewers of *Imitations* were disturbed by Lowell's attempts to exceed his originals in some quality peculiar to his poetic, some quality they claimed was not in the originals.

Lowell had published several translations or imitations in *Lord Weary's Castle*, but *Phaedra* (his spelling for his English version) and *Imitations*, both published in 1961, were his first sustained attempts to present himself as a translator. Reviewers who assumed a view of translation similar to Tate's, and who likely considered Pound a model translator, admired *Imitations;* those who assumed that more literal translations indicated greater respect for the original castigated Lowell for lack of humility and general bad taste. Both *Phaedra* and *Imitations* had explanatory forewords, but these may have exacerbated, rather than allayed, the doubts of some readers. *Phaedra* is written in heroic couplets. Lowell explained his procedure by admitting, "Racine's plays are generally and correctly thought to be untranslatable," so that, without using the word, he claimed rather to have imitated him.[18] In laying his claim, Lowell laid himself open to the charge of believing that he had in some way improved on Racine: "He has few verbally inspired lines, and in this is unlike Baudelaire and even La Fontaine. His poetry is great because of the justness of its rhythm and logic, and the glory of its hard, electric rage. I have translated as a poet, and tried to give my lines a certain dignity, speed, and flare." [19]

While "dignity, speed, and flare" are not synonyms for verbal inspiration, Lowell seemed to suggest that he had given Racine's uninspired verse a life that it had lacked in the original. Further, Lowell did not claim to have produced a very loose translation; rather he pointed out that he had "used every speech in the original, and almost every line is either translated or paraphrased." George Steiner, for one, felt that, despite this claim, Lowell's version was only nominally connected with Racine and was actually "a variation on the theme of Phaedra, in the manner of Seneca and the Elizabethan classicists." [20] Although Steiner accused Lowell of immodesty, linking him to the Elizabethan classicists came close to Lowell's own comment, "I inevitably echo the English Restoration, both in ways that are proper in my sometimes unRacinian humor and bombast"—Restoration because of his couplets and perhaps Elizabethan in humor and bombast.

Imitations drew more fire, and Lowell's introduction, even though a straightforward argument for his method, fueled the flames. "I have tried to write alive English and to do what my authors might have done if they were writing their poems now and in America," he said, but many of the reviewers took this as another expression of his lack of modesty. [21] The licenses Lowell took—"Many," by his own account—inflamed critics who considered the poets they admired to be inviolate although, as Lowell correctly argued, most strict metrical translations "are likely to be stuffed birds." [22] Hamilton has accurately characterized some of the criticism by pointing out that "respect for the original was spoken of as if it were something like respect for a parent, or a grown-up." [23] The problem was seen as more than merely disrespect; some of Lowell's translations were also stuffed birds—or worse. Hamilton has argued that Lowell wrote a number of the imitations in "limp translatorese." [24] Some of the poems certainly are not good by Lowell's own standards, and for these failures, his introduction was no defense at all. Some imitations, particularly those of Baudelaire, inspired extremes of praise and condemnation from critics of differing views, but others inspired praise from no one.

Tate, though, preferred to judge Lowell on his own terms, especially since Lowell's standards of translation were similar to his own. On 26 February 1961, after seeing the manuscripts of both *Phaedra* and *Imitations,* he wrote at length to Lowell about each, first about *Phaedra:* "I don't know whether your Phaedra is close to Racine. . . . But close or not, your version is very powerful. Phaedra's magnificent speech on page 44 gets its effects through the suppleness of your couplets and your modulations. By the latter I mean the subtle shift, back and forth, between high rhetoric and colloquial speech. I would cite as an example the six lines beginning with "Am I a Gorgon. . . ." The overall effect of your versification is to carry the reader as on a boat shooting the rapids: it moves with great speed." [25]

Actually, the versification of *Phaedra* varies considerably in quality. At times it is sluggish, bombastic, artificial, and in performance sounds bookish and clotted, a mouthful for the modern actor, but Tate's praise accurately characterizes Lowell's couplets at their best. Phaedra speaks the lines Tate admires in act three, scene three:

> Am I a gorgon, or Circe, or the infidel
> Medea, stifled by the flames of hell,
> yet rising like Aphrodite from the sea,
> refreshed and radiant with indecency?
> Can I kiss Theseus with dissembled poise?
> I think each stone and pillar has a voice.

Lowell's skill in flexing his syntax from line to line serves him well in these couplets in which the enjambed rhymes occur smoothly and enforce the flow of feeling by linking related nouns ("infidel" / "hell"), emphasizing sensuality ("sea" / "indecency"), and in the half-rhyme of "poise" and "voice," which undercuts the insincerity of the first with the metaphorical solidity of the second. He takes greater liberty with his rhymes than either Dryden or Pope;

rhyming masculine and feminine endings and the vowel rhyme of "poise" and "voice" would have incurred their suspicion, but by bending prosodic rules, Lowell gives his verse the range of options necessary to sustain such an intense effort in an age that is no longer enamored of the heroic couplet. Similarly effective lines occur throughout the play, such as these from act two, scene five:

> I grew so wrung and wasted, men mistook
> me for the Sibyl. If you could bear to look
> your eyes would tell you. Do you believe my passion
> is voluntary? That my obscene confession
> is some dark trick, some oily artifice?
> I came to beg you not to sacrifice
> my son, already uncertain of his life.
> Ridiculous, mad embassy, for a wife
> who loves her stepson! Prince, I only spoke
> about myself! Avenge yourself, invoke
> your father; a worse monster threatens you
> than any Theseus ever fought and slew.

Neither the efficacy of individual passages nor the relative success or failure of the whole is as important as the propriety of the enterprise. Tate, by his own approach to translation (and even imitation in some instances), was predisposed to approve of Lowell's methods, even though he retained the right to criticize the actual results. In the same letter, he goes on to *Imitations* (which, like *Phaedra*, had not yet been published) and praises Lowell for particular poems: "I have not read all the Imitations with equal attention, but confined my closest reading to the renditions of Baudelaire. These I think are supremely good. Voyage to Cythera, The Swan, and Au Lecteur bring these poems to life for me again. The version of Au Lecteur is masterly, possibly it is better than the original; it is certainly more powerful."

This last comment is consistent with what he would later write about the same poem in "Translation or Imitation?" but here he is not concerned with the implications of a translation being better than its original. The general praise of this letter is consistent with his later argument about the translator's status and role: "I believe that generally you are making the art of translation an original art.

150

The best of these versions are yours quite as much as theirs. May I suggest that you consider some other title? 'Imitations' under- states your achievement. Why not 'Versions: a book of free Trans- lations.'"

Tate's proposed title probably would not have mollified the critics, but it does better describe what Lowell had done. A poem such as Tate's "Death of Little Boys" might better be described as an "imitation" in relation to Rimbaud's distant original. Perhaps, as already suggested, even Lowell's "For the Union Dead" could be regarded as an "imitation." No term exists for such remote der- ivation of one poem from another. Lowell's imitations, however, could not escape being regarded as some form of translation, so by appending the word "free," he might have better prepared the critics for the loose yet definite ways in which these poems are linked to their prototypes. Lowell's predisposition to "imitate" both poems of foreign literatures and those by his mentor suggests how deeply indebted he felt toward his predecessors and rivals and how willing he was to make their poems his own. What Harold Bloom has named the "anxiety of influence" Lowell at- tempted to make an integral part of his poetic.

In November, Lowell wrote a touching but humorous letter that had nothing to do with Tate's praise of *Imitations:* "The years of our friendship seemed to roll through me the other night as the hours went and I hope my sobriety didn't hide my strong feelings. Your account of Gettysburg at the dim end was like some appari- tion and haunted me. I thought too at that moment, when there was just the family left, and we were all joking and interrupting that everyone loved you and that it must be very fine to have Belle take you just as you are, and that all the talk of Caroline that might have been embarrassing made everything more natural and was a relief." [26]

Their friendship was relentlessly literary, however, and the next month, on rereading *Imitations* after publication, Tate felt more predisposed to pick and choose, so he wrote to Lowell outlining his dislikes and preferences: "I wish you had done without the Homeric fragment, the Hebel and the Heine, and perhaps even Valery's Helen. This last is fine, but perhaps one of the big poems

151

might have been expected of you. I can say little of your Paster-
nak, except that they don't hit me hard. . . . (you are a better
'translator' than Pound). . . . There are exciting things in your Villon. I feel that perhaps your ballade stanza might have been a little
more stiff and formal. Nobody has done the magpies and crows in
the Epitaph as well as you."[27]

The Hebel ("Sic Transit") does appear to be a victim of "translatorese," as does "Heine Dying in Paris," but the passage that Tate
praises from Villon is vivid and effective:

> The rain has soaked and washed us bare,
> the sun has burned us black. Magpies
> and crows have chiselled out our eyes,
> have jerked away our beards and hair.
> Our bodies have no time to rest:
> our chains clank north, south, east and west,
> now here, now there, to the winds' dance—
> more beaks of birds than knives in France!

Lowell's strong verbs—"soaked," "chiselled," "jerked,"
"clank"—suggest the harshness of the situation and, in particular,
mimic the quick, rough gestures of the feeding birds. Much of the
Villon piece is effective, and the general consensus was that the
imitations from French poetry were stronger, in general, than
most of the others.

In "Translation or Imitation?" when he reprints Lowell's and
Kunitz's versions of "Au Lecteur" to demonstrate how two varia-
tions on the same original can sustain interest, Tate argues, "The
versatility of translation is without limit."[28] Although a number of
reviewers thought that Lowell had transgressed a nonexistent
limit and others, such as Edmund Wilson, were as sympathetic as
one might wish, Tate probably understood better than anyone
what Lowell had hoped to accomplish, and his praise was offered
in full understanding of the risks run and the difficulties incurred.

After "For the Union Dead," Lowell wrote no original poetry for
more than a year, but late in 1961, he began producing new work,
mostly in brief, orderly free-verse stanzas. "Water," "Eye and
Tooth," "The Scream," and "The Old Flame" were among the

poems that would later become part of *For the Union Dead.* Each of these is of particular interest here. "Eye and Tooth" (along with "Middle Age") responds to Tate's "The Eye" by explaining the results of Tate's dicta,

> The happy child becomes the man,
> The elegant man becomes the mind,
> The fathered gentleman who can
> Perform quick feats of gentle kind . . . ,

in terms of present physical suffering (ironically, according to Lowell, caused by ill-fitting contact lenses) [29] and flawed vision ("I saw things darkly, / as through an unwashed goldfish globe"). Both difficulties, the poem implies, derive from the child's little sin:

> No ease for the boy at the keyhole,
> his telescope,
> when the women's white bodies flashed
> in the bathroom.

The consequences were immediate: "Young, my eyes began to fail." If Tate's poem, as Robert Dupree argues, "depicts a world that has misused memory," Lowell's response depicts a man physically flawed by memory.[30] Tate's eye may well represent the ego, but Lowell's represents the ironic failure of the ego. He said at a reading that "Eye and Tooth" referred to a failed attempt to wear contact lenses. New York grit got under them and abraded the corneas. He wore the contacts, he said, to look younger. The humor of "Eye and Tooth" is oblique and not inherent to the poem (one needs to know the story of the contact lenses), but with its ending is humility itself and accords, in a more personal way, with Tate's poem in which the death of the spirit is an issue. In Lowell's poem, even the spirit is temporarily blinded by the corneal pain, so the entire world is reduced to the physical, and all of the speaker's memories are of the body—first the tooth "noosed in a knot to the doorknob," then the glimpsed "women's white bodies" that caused his young eyes to falter. "Everyone's tired of my turmoil," he claims, and this personal chaos is incurable in part because it is the product of a lifetime of concentration on the physical world that has failed him in great and small ways.

"Water," which would become the first poem in *For the Union Dead*, probably derives from Lowell's visit to Bishop in Stonington, Maine, in 1948. (Revised and reprinted in *History*, it bears the title "For Elizabeth Bishop 1. Water") The poem's landscape is specific and geographically correct; Stonington's island granite quarries remain visible (some worked even in recent years):

> dozens of bleak
> white frame houses stuck
> like oyster shells
> on a hill of rock

These word portray the village almost as effectively as John Marin's famous watercolors do. After discouraging Mrs. Dawson, Lowell stayed with Bishop in the rented house in Stonington and, at some point, asked her to marry him. In the fiction of the poem, the woman and the speaker apparently agreed that, because "the water was too cold" for them, they would renounce marriage or romance for friendship. Bishop was a lesbian and unlikely to consider marriage, but the biographical accuracy of the poem is not so important as the fact that Lowell, in the early 1960s was returning to his life of the 1940s as a source of inspiration. Even though the poem is set in an identifiable place, the effective imagery is the result not of geographical precision or specificity but of Lowell's tactile language, which appeals to the senses of touch and texture as well as sight.

> Remember? We sat on a slab of rock.
> From this distance in time,
> it seems the color
> of iris, rotting and turning purpler,
>
> but it was only
> the usual gray rock
> turning the usual green
> when drenched by the sea.

Anyone who has sat on a rock by the sea feels those colors—purple, gray, green—as textures of barnacle and weed. The modest free verse, with its occasional rhymes (usually ABCA), allows the carefully linked sea-images of islands, oyster shells, weir, rock, mermaid, wharf-pile, and barnacles to give the poem its structure so that the last line—"the water was too cold for us"—renounces everything physical and sensuous in the poem's world and offers a perfect, negative image of chastity. The paradox that sensuous— or sensual—indulgence should be potentially "too cold" is a consequence of the poem's chilly Maine atmosphere, and in context it is convincing.

Bishop clearly was on his mind at this time. "The Scream" is an imitation or translation of her story "In the Village," which had appeared in the *New Yorker* some years before. Lowell's poem isolates the elements or symbols of madness and abnormality to present, in the context of childhood memory, a sense of loss beyond that vague nostalgia we all feel for our past. In "The Scream," everything is linked to madness, everything is strange or unsightly or disgusting, even the "unlovely" books sold by drummers. Although the voices of the mad and the dead were "too frail / for us to hear [them] long," the poem preserves them and demonstrates how, in memory the mere "echo of a scream," a "thinning scream," can shape forever the variety of unrelated images, even of the most ordinary domestic scenes:

A cow drooled green grass strings,
made cow flop, *smack, smack, smack!*
and tried to brush off its flies
on a lilac bush—all,
forever, at one fell swoop!

In the blacksmith's shop,
the horseshoes sailed through the dark,
like bloody little moons,
red-hot, hissing, protesting,
as they drowned in the pan.

Nothing of the gentleness of Bishop's story remains, none of its leisure and fluency, only the cruellest or harshest images. The poem is almost as different from the story as Tate's "Death of Little Boys" is different from Rimbaud's "Le Chercheuses de poux." Lowell's derivation is more deliberate and is acknowledged, as is only proper, but the acknowledgement invites the reader to compare the poem to the story, and in that comparison, the poem seems wanting because it has rejected so much of Bishop's humanly ambiguous context.

"The Old Flame," another poem derived from his life in the 1940s, addresses Jean Stafford and refers to their time in Damariscotta Mills. The speaker drives through the village and notes that a new landlord, disregarding whatever decline or suffering Lowell and Stafford may have undergone since they lived there, has renewed their old house. "Everything's changed for the best," he bravely asserts, the "ghostly / imaginary lover" long departed with their younger selves, then "quivering and fierce . . . simmering like wasps" in their "tent of books." Like her imaginary lover, Stafford is now a ghost (not actually deceased, but a ghost of memory), but the poem asks her to "speak" again (like Hamlet's father) with her "voice / of flaming insight." The poem concludes by implicitly acknowledging their essential separateness even at that time:

In one bed and apart,

we heard the plow
groaning up hill—
red light, then a blue,
as it tossed off the snow
to the side of the road.

The careers of Lowell and Stafford, "groaning up hill" like that plow, were then a single unit, but like the red light and the blue, the poet and the novelist were opposites in some spectral way and were destined to finally separate. Momentarily united in the single task of forging their careers (tossing "off the snow / to the side of the road"), they parted as soon as those careers were established. Again, reading the poem in this light requires biographical information that is not included in the poem, but Lowell, by introducing the ghostly imaginary lover, directs the reader toward one of the sources. Stafford's "A Country Love Story" concerns a woman whose unhappy marriage to an ailing, selfish intellectual is slowly failing, and it includes a ghostly imaginary lover. The story, which is set in a spot much like their lost Maine paradise of Damariscotta Mills, is the source of both the lover and the image of the plow groaning uphill with its red and blue lights.[31]

Of interest here is Lowell's apparent obsession with the 1940s, illustrated by a poem responding to one of Tate's from the period, two poems related to his early years of friendship with Elizabeth Bishop, and one reviving images from his first marriage. A number of others written in the next two years would derive from, or refer to earlier works by friends or would dramatize events in Lowell's life that occurred twelve or more years earlier. Scattered or grouped among the varied poems of *For the Union Dead*, they lend a sense of autobiographical continuity to a book that is mostly written in the domestic or public voice of the quotidian.

In the fall of 1964, *For the Union Dead* appeared to generally laudatory reviews. The book appealed to many critics for its forthright public poems like "Fall 1961," an expression of collective terror of nuclear war, and the title poem, which addressed a variety of contemporary concerns including war, segregation, the deterioration of urban life, and the helplessness of the individual. The book was well-balanced between autobiography and public statement, offering something for critics of most persuasions. Robert Bly disliked the book, but Stanley Kunitz, Richard Poirier, and a number of others practically canonized Lowell. The poet was amazed, and wrote to Tate, "My book is getting astonishing attention, and I suppose I enjoy it all to the limit—a head of uncertainty curdled with vanity. You see, it all comes on top of a stretch of dark, post manic and pathological self-abasement. Well, no moral—it's a good life for all its excessive shine and wriggling."[32]

Lowell was responding to a letter Tate had written to him just a few days before. Tate focused on the poem that, as Lowell would acknowledge, owes the most to Tate's own work, but he found much else to praise as well:

> I have been reading and reading For the Union Dead. It is a very fine book. Comparisons with Lord Weary or Life Studies might be profitable, but they would not define the quality of the newer work. After my first reading of For the Union Dead I had the unhappy suspicion

that, as a *book* of poems it might not be as impressive as Lord Weary. I had checked the titles in For the Union that I thought are first-rate. There are more fine poems here than in Lord Weary. I am not considering chronology or "development," merely two books of poems.

Here is my list:

The Severed Head. This may be your most powerful poem. I can find no flaw in it.

Beyond the Alps. From all your books this is one of the four or five best. (Since you reprinted it from Life Studies, I could wish you'd reprinted To the Reader—your poem, not Baudelaire's—from Imitations.)

The Old Flame. This makes me dizzy on the brink of a chasm.

Tenth Muse. Your formal verse is still masterly.

The Drinker. This is very fine; but I feel it would be even better without lines 13–18.

Those Before Us, Eye and Tooth. Law and Middle Age are fine, but not your top level.

The Flaw and Night Sweat are in your best vein, but just a little below The Severed Head.

For the Union Dead I still greatly admire but it suffers from being in competition with your very best.

The only rival you had in your literary generation was Ted Roethke (he was actually ten years older than you). The rivalry was strictly in excellence: you and Ted are as different as night and day, both of you being night *and* day.[33]

Tate seized upon "The Severed Head," not only for its excellence, but because it reworked a persistent theme in his own work, the confrontation with the alter ego or the double, usually in some mutilated form. The particular mutilation here, the severed head, derives from Tate's "The Maimed Man," but where Tate shows us "a young man . . . headless, whose hand / Hung limp," Lowell gives us a head without the body for a title. The confrontation of the dreaming speaker is with his deepest creative self, whose words, although written in blood, fed directly from his heart and "left no markings on the page." The vision of himself as being reduced to a futile writer, who says, "Sometimes I ask myself, if I exist," leaves the speaker contemplating his cruelty and indif-

158

ference to his wife, who in the dream is merely a paper figure. The poem then concerns itself with the ruthlessness of the writer's self-obsession. Another interpretation, as Stephen Yenser has pointed out, reveals the poet's "relationship to his material," his escape from the confinement of his early career through the confrontation with the mystery figure. This figure is tutor, alter ego, or both; his link between heart and pen "represent[s] an intimate, immediate sort of poet."[34] Any reading of this complex poem has to confront the enigma of the alter ego, the mystery self that, like Tate's headless young man, bears a significance beyond mere paraphrase. The poem's terza rima is subtly handled. No doubt it appealed to Tate as homage to his own terza rima and as proof of Lowell's continued allegiance to, and mastery of, formal verse.

Lowell's reply left no doubt of the link between Tate's work and his own, but he does not mention "The Maimed Man" and, instead, suggests two other poems that resemble "The Severed Head" in tone and syntax:

> Thanks for liking what you like, and for being pointed and generous as always. Nothing could please me more than your picking the Severed Head. For years after reading your terza rima poems, I"ve wanted to try the meter. I've always found I could not even make sense, and somehow lacked the energy to bend the rhymes to anything. When I finally did, it nearly killed me. The poem owes a lot to you in general. Wolves, the Autumn section of Seasons and elsewhere. I wanted to dedicate it to you, but thought it dull and monotonous in comparison with your much stronger and more original Swimmers.
>
> P.S. It's curious how the form makes possible and almost demands some sort of allegorical narrative.[35]

"Allegorical narrative" is a reasonable term for both "The Buried Lake" and "The Severed Head," neither of which attempt the greater naturalism of "The Swimmers." Since the *Divine Comedy*, the grandparent of all terza rima poems, might be called an allegorical narrative, Lowell's footnote may be a shy way of linking Tate and himself to their ancestral source. Dante had been one of Lowell's favorite poets from the early 1950s on; his modest success

159

with "The Severed Head" may have lent him the courage to attempt a translation of Canto XV of the *Inferno*, which he did the following year.

"The Wolves" is another allegory, a dramatization of various nightmarish, inescapable situations. Like so many of Tate's poems of the 1930s and 1940s, it deals with the sufferings of a life in which fear has displaced faith. Lowell's response in "The Severed Head" uses none of Tate's pointedly archetypal imagery. Tate's closing statement that "man can never be alone" may have suggested to Lowell the persistent presence of the dream-figure, the alter ego. Too human to actually resemble Tate's wolf, "a savage beast / Maybe with golden hair, with deep eyes / Like a bearded spider on a sunlit floor," Lowell's dream-figure nevertheless sports a moustache that is "too brown, too bushy," possibly a very oblique parody of Tate's bestial archetype. The threatening, nightmarish atmosphere of "The Wolves," effective despite the slightly melodramatic allegory, was probably what most impressed Lowell and was certainly what he tried to reproduce in "The Severed Head."

The "Autumn" section of "Seasons of the Soul" is a dream of a descent into a private hell, a kind of nightmarish version of Alice's descent into Wonderland:

> The round ceiling was high
> And the gray light like shale
> Thin, crumbling, and dry:
> No rug on the bare floor
> Nor any carved detail
> To which the eye could glide;
> I counted along the wall
> Door after closed door
> Through which a shade might slide
> To the cold and empty hall.

Although the speaker resolves to leave this place, he must walk "years down / Towards the front door / At the end of the empty hall," where he finds that the "door was false—no key / Or lock." No escape, only confrontation with figures from the past, none of whom, not even his father, recognizes him. Lowell echoes this entrapment in an even bleaker picture:

160

Translation or Imitation?

> What
> I imagined was a spider crab, my small
> chance of surviving in this room. Its shut
> windows had sunken into solid wall.
> I nursed my last clear breath of oxygen,
> there, waiting for the chandelier to fall,
> tentacles clawing for my jugular.

Despite Lowell's acknowledgement, the echoes are oblique and the originality of his poem far outweighs its small debt to Tate. Lowell was conscious of that debt largely because Tate, unlike most of his predecessor poets, was a living presence in Lowell's life, a figure that, through the years of their friendship, linked him to his own past and continually reminded him of his early efforts and influences.

Immediately following the publication of *For the Union Dead*, Lowell was caught up in the production of *The Old Glory*, which opened at the American Place Theater in November 1964. He suffered another breakdown that winter but, by summer, had recovered and was ready to begin a new stage of his career. Invited in June to attend a White House Festival of the Arts, he at first accepted then changed his mind. In a letter sent to President Johnson and the *New York Times*, he objected to America's growing war in Vietnam, then in its early stages, and explicitly linked art to politics by arguing that "every serious artist knows he cannot enjoy public celebration without making subtle public commitments." This stance differed from Tate's and his own position of the 1940s; if applied to the Ezra Pound situation, it might have made the Bollingen controversy appear somewhat different.[36] Tate and Lowell both saw a role for the poem as a critic of culture and society, but "To Our Young Pro-Consuls of the Air" specifically rejects the more directly activist role fostered by MacLeish and others, and Lowell, in *Land of Unlikeness* and *Lord Weary's Castle*, ignored the possibility of direct political statement in favor of a more general critique of contemporary society. Since both poets had more or less disavowed any direct role in political affairs, they could deny Pound the same role, deny that his radio broadcasts and unsavory political opinions corrupted his poetry or violated

161

his aesthetic standards. Of course, the case for *The Pisan Cantos* could have been argued on other grounds as well, but in 1948, Lowell did not see the poet's role as political as he would in the late 1960s.

Lowell's revised stance—that even an appearance at a public event could make the artist complicit in political machinations from which he should remain aloof—implied that the artist's actions count in political terms, that these actions assume a more precise and deliberate role in which resistance to unethical government behavior had to be explicit. Lowell's letter enjoyed wide publicity and, in one stroke, made him a leader among intellectuals who were opposed to the war. The consequences for his poetry were considerable; musing on this event and on the role of poets in world affairs in general during the summer of 1965, he drafted his most public poem (public in both topic and voice) to date, and he turned to Horace and Dante as examples of poets who spoke to the issues of their day in a way that made them timeless.

Public Voices

The eruptive decade of the 1960s confirmed Lowell's determination to bring poetry closer to both personal experience and the larger experience of America. The collective agony of the era began with the assassination of John Kennedy but found its apotheosis in the public struggle over the Vietnam War. Earlier than many artists and intellectuals, Lowell committed himself to a role of opposition. The publicity generated by his refusal of President Johnson's invitation initiated a new public presence for Lowell during the months that he was working on the poems of *Near the Ocean* and in the three or four years following.

Although the war and the politics surrounding it began to obsess Lowell, in 1965 and 1966 the most immediate source of grief was the deaths of friends. Delmore Schwartz died in July 1966. He had been ill for years and lived alone in a seedy hotel, his reputation dimmed, his paranoia alienating him from even the most loyal friends. Lowell had secured him a job at Syracuse University, but Schwartz's strange and sometimes nearly violent behavior had rendered him almost unable to function. Early in 1966, without waiting for a decision from the administration on his tenure bid, he left Syracuse for New York and took a room at the Hotel Dixie.

163

He died of a heart attack while carrying his trash into a back hall-way and lay there unnoticed for some time. His body remained unclaimed for several days in the morgue.

This was the third (after Roethke and Jarrell) of the premature deaths that haunted Lowell's generation. The first, and perhaps the hardest for Lowell to bear, had occurred the previous October. Randall Jarrell, who like many of the other poets of his generation had been suffering some mental instability, had been struck and killed by a car while walking on a dark, busy highway. Lowell's papers at Harvard contain a collection of newspaper clippings from North Carolina; he apparently examined the tragedy as closely as possible. Whether Jarrell had died accidently or whether he had leaped into the path of the oncoming car was—and is—uncertain, but Lowell was convinced that the death was suicide. In *History,* he memorialized Jarrell in terms that make clear his belief that Jarrell killed himself. Making no attempt to explain Jar-rell's fate, the poem contrasts the crude glory of his death with the memory of their college days in Ohio:

I grizzle the embers of our onetime life,
our first intoxicating disenchantments,
dipping our hands once, not twice in the newness . . .   (*Lowell's ellipsis*)
coming back to Kenyon on the Ohio local—
the view, middle distance, back and foreground, shifts,
silos shifting squares like chessmen—a wheel
turned by the water buffalo through the blue
of true space before the dawn of days. . . .   (*Lowell's ellipsis*)
Then the night of the caged squirrel on his wheel,
lights, eyes, peering at you from the overpass;
black-gloved, black-coated, you plod out stubbornly
as if in lockstep to grasp your blank not-I   (*Lowell's ellipsis*)
at the foot of the tunnel . . . as if asleep, Child Randall,
greeting the car, and approving—your harsh luminosity.

Disenchantments are intoxicating at first, but later they turn deadly. Yet Jarrell always retained something of the child's love of wonder, if not the capacity to experience it. Dressed as the very embodiment of death, he stepped into the highway to enter everything that was not himself. His love of children may have, in some way, alienated him from the adult world. Tate noted, "When he came to see us in Tennessee, and later at Princeton, he would leave the company to play with my small daughter and her friends, whom he enjoyed more than he did us."[1] Tate's uneasiness with Jarrell pervades the brief memoir written for a memorial volume that was edited by Lowell, Taylor, and Robert Penn Warren. The intimacy he felt with Lowell, the equal freedom to criticize or to praise, was lacking in his relationship with Jarrell, although he admired his work. Reading Tate's memoir, one senses that, for him, Jarrell remained "a proud and difficult young man who studied all the time," who avoided the relative relaxation of maturity. Lowell, who obviously loved Jarrell, also found him distant and elusive in some ways and, in his own memoir, fixed him in a series of images and contexts:

> Poor modern-minded exile from the forest of Grimm, I see him un-bearded, slightly South American-looking, then later bearded, with a beard we at first wished to reach out our hands to and pluck off, but which later became him, like Walter Bagehot's, or some Symbolist's in France's *fin de siècle* Third Republic. Then unbearded again. I see the bright, petty, pretty sacred objects he accumulated for his joy and solace: Vermeer's red-hatted girl, the Piero and Donatello reproductions, the photographs of his bruised, merciful heroes: Chekhov, Rilke, Marcel Proust. I see the white sporting Mercedes-Benz, the ever better cut and more deliberately jaunty clothes, the television with its long afternoons of professional football, those matches he thought more graceful than college football. . . .[2]

Lowell concludes by referring to Jarrell's "noble, difficult, and beautiful soul," but glimpses of that soul seem oblique and distant. The imagery of Jarrell, with and without beard and surrounded by his art objects, is a series of still lifes, unlike the portrait of Tate in Lowell's 1959 memoir in which the imagery serves to animate Tate's brilliant conversation.

This digression into Jarrell's relations to Tate and Lowell is intended to suggest that the friendship between Lowell and Tate was unusually open in some respects. Little in the correspondence between Jarrell and Lowell invites comparison with the warmth of Tate and Lowell's friendship. Despite their natural reticence, Tate and Lowell were consistently frank and affectionate. Lowell's correspondence with Jarrell and with most other poets of his generation shows less of this warmth; his correspondence with Elizabeth Bishop, who also was a poetic model for him, is the major exception. This does not diminish Lowell's affection for Jarrell, which plainly was sincere, but Tate and Bishop offered him more as a poet, and his particular interest in their work, fond as he was of them as friends, was often what animated their correspondence.

The deaths of Jarrell and Schwartz dismayed Lowell, and his poetry from then on would have a new elegiac undertone. Theodore Roethke had died in 1963. Even though, or perhaps because he was not as close a friend as either Jarrell or Schwartz, he was the first Lowell eulogized in verse. "For Theodore Roethke" (in *Near the Ocean*) emphasizes the primal quality of Roethke's poetry, its closeness to elemental forms of life, rather than centering on their rather distant friendship. The elegies in *History*—to Jarrell, Schwartz, and Roethke again—are more concerned with friendship, as is the fine elegy to Berryman in *Day by Day*. Elegy stimulated some of Lowell's finest work. "The Quaker Graveyard at Nantucket," "In Memory of Arthur Winslow," "For the Union Dead," and "Soft Wood" demonstrate how well he could handle the genre over a varied range of formality. The deaths of the poets of his own generation eventually brought a new note of personal sadness into his work, possibly confirming Tate's fear that Lowell could not achieve sufficient distance from his subject. To some readers, however, this sadness seemed a fresh mood in poetry, one that, however personal and distant from the grander emotions of tragedy, gave appropriate voice to the long decline of twentieth-century America.

At the end of 1966, Lowell suffered his annual winter breakdown and entered McLean's for another stay, but this time the psychiatrists were more helpful. They prescribed lithium, which had been tested in Europe as a treatment for manic-depressive syndrome and found somewhat effective. Lithium helped Lowell for a few years, but it requires careful monitoring and does not mix well with other drugs, including alcohol. It would not provide a permanent cure, but it did help Lowell get through several winters without what had become a serious annual breakdown. It enabled him to get more writing done, giving him the freedom from illness that made *Notebook* and the subsequent sonnet volumes possible. Lowell was at first cautious about the efficacy of the drug, but when he had enjoyed a whole year without problems, he wrote about it to Tate, who responded with further encouragement: "The best news in your letter is the new pill you are taking. It's not at all *so late!* You have thirty years ahead, if not more. That you missed this last December crisis is a wonderful sign."[3]

The respite provided by lithium, though temporary, was welcome. The first result was the publication of the much-delayed *Near the Ocean*. Its composition, revision, and publication had been a drawn-out process; despite the time and effort, it would be Lowell's slimmest volume. With only seven new poems and imitations of Horace, Quevedo, Gongora, and, most significantly, Dante and Juvenal, the book appeared that spring. But the ambition and grandeur of its attempt to link imperial Rome and imperial America in a unifying poetic vision make it seem larger than its modest bulk and its somewhat pretentiously illustrated format suggest.

Politics and power were on Lowell's mind and had been topics in his poetry for years. In keeping with his now well-defined aesthetic dedication to the linking of art and experience, he faced the problem of finding a fresh voice to express a dismay that was both personal and social. In *Life Studies* and *For the Union Dead*, he had invented a poetic that would not only accommodate a variety of public and private experience but would link, and perhaps eventually obliterate, the distinction. In writing "Waking Early Sunday Morning," a major effort in the new public mode of his poetic, he turned to a source of inspiration that he had first attempted in the 1940s. Following Tate's example, he borrowed a stanza from Marvell that demonstrated flexibility yet sufficient formality for the seriousness of his topic. "Waking Early Sunday Morning" is important—although Tate left no comment on it—because it embodies a recurrent aspect of Tate's poetic, one that Lowell adopted and used throughout his career: the revitalization of poetic forms and strategies from the past. Alan Williamson has traced the evolution of this poem through various drafts, from one concerning the poet's consciousness of personal and poetic inadequacies to one that links personal flaws with the collective guilt of a nation that, through the abuse of power, threatens the entire planet. He argues that "Lowell associated his own more formal high style with political engagement."[4]

The choice of a stanzaic form from Marvell for "Waking Early Sunday Morning" would seem to confirm that argument, but the political poems in *For the Union Dead* are all in free verse, and the political poems of *Notebook* are written in the informal unrhymed sonnet-shape to which Lowell committed six years of his writing life. In the act of rewriting "Waking Early Sunday Morning," however, the formality of Marvell's stanza pushed him farther from the personal voice of the early versions and into the public subject matter and more strident voice of the final version that appeared in *Near the Ocean*. The tetrameter octet rhymed in couplets was one of Marvell's favorite forms. He used it for "Upon Appleton House," "Upon the Hill and Grove at Bill-borow," "Damon the Mower," "The Unfortunate Lover," and, most importantly, "The Garden." Lowell's poem revolves around the theme of the machine in the garden, the intrusive presence of technology—in this case, the technology of war—in an idealized pastoral setting, and the cruel phallocentrism of American and Christian culture that encourages the abuse of power by centering it in a Freudian misapplication of sexuality.

Apparently Lowell neglected to send Tate "Waking Early Sunday Morning," so his mentor's reaction to it is not clear. Two years after *Near the Ocean* appeared, Tate commented only, "I was worried about *Near the Ocean* except for about three poems."[5] Whether those three included "Waking Early Sunday Morning" is unknown, but a poem as richly inclusive, as gracefully and formally argued, and as dependent on a borrowed but time-honored formal stanza must have caught Tate's interest. As it appeared in *Near the Ocean*, it was the most political of Lowell's important poems, but its complexity, Freudianism, reference to the pastoral tradition, outrage at human and environmental abuse, and anger over lack of faith must have won Tate's sympathy. Whether his ear was fully engaged by the Marvellian stanzas is another matter. He may have found them too obvious and insistent for such a strident and horatory poem. What would have been appropriate in Marvell's time might have seemed heavy-handed to a poet schooled in T. S. Eliot's more oblique use of borrowed formalities. Yet, on the whole, it is hard to believe Tate did not approve of the poem, which skillfully debates in its own terms the problems of the poet's responsibilities, ambition, and relationship to the world of power and politics.

"Waking Early Sunday Morning" appropriately opens with a highly conventional invocation that appeals to nature as the only source of adequate metaphors for the proper linking of power and sexuality, a stanza that sets the tone of longing that dominates the poem. In the literary formality of its conventional apostrophe and its declaration of allegiance to a rigid verse-form, the first stanza suggests the shape and boundaries of the cultural and social restraints from which the poet longs to free himself:

> O to break loose, like the chinook
> salmon jumping and falling back,
> nosing up to the impossible
> stone and bone-crushing waterfall—
> raw-jawed, weak-fleshed there, stopped by ten
> steps of the roaring ladder, and then
> to clear the top on the last try,
> alive enough to spawn and die.

Because the poet cannot achieve this heroic dream of the conquest of obstacles and the fulfillment of the reproductive urge, he is forced to grope about in his waking moments for a metaphor, from either memory or the present, for some other embodiment of healthy sexuality and the non-destructive use of power. First he reenters for a moment the sexual innocence and timelessness of childhood:

> Stop, back off. The salmon breaks
> water, and now my body wakes

169

to feel the unpolluted joy
and criminal leisure of a boy. . . .

The poem then darkens. The expression intensifies and the mood changes to one of potential tragedy as the poet confronts his failure to find an adequate outlet for his own energy and creative drive. "Vermin run for their unstopped holes," and other "creatures of the night . . . go on grinding," their obsessions unsated, insatiable, their tasks pointless and repetitive. In facing this microcosmic actuality, the poet also faces his knowledge that memory will not suffice, that another day of pain, lack of faith, and failure of self-expression lies ahead; the "sun's / daily remorseful blackout" is another trial by fire. The pastoral imagery takes an ironic turn in this third stanza. "Vermin" are not the dignified creatures of natural symbolism; they represent a declension from the dream-image of the falls-leaping salmon. In similar declension, the sunrise that is dimmed by the poet's sense of inadequacy becomes a paradoxical blackout rather than a fresh illumination.

The poet then turns that "Fierce, fireless mind," its powers waning, to the ordinary harbor scene of expensive yachts. Their Homeric "wine-dark hulls" are the first of a series of phallic images that obliquely, and then more explicitly, equate money and power (both political and spiritual power) with the abuse of sexuality. Ironically, instead of men going "down to the sea in ships," it is "business as usual in eclipse" that makes this journey. The sea is now the private domain of the rich and privileged.

Since his glance toward the harbor proves unsatisfying, the poet tries to find himself in an object near at hand. He watches "a glass of water wet / with a fine fuzz of icy sweat" and imagines that its "silvery colors touched with sky" represent a "neutrality" that will calm him, but behind this neutral color lies something darker, more obdurate, and gloomier:

yet if I shift, or change my mood,
I see some object made of wood,
background behind it of brown grain,
to darken it, but not to stain.

The poem then returns to the high rhetoric of the opening stanza and, for two stanzas, mourns the death of spirit and the

170

failure of religion. Once faith "gave darkness some control," but it is no longer available to Lowell because, as the poem eventually argues, "His vanishing / emblems" are so phallic and so useless that they have become emblems without significance, "sad / slight, useless things to calm the mad." The poet realizes this only when he has confronted the "dregs and dreck" of his own life, pathetically and uselessly phallic "tools with no handle, / ten candle-ends not worth a candle, / old lumber banished from the Temple." The Christian references might seem to be matters of association, but they are calculated to link the personal impotence of the poet (not a literal impotence, but one that is political and rhetorical) with the faded rhetoric and lost aspirations of the church.

The next stanza yokes the church to Goliath's "military splendor" as a further study in failed rhetoric and aborted power. It concludes with an image that explicitly allies the failure or abuse of power ("elephants and phalanx") with sexual frustration: "a million foreskins hit the trash." Yet having presented this harsh juxtaposition, the poet rebukes himself for raising his voice, even though he is aware that a lowered tone will not resolve his dilemma and may open his meditation again to obsessions with power, sexuality, religion, and other sources of excessive rhetoric. In the ninth stanza, in which God's "vanishing emblems" occur, the poet refers for the first time to "we." This first-person plural indicates that the poet now sees his voice as a public one that speaks both for his own obsessions and failures and for those of the larger community.

The three remaining stanzas constitute Lowell's strongest public statement. The first of these returns to the opening stanza, reiterating its desire to "break loose" from the demands of self and others, from the abuse of power, rhetoric, and sex. It argues beautifully, perfectly, that "all's life's grandeur / is something with a girl in summer." The speaker then turns to the president (Johnson at that time) a figure of phallocentrism "swimming nude, unbuttoned, sick / of his ghost-written rhetoric." The president has tired of his own words partly because they are written by others; the poet, on the other hand, is tired of his own words because they speak to aspects of himself that disgust him: "everyone's tired of my turmoil" as he said in "Eye and Tooth."

The cruelty, obsession, and ambition of war dominate the penultimate stanza. It closes with a metaphor that echoes the pastoral source of this stanza form, a gardening image that is fused to an Old Testament sense of fate and finality:

No weekends for the gods now. Wars
flicker, earth licks its open sores,
fresh breakage, fresh promotions, chance
assassinations, no advance.
Only man thinning out his kind
sounds through the Sabbath noon, the blind
swipe of the pruner and his knife   (*Lowell's*
busy about the tree of life . . .   *ellipsis*)

The closure assumes a new diminuendo, the lowered tone and pitch of prayer; but in a poem that has more or less dismissed faith as a failed attempt to give "darkness some control," this ending is ironic and tragic, appealing for "peace to our children" to a god that is as diminished in power and as girdled in rhetoric as are the poet and the president:

Pity the planet, all joy gone
from this sweet volcanic cone;
peace to our children when they fall
in small war on the heels of small
war—until the end of time
to police the earth, a ghost
orbiting forever lost
in our monotonous sublime.

This final note of pain and loss are truer and more heartfelt than anything a more insistent rhetoric could offer. A change of tone would seem unjustified except that striking such an elegiac note (like contriving the opening apostrophe to nature) requires mastering a certain literary tone. That is, the poet had to realize the pervasiveness and conventional nature of rhetoric and risk the possibility that even finding the right voice would fail to free him for the heartfelt closure unless he were first to free himself from self-obsession and direct his gaze outward beyond the president and the suffering public world. The argument seems to be that

172

rhetoric demands to be tempered to its subject, that self-obsession must give way to empathy—even empathy with the president—to induce the proper note of unsententious grief. The discovery of this sentiment in a poem so profoundly distrustful of its own shifts of mood, so willing to link rhetoric and the drive for power with impotence, castration (according to Williamson), and other unpleasant, unhealthy, or maimed states of sexuality is a miracle of some sort and makes the poem for some readers indescribably moving.

"Waking Early Sunday Morning" first appeared in the *New York Review of Books* in a version that emphasized somewhat more forcefully Lowell's disappointment with his own writing, and Tate may have seen this as another unhealthy sign of self-obsession. Some readers have preferred the *New York Review* version, but for others, the version that appeared in *Near the Ocean*—which avoids the topic of failed verse and instead moves into such issues as the links among power and sexuality, politics, rhetoric (not poetic, but general), and the loss of faith—seems stronger. Certainly Tate should have admired it, and perhaps he did, but unless letters have been lost, it is strange that he did not express his opinion of the poem more directly. Although Tate and Lowell visited each other several times from 1965 to 1967, and probably talked on the phone, they characteristically shared their comments on each other's work in letters, perhaps to give their criticism a degree of permanence, perhaps simply because they both had grown up in an age in which people still wrote letters. It is unfortunate that so little passed between them on the subject of this and the other *Near the Ocean* poems.

By 1967 much of America was caught up in debate or protest concerning the war in Vietnam, and grass-roots leaders of all sorts were emerging. Power was on their minds too, sometimes the power of numbers, sometimes that of violence. In this context, Lowell began in June to write the unrhymed sonnets that would become *Notebook 1967–68*. The majority of these brief poems would be concerned with domestic matters and personal memories, but many would deal with the uses and abuses of power and other contemporary topics, as well as some events that directly involved Lowell.

In September, Lowell signed a public statement that was published in the *New Republic* and the *New York Times* promising to raise funds for draft resisters. In October, he participated in a huge demonstration in Washington at which many young men publicly burned their draft cards and thousands more participated in a march to the Pentagon. Lowell, who read "Waking Early Sunday Morning" for the crowd of draft resisters, was one of several invited speakers, all well-known writers. The sonnets that Lowell wrote shortly after the event recapture much of its flavor and atmosphere. The first of them (both are entitled "The March") contrasts the cold monuments of Washington's overscaled landscape with the intimacy of the participants, and contrasts the marchers, who share the old-fashioned ideals of the Civil War soldiers, with their opponents, who are an alien and impersonal army of apes and heroes:

> Under the too white marmoreal Lincoln Memorial,
> the too tall marmoreal Washington Obelisk,
> gazing into the too long reflecting pool,
> the reddish trees, the withering autumn sky,
> the remorseless, amplified harangues for peace—
> lovely to lock arms, to march absurdly locked
> (unlocking to keep my wet glasses from slipping)
> to see the cigarette match quaking in my fingers,
> then to step off like green Union Army recruits
> for the first Bull Run, sped by photographers,
> the notables, the girls . . . fear, glory, chaos, rout . . .
> our green army staggered out on the miles-long green fields,
> met by the other army, the Martian, the ape, the hero,
> his new-fangled rifle, his green new steel helmet.

While the marchers are "green," untested and undisciplined, the only thing "green" about the professional soldiers meeting them is their helmets of green steel, an emblem of strength, not (as with the marchers) weakness. The poem underscores quixotic idealism and physical frailty (his "wet glasses . . . slipping"), but Lowell speaks as a participant in a political attempt to wrest some degree of power from a government that he had recently described (at a highly-publicized reading at the YMHA) as "really terrible." For Lowell, poetry and life had moved into more immediate proximity. The journalistic sprawl of *Notebook*, the brevity and relative informality of his unrhymed sonnets, provided the immediacy and flexibility of prose notes, yet Lowell had so perfected his grasp of poetic strategies that he was able to write with the compression, metaphorical power, and strong feeling for imagery that had always characterized his work. The fact that these strategies would appear at times to be mere mannerisms was inevitable in such a lengthy work written (for him) so hastily, but poems like "The March" are more than offhand responses to the pressures of reality. They draw upon a lifetime of reading and experience and combine disparate elements (the Civil War, "the Martian," the "marmoreal" monuments, the slipping glasses) into a new whole, a moment of revealed experience as self-contained and complete as any previous Lowell poem, yet linked and knit by sequence into new significances.

To assert that Lowell now has moved decisively toward a "documentary" or "snapshot" aesthetic would be misleading if we think of this as a pictorial or neoimagist aesthetic. Instead, he creates a verbal approximation to the visual aesthetic that takes objects, scenes, persons as they are at a given moment and presents them in a relatively undistorted manner (except by abrupt juxtaposition), as though their actuality were their significance, as though the meaning inhered there rather than in the wrenchings of art. Lowell, no imagist, has come to respect Pound's injunction, "The natural object is always the adequate symbol," an injunction he ignored in the poems of *Lord Weary's Castle*. Of course, Lowell never abandoned art or a commitment to the individual imagination; both his subjective stance and belief in craft precluded any endorsement of so extreme a "snapshot" aesthetic as that of the "found poem," or even Williams at his most objectivist, as in "The Red Wheelbarrow."

After *Life Studies* and certainly in his *Notebook* period, Lowell had become intrigued by the phenomenology of the imagination. He became aware and wary of how the mind manipulates objects

175

and even violates their integrity. To call his aesthetic "documentary" at this point suggests the direction he was taking, but it requires qualification. It became documentary only in the sense that, with an increased awareness of the imagination's manipulative power, he grew more conscious of his subjectivity—although aware that, for the meditative lyric poet, subjectivity is the essential stance—and more deliberate in his depiction of things outside himself. *Day by Day* most starkly delineates his wrestling with the virtues and limitations of this more objective type of seeing, but the *Notebook* sonnets dramatically juxtapose objective images by means of the sudden leaps and thrusts of the uneasy associative mind.

Lowell's new commitment to political action must have contributed to (or resulted from) his shift from a symbolist to a more objective aesthetic. For anyone less obsessed with poetry, such a statement would seem exaggerated, but Lowell, especially, wanted to link his art and his life, not only by means of a poetics of experience, but with declamatory actions that would be to ordinary life what poems were to ordinary language. His "Declaration of Responsibility" and, even more so, his jail term of 1943–44 were the first such actions. His attack on Agnes Smedley, although misdirected and regrettable, was the second. Beginning with his public rebuke to President Johnson, the 1960s brought opportunity for many such public gestures.

Concerned with the direction events were taking, Lowell, in February 1968, began to work with the presidential campaign of Eugene McCarthy and began a correspondence with Robert Kennedy, whose campaign manager was Blair Clark, Lowell's old friend from his St. Mark's days. During that spring, he traveled and spoke on McCarthy's behalf and, in June, met with Kennedy shortly before his assassination. Even though professional staffers thought that Lowell was a distraction rather than an asset to McCarthy's campaign, his presence further publicized McCarthy's nearly successful effort to win the nomination. If Kennedy had not entered the race late and beaten McCarthy in California, McCarthy might have had an excellent chance at the presidency, and Lowell would have witnessed that ascension to power firsthand.

Such public appearances and public uses of poetry were beyond the experience of Tate. At another time, he might have taken considerable interest in Lowell's newly emerged political persona (although, perhaps, looking at his interest in power with skepticism since such interests had often surfaced when Lowell began to lose control), but he was otherwise occupied. Almost seventy years old, he had become a father again. In August, Helen Tate, his third wife, had given birth to twin boys, Michael and John. Acting not so much on impulse but on a lifelong recuring desire, Tate decided to return permanently to the South and built a house on Running Knob Hollow Road at Sewanee. He had been teaching at Vanderbilt the previous semester and, although he had always liked Minnesota in many ways, had decided that he had had enough of wandering and the alien, if congenial, world beyond the territory of his ancestors. He formally retired from Minnesota in June of 1968 and settled in Sewanee for good.

Tate's literary activity continued. Withdrawal from the peripatetic life of the visiting professor did not mean withdrawal from the world of letters. In 1967 he was preparing his largest prose collection, *Essays of Four Decades*, to be published in 1968. A year before, he had edited *T. S. Eliot, the Man and His work* and, in his postscript to this volume, touched on the complex issues of literary friendships:

> On the death of a friend one may meditate the Thankless Muse, even if the friend was not a poet. The meditation becomes more difficult, and one almost gives it up, if the friend is not only a poet but perhaps a great poet. The Poet-as-Greatness is not, as our friend might have said in his Harvard Dissertation on F. H. Bradley, an object of knowledge: it is only a point of view. Private meditation at best must land one in the midst of The Last Things, beyond the common reality; but poetry begins with the common reality, and ends with it, as our friend's friend, Charles Williams, said of Dante.[6]

So the claims of friendship and the claims of poetry do not equally command our attention, and poetry is, in the end, committed only to the "common reality." Friendship, on the other hand, touches on the soul or the spirit or, at least, on spiritual aspirations. The immortality of great poetry depends merely on a "point of view," but to reach "beyond the common reality" is a private matter.

Tate's considered distinction between life and art is characteristic of his later criticism. Although derived from an intelligent appraisal of the place of art in society and the relationship between art and religion, this distinction sets definite limits on the influence of art and, perhaps, suggests why the fever of poetry, which does not thrive under such an awareness of limitations, cooled in him after the early 1950s. He would publish two more brief poems in the 1970s, but he had come to see people—their spiritual selves, at least—as larger than poems and could no longer generate sufficient faith in the poetic process as a route to knowledge. Tate had never advocated poetry as a substitute for religion. Instead, he had argued that the context of a spiritually confident culture was necessary for poetry, but in "Literature as Knowledge," he concluded that "in the poem, we get knowledge of a whole object" and that knowledge was not fully subject to rational inquiry and delineation.[7] Tate never recanted his belief that poetry offered a unique form of knowledge, but it is possible that the glimpse of the mysteries offered by Catholicism made the writing of poetry appear to be a comparatively limited approach to the unknown. It is difficult to say, since Tate never explained his long poetic drought, but in 1929 in "Humanism and Naturalism," he had written "Religion's respect for the power of nature lies in her contempt for knowledge of it; to quantify nature is ultimately to quantify ourselves. Religion is satisfied with the dogma that nature is evil, and that our recovery from it is mysterious ("grace")."[8]

Perhaps having experienced grace, Tate could no longer take sufficient interest in nature (the mundane Not-I) to continue to "quantify" it in that oblique way that is poetry's. Although he had sought some kind of Christian humanism for many years, his finding it coincided with—whether it precipitated it or not—the decline of his poetic inspiration. If anything, it stirred the critical faculty to fresh exertions, and the last three decades of his life produced much of his best prose.

The happiness occasioned by the birth of his twin sons did not

178

last. Tate had moved permanently to Sewanee in June 1968, and on 16 July, Michael, one of his sons, died in a cruel accident. Tate wrote to Lowell a few days later: "Michael died last Tuesday the 16th. He had a plastic toy telephone receiver in his mouth. We infer that he fell face down and choked to death, the toy being forced down his throat. The nurse was running the water for John's bath and couldn't hear Michael's groans. We were at Monteagle for dinner. He died before he could be taken to the hospital."[9]

Lowell's replies, though heartfelt, may seem perfunctory. He had just agreed to edit a collection of essays about Tate and his work, which was to be published by the University of Minnesota Press as a surprise for Tate. John Ervin, Leonard Unger, and Dick Foster had planned the collection and invited Lowell to edit it before informing Tate. Unfortunately, Ervin wrote to Tate in early July, so Tate's pleasure in the project was soon blunted by Michael's death. Lowell responded twice to Tate's grieving letter. Each time he apparently thought it kinder to direct Tate's attention toward literary matters than to commiserate at length over a painful topic. His first response (July 24) was brief, dazed, and empathetic:

> I don't know what to say. When the twins were born, it seemed a gay miracle. Good, one is left. Good, I was about to write, that the child is so young. But nearly a year isn't young. I remember my Harriet at much the same age going down Marlborough Street in her carriage; she wore a cumbersome ribbed hood like Charles Bouvary's famous hat; she had a hideous, heavy frown that probably meant she wanted sleep—and she was everything!
>
> Poor Allen, poor Helen, poor little lost boy! I am almost crying myself, and wish I could help.[10]

The postscript turns to the subject of essays for the projected book, "It will be a useful and readable book, and tho you know the contents, I hope, a joy to you." In the second letter, written six days later, even his words of consolation are vaguely literary-historical: "What can I say to you about Michael? Some things seem humanly impossible, alas, all too possible in nature. A child's death is the worst; even the very old gravestones with their brief dates are impossible to look at. I wince from what you and Helen

179

have been going through; I think I who have never seen Michael, will not forget him."[11]

Again, as with the first letter, he then directs attention to the more cheerful subject of the festschrift:

> About the essays: I have the bibliographies, tho I don't have the texts of the pieces. I think Minnesota will mail them to me. If not I would be grateful for your copies. I probably won't do much before October, so it would be better to have them in New York. I want to do the choosing, of course, but also of course anything you really want will go in. The book is for you. I'm numb to academic explanation that I can't understand, on poems I can understand. "The comment does the text confound." Still, the selection shouldn't be entirely graceful belle letters.

He then closed with a lighthearted reference to his own work and his own child, the sad occasion seemingly consigned to the irredeemable past: "Oh dear, summer gone before it came. I'm finishing a huge poem for me 1900 lines. We've been without history, but Harriet has had a good summer at camp, her first time of any length away." .

Michael presumably is "history," but he would not be forgotten by either Tate or Lowell. Tate had already (on July 28) written another letter about his death: "The Negro nurse panicked and forgot where we had gone for dinner. She wasted half an hour trying to locate *us*, instead of calling the hospital or doctor."[12]

Tate also was anxious to move on to other matters, as best he could, and this letter concludes with notes on materials for the projected volume. Neither he nor Lowell were unnaturally anxious to avoid dwelling on Michael's death, but both, especially Tate, needed time to assimilate it. The shock to the Tates must have been devastating. It is doubtful that a parent could ever get over such a blow. Lowell, who in the 1940s had apparently disliked children (Gertrude Buckman had chastised him for this) had become a loving parent who was capable of empathizing with the Tates in their grief.

For both of them, however, literature was central. More than a refuge from life, it was life. To console each other with subtle reminders that their literary lives would go on was natural to them. For Lowell, poetry had become a daily occupation. His unrhymed sonnets absorbed all of the minutae of his daily life and were the receptacle of the miscellaneous, but crucial, flux of his reading. It was only natural that Michael's death should become the subject of a sonnet that demonstrates Lowell's deep empathy for Tate, whom he knew so well and for whom he had such complex feelings. The poem echoes phrases, an image, and an idea from his consolatory letter, referring to the ancient gravestones, reversing the syntax of "A child's death is the worst," and revising the distinction drawn between human and natural possibilities. It also uses Tate's letters, repeating "groans" but making the bath being drawn Michael's instead of John's. Like so many of these sonnets, "For Michael Tate: August 1967–July 1968" has something of the immediacy of the personal letter fused with Lowell's associative imagery, and it concludes with a telling paradox:

> Each night, a star, gold-on-black, a muskellunge,
> dies in the highest sphere that never dies. . . .
> Things no longer possible to our faith
> go on routinely usable in nature;
> the worst is the child's death. Even his stone,
> the very, very old one, one century, two,
> his one-year date common in auld lang syne
> is no longer for faith's eye-scale. And, Michael Tate,
> gagging on your plastic telephone,
> while the one night sitter drew water for your bath,   *(Lowell's*
> unable to hear your groans. . . . They think: if there'd been   *ellipsis)*
> a week or two's illness, we might have been prepared. . . .   *(Lowell's*
> Your twin crawls for you, ten-month twin. They are no longer   *ellipsis)*
> young enough to understand what happened.

Apparently Tate did not see this poem until the book was in proofs. His reaction to this and three others about himself and his family has been the subject of some misunderstanding. C. David Heymann has claimed that Tate was so upset by the poems that "he broke with Lowell over them, mending their friendship only after a duration of several years."[13] Lowell was certainly appre-

181

hensive about Tate's reaction, and Tate may have been quietly disturbed, but no trace of anger over this poem survives in their correspondence. The real cause of their temporary estrangement had nothing to do with the Michael poem or any of Lowell's other poems. Tate's reaction to *Notebook 1967–68* was, in fact, as favorable as it was to *For the Union Dead*, and his comment on the Michael poem was warm.

Before dealing more fully with Tate's response to *Notebook*, it would be useful to look at an important letter that Lowell wrote to him in December of 1968. Tate had written to inform Lowell that he was writing a memoir: "It makes haste slowly. It's much harder to write than *The Fathers*. The memoir, like all memoirs, is fiction too, but stubbornly bound to shadowy fact." [14]

Tate had touched upon a central tenet of Lowell's historically oriented aesthetic. Lowell responded first by describing the grip his new poem-in-progress had upon him, then by extending Tate's contention about the role of fiction in supposedly nonfictional writing: "My poem possesses and obsesses—like whiskey that other inspirer. When I know I'm through, another small section pushes out. This says nothing about the true inspiration one always hopes for. I think I have almost more discarded versions than I can lift. Wonderful your memoirs are 'fiction too, but stubbornly bound to shadowy fact.' I've always thought history (the best history) was this too. Much of it would be more philosophic if historians knew this." [15]

This reopens the question of what *fiction* meant to Lowell. Clearly, it meant compressing, editing, selecting, but it also apparently meant *personal*, something generated by private inspiration and enthusiasm. To write fiction, prose or poetry, romance or history is to render up a version—no more than that—of an experience or a life. Lowell would later identify himself with Wordsworth in this effort of writing fiction and autobiography. In 1977 he wrote, "Looking over my *Selected Poems*, about thirty years of writing, my impression is that the thread that strings it together is my autobiography, it is a small-scale Prelude, written in many different styles and with digressions, yet a continuing story. . . ." [16]

Notebook would be "fiction . . . but stubbornly bound to shadowy fact." In the instance of the poem about Michael, the facts are
clearly presented but the poet's voice casts the shadow. To read is
to fictionalize, to read one's own life commits one to a single version not to its totality. Tate understood this well. The mystery is
not his lack of resentment at the appearance of the poem in *Notebook* but that he suspended his understanding when faced with
the *Life Studies* poems. Why should he or anyone, for that matter,
resent the incorporation of facts in a poem? It was in the area of
fancy, not the manipulation of fact, that Lowell had already stirred
resentment. A few years earlier, Peter Brooks had chastised Lowell
for writing about Brooks' wife Esther as though she were Lowell's
mistress.[17] No one could blame Brooks for this. Lowell and Tate
agreed, for the moment, on how incompletely, therefore fiction-
ally, the literary process rendered the experiences of the imagination and the quotidian. Yet such agreement is never universal,
and their easy colloquy in these letters fails to resolve completely
the vexing problem of the relation of literature to life. Lowell would
have to deal with this again and again. Adrienne Rich would make
no allowance for Lowell's fictionalizing when she attacked *The
Dolphin* in 1973, and Elizabeth Hardwick would resent Lowell's
treatment of their daughter in the same book.

These reactions, however, have a history and context of their
own. *Notebook 1967–68*, while it received mixed reviews, aroused
no particular outrage for its manipulation of autobiographical and
historical materials. The sonnets are sometimes too domestic, too
focused on the trivia of daily meditations, but although they sometimes refer to Lowell's affairs with various young women in Cambridge and Mexico, their main subject is the associative moment
of the author's mind and the way his imagination links art and life
in a texture of perception so dense and complex that they become
one. In poems like "Cattle," the poet's associative powers are at
their peak, linking history, contemporary events, landscape, and
bestial metaphor in a single version of localized apocalypse:

The moon, invisible behind a cloud-ledge,   (*Lowell's
briefly glitters its bonfire on the harbor. . . .*   *ellipsis*)

183

Machiavelli despised these furiously fought
mounted Tuscan mercenary battles:
lines rushed, and Greek met Greek; one man was killed,
men died of a stroke, but not the strokes of battle.
Our police hit more to terrorize than kill:
a hundred riots, nobody left dead;
clubs break and brains, women are rooked on curbs—
none killed or crippled visibly forever.
Is this tidal wave blown from a bubble of soap?
Why do we always undersell the weak?
Cattle have guts, but after the barn is burned,
they will look at the sunset and tremble.

The problem Lowell posed for himself in this long sequence of identical poem-units was finding a rhetoric and syntax adequate to his unifying and image-making imagination. Simply stringing together perceptions in a version of Poundian association, one image or perception after another, would have produced a numbing monotony. Occasionally and momentarily, Lowell slips into such a listing of rhythmically similar phrases, but his reliance on syntax as a shaping force saves him from a false rhythmic harmony that would render the book too easy and too stupefying to read. The series of complex sentences that makes up "Cattle" is rhetorically interesting enough to substitute for a conventional rhyme-scheme and to lend some tension to the irregular iambic rhythm.

Lowell finished *Notebook 1967–68* in January 1969, and it was published in June. The reviews were generally muted, respectful, and somewhat uncertain. One was both laudatory and perceptive: William Meredith's in the *New York Times* called the book "complex and imperfect, like most of the accomplishments of serious men and women today . . . a beautiful and major work."[18] But the comments that may have meant the most to Lowell came a month before publication from Tate, who wrote on 15 May, "I'm not worried about *Notebook*. Until my next reading, and perhaps after it, this work is your finest to date—uneven, of course, but most impressive. Not at all uneven is "Long Summer," the entire sequence of fourteen "sonnets." I'm inclined to think *this* is your finest work to date: not a word out of place, the "confessional" material controlled and formal."[19]

That Tate should single out "Long Summer" as Lowell's "finest work" is not entirely eccentric. This sequence of fourteen sonnets is, as he says, "controlled and formal," its autobiographical content depersonalized. The first-person speaker is not even vocally present in a few of the sonnets, his associative voice reaching beyond personal concerns to give order and significance to more local imagery and events. The sequence opens by depicting a humble attempt by the speaker to make sense of his brutality, alcoholism, ironic uxoriousness, and the poignancy of a quarrelsome, yet still loving, relationship:

> Each day more poignantly resolved to stay,
> each day more brutal, oracular and rooted,
> dehydrated, and smiling in the fire. . . .

The sequence ends by returning to the topic of alcohol and the attempt to preserve a faltering relationship. Lowell finds the perfect objective correlative for the evenings of quarreling and drinking:

> the neverness of meeting nightly like surgeons'
> apprentices studying their own skeletons,
> old friends and mammoth flesh preserved in ice.

Between these passages, the poem explores a summer in Maine, every sonnet evocative, specific, powerfully sensuous. The most obvious precedent for this kind of sonnet in American literature is in Frederick Goddard Tuckerman's work, but Lowell outdoes even that neglected master of natural description in his stark portrayal of a marred Eden, a natural (and marital) paradise gone awry:

> The shore is pebbled with eroding brick,
> seaweed in grizzled furrows—a surf-cast away,
> a converted brickyard dormitory; higher,
> the blacktop; higher yet, a fish-hawk's nest,
> a bungalow, view-hung and staring, with wash
> and picture-window—here, like offshoots that
> have taken root. Grass shooting overnight,
> sticks of dead rotten wood in drifts, the fish
> with missing eyes, or heel-print on the belly,
> or a gash in the back from a stray hook;

the lawns, the paths, the harbor—stitched with motors,
yawl-engine, outboard, power mower, plowing
the mangle and mash of the monotonous frontier,
bottles of dirt and lighted gasoline.

The closing image embodies the dualisms that empower the
sequence—earth and fire, marriage and alcohol, nature and ram-
shackle civilization. That Tate so admired this powerful sequence
is hardly surprising, but Lowell's dismemberment of this nearly
perfect poem, scattering the individual sonnets through *History*,
seven of them placed in a series of "1930's" sonnets as if to destroy
the relative autobiographical immediacy of *Notebook*, seems peculiar. This destruction was part of the general reordering that resulted in *History*, in which the poems are no longer grouped in
separate sequences but are individually titled and subsumed into a
larger chronology. *For Lizzie and Harriet* retained the original idea
of the sequence within the larger sequence but preserved only a
few of the original sequences from *Notebook*, and these are in
much-altered form. To disrupt the poem and disregard Tate's high
praise, Lowell must have felt strongly that *Notebook* was essentially
faulty in its ordering. It is possible that he worried about the minor
autobiographical revelations of "Long Summer," but this seems
unlikely given the greater frankness of some of the other material.
He could have chosen to leave the sequence intact in *For Lizzie and
Harriet*, where, in its original form, it would have a place and
function similar to that in *Notebook*. That is, it would portray him
as committed to his marriage despite quarrels and his drinking,
and it would help prepare for the disruptions, indecision, and turmoil of *The Dolphin*.

Tate then turned to the poems about friends, including the poem
about Michael and the three about himself, and offered a few
minor corrections in the spirit of preserving factual accuracy in a
fictional context:

> Naturally, I read first the poems to your friends, including me. Helen
> is greatly moved by the one about Michael. I suspect that "Tom" in
> heaven, leaning from the golden bough, can like the poem about him
> better than if he were still on earth. (Did he ever say "It's balls . . . ?")

As for me, I didn't write you "alert"; I said "harassed." And Ford said, "It's not done," not "It's rude." These corrections are due the poet who writes *poesie a clef*. I take it that my little scene with Harriet (Southern belle, etc.) is fictitious; I can't say it's inaccurate because if true, I don't remember it.

Tate clearly had no objection to being fictitiously portrayed but was only concerned with accuracy in recounting what was actual. The "Tom" poem ("T. S. Eliot") is one of several in which Lowell reconstructs conversations with other writers to affirm the value of talk as the way of redeeming the speaking self from what the poem calls "the everlasting dross." Although the sequence "Writers" contains two sonnets entitled "To Allen Tate" and a poem about Ford, Tate was referring to "To Allen Tate I," a poem about Lowell's 1937 summer visit during which Ford is made to say, "You must show your cards, dear Tate . . . it's so rude, you know." Clearly "it's not done" is metrically identical to "it's so rude," but Lowell's misremembering underscores Ford's belief in the importance of manners. Since Ford, from all accounts, treasured manners, the choice of "it's so rude" might have rendered a more accurate portrayal of him than dogged adherence to historical fact would have done. Lowell acknowledged the accuracy of Tate's memory, decided he preferred the sound of "it's not done," and revised the poem accordingly. The second Tate poem depicts him in all his eccentricity, but with affection and humor:

> On your enormous brow, cannonball head of a snowman,
> is a ripped red tissuepaper birthday hat;
> you squint, make out my daughter, then six or seven:
> "*You* are a Southern *belle;* do you know why
> you are a *South*ern belle?" (Stares, stupor, thumb in her mouth)
> "Because your *mother* is a Southern belle."
> Your attention wanders, "I love you now, but I'll love you
> more probably when you are older." Harriet whispering,
> "If you are still alive." We reach Gettysburg;
> both of us too much the soldier from Sourmash:
> "I don't know whether to call you my son or my brother."
> Ashtrays and icecubes deployed as Pickett's columns:
> a sloping forest of flashing steel. You point:
> "There, if Longstreet had *moved,* we would have *broke* you."

187

Son or brother, ephebe or peer, Lowell had this time written a book that seemed to satisfy Tate more than any other. Tate concluded his letter by saying, "Well, it's a fine book. Your arbitrary fourteen-liners serve you well."

Lowell's response showed relief and acknowledged Tate's recollection of historical matters. He had not yet decided to extensively revise *Notebook,* so he foresaw no problem in continuing with the Tate book:

> Thanks for your generous, amusing letter. I was afraid you might be chafed by my joking, and still more afraid the poem about Michael might offend. Yet I trusted my hand and intentions and didn't invite the embarrassment and trouble of sending the poems to you before publication. I meant to change "harassed" to "alert," I had to make some slight alteration and interpretation of my own. Eliot did say "Balls" but I don't entirely build up the plausibility. In my second printing, I'm changing, "it's so rude, you know" to "it isn't done." I wouldn't mind tinkering with what Ford had said but I kept feeling he had in fact said something a good deal more interesting than I could remember.
>
> After about two years' joyful and relentless work at writing, I am released, and feel a little, I think, as you do retired for teaching—airy, empty, melancholy, retired. I'll soon be starting on your volume. You put in anything you want, and I'll put in anything I want. We'll overlap mostly tho not entirely. How can I get a copy of your old biographies and political essays? [20]

Lowell's fears must have been quite real to have prevented him from sending the poems to Tate in manuscript (which he had done with so many other poems), but the response indicated how justified he was in trusting his own judgment. In many respects, their relationship apparently had reached its peak. Tate had found Lowell's new poems his best work, and Lowell was about to prepare a book celebrating his early mentor and valued friend. Following *Life Studies,* Tate had learned to accept Lowell's formal vagaries and experiments on their own terms. Their friendship, as depicted in Lowell's poem, was too firm to be disrupted by minor quarrels. Although a more serious quarrel loomed—the most serious of their friendship—they would survive that one too.

Lowell had accepted the assignment of editing the Tate festschrift in the summer of 1968. By September 1969, the task had come to seem onerous. He was busily revising *Notebook* for its British publication (and later, its revised American edition), and the problem of writing a suitable preface for the Tate book weighed heavily. He had gathered a good deal of material, some sent by Tate, some by John Ervin, and had read much of it, but now he was preoccupied with rewriting and adding to the book he had just so thankfully completed. As he wrote in a note at the conclusion of the third edition of *Notebook* (1970), "I couldn't stop writing, and have handled my published book as if it were manuscript."

Caught up in this revision, he wrote an apologetic letter to Tate to explain his neglect of the festschrift: "I have humble apologies to write you and have put off this letter several weeks in hopes that I wouldn't have to. I have nothing, except notes, written for your volume. The trouble is that I got working on what will be the first English edition of my NOTEBOOK—time to add, time to revise before my late September deadline. I suppose this summer was my last chance to do anything on it. After this the year and one's concerns, temper etc. change. I feel I've done myself a good turn but a very dirty trick on you." [21]

Tate's response was generous but betrayed his growing impatience: "Don't give the 'book' another moment's thought. Your English edition obviously came first. I have been hoping for some time that you would give the project up. . . ." [22]

Whether Tate had really been "hoping for some time" that Lowell would withdraw from the editing, or whether it occurred to him when he received Lowell's letter that it would be a good idea, he conveyed his doubts to John Ervin, who would write to Lowell and formally request that he give up the task. As late as 5 November, Lowell wrote to Tate as though he still considered himself to be on the job even though he had been spending most of his time revising *Notebook*. His proposal for continuing sounds unrealistic and perfunctory: "I have been dilatory about your essays because I have been trying to finish my poem, my endless poem, 3000 lines, polishing, cutting, adding. Now it's off (I won't say finished) to galleys. All fall, it's all I can do to decently, or even indecently, prepare my Shakespeare classes. Well, I will have the selection made and I hope the preface by Christmas."[23]

Since Lowell had been delaying this task since the middle of the previous year, it seemed obvious that he could not accomplish in a month what he had failed to do in fifteen months.

The problem, as he would explain to Tate, was largely with writing the preface. Since his earlier *Sewanee Review* piece, Lowell apparently had grown more self-conscious in trying to write about Tate. The fragmentary draft of his attempted preface illustrates his difficulty in focusing on Tate's work without either delving into private matters or becoming glib and superficial: "The pressures to be polite and empty are almost irresistible. But not from Allen Tate who on such occasions has a talent for being most gracious and generous without giving upon impertinence and even rudeness, without which friendly criticism would [be] unreadable, inconsequential. . . ."[24]

Lowell suggests that the "pressures to be polite" come from within, but this is disingenuous since any "impertinence" in writing this preface would have met with severity. Matching Tate's graciousness was possible for Lowell in his earlier essay, but now he stumbles over his own attempt to justify the "impertinence" (a favorite Tate rebuke) of trying to summarize a lifetime of personal and literary friendship with all its attendant complexities. Lowell refers to his first meeting with Tate in an attempt to define the older poet's importance to him, but in this rough draft, the argument seems forced and overly apologetic: "When I met Allen Tate in 1937, I think I must have [had] a bias toward his temper and ideas. I had a temper, but no distinct ideas. I still have too little interest in sustained argument, sustained polemic, to much want to write a critical essay. In this instance, I shall try to be erratic and conversational."

Instead of going ahead and writing his essay, Lowell has already conceded that his effort will be radically imperfect, insofar as "erratic and conversational" are not necessarily what a reader expects of the formal introduction to a collection of essays. His lack of "interest in sustained argument" suggests that Tate's influence was not as helpful as it might have been. This admission of weakness is prophetic since the draft now turns to Tate's criticism, which

190

requires an interest in, and understanding of, argument and polemic. The attempt to comment on the essays begins with a relatively straightforward comparison with Eliot and an insight that Lowell might have developed into a useful argument, but it then veers into haphazard personal commentary: "First the form. I like the way Tate . . . confesses that he has no plan or system and hardly knows how or what sentences will follow the last. In this he follows Eliot and still earlier Arnold. He is close to both in his interest in society, in his mingling of literary judgment, morality and religion. In this last and of course in his specific literary likes, Tate is closer to Eliot. Both perhaps use religion to hedge off the graceless, verbally graceless expert in modern science and part science."

This insight into the use of religion might apply to the early Lowell as well as to Tate, but instead of developing this useful argument, Lowell allows the comparison to lead to a characterization that seems dangerously close to caricature:

> Tate sometimes seems a Tennessee version of Eliot, so close are their prejudices, so close are their discoveries. Tate is much the more overt and direct and chivalrous. I mean this as a tribute and a limitation. Tate is much the physical, open and simple-minded. He is much closer to the body with its colors, habits, sudden angers and courtesies. Often, I feel Tate is hammering some belief or obsession to death. Then he suddenly switches with some flashing, inconsistent figure of speech, makes some gay, destructive concession, admits confusion, complexities beyond his argument—or nails down an opponent he has merely been nagging. The New Englander, fulfilling Tate's prejudice about us, may find him naive, only to be amazed by some instant, off-hand [display of?] an accurate mind. What a good mind, I say, thinking less of the long reasoning as of the humor, the quick terms, the relaxed hit.

Patronizing Tate would be the ultimate impertinence and was surely not what Lowell intended, but when he found himself moving in that direction, he probably realized there was more "limitation" than "tribute" in this profile, and so he broke off his attempt at this point. On 21 November, Ervin wrote to Tate and informed him that he had asked Lowell to withdraw from the project.

191

Lowell had been offered a visiting professorship at All Soul's College, Oxford, to begin in April 1970. With his recently revised book and his residency in England on his mind, he was, no doubt, relieved to be free of the burden of the Tate book. He cheerfully wrote to Tate on New Year's Eve, teasingly suggesting that he write some new poetry: "I've been drifting through a light bout of flu. In the midst came a doctor's thesis on me, you and Crane. The writer almost demonstrates by logic that The Buried Lake is your best poem. Maybe it is, along with Swimmers; could that jog you into more parts? It's as tho you stopped sail-up with a full wind."[25]

Tate had published no poetry since "The Buried Lake," but in February 1969, he had written to Lowell, "I took a vacation the other day from terza rima and wrote a sonnet—the first in 30 years."[26] So, apparently, he was still working on the terza rima sequence begun seventeen years before, although he would publish no more of it.

Tate was caught up in the recent birth of Benjamin Lewis Bogan Tate. It may have been a sign of his anger at Lowell's failure to pay sufficient attention to his book that he neglected to inform Lowell of this important event, which occurred on 18 December. Lowell had to inquire: "Tony Hecht says your child must be born now, but I doubt if you would fail to say so in your letter. But maybe, by now."[27] Tate's unresponsiveness must have bothered Lowell, but he was caught up in his plans to travel abroad with Elizabeth and Harriet, beginning with a visit to Italy and then proceeding to Oxford.

Shortly before Lowell left for Italy, Tate casually requested the return of the material he had lent Lowell for the book. The press had asked Radcliffe Squires to replace Lowell as editor, and Tate needed the material. Lowell responded with a mixture of embarrassment and feigned offhandedness that must have outraged Tate: "I tried to get you on the telephone but was told you had gone to Nashville. I know I can't apologize adequately. Somehow all the Tate material has been lost. I brought it back from Maine in a special carton, then placed it on a shelf in my study bookcase, then back in a carton. When I was away recently, my study was cleaned all too thoroughly by the maid, and she threw out the carton. When your letter arrived, I remember telling Lizzie that I'd have the stuff off to you in a minute because it was all collected in one place. Hell!"[28]

Obviously Tate would find this difficult to believe. Why would a maid throw away a box of books and journals without permission? Lowell continued with his apology, which, though no doubt well-intentioned, was literary enough to appear staged if not insincere:

> I feel like Mill with Carlyle's French Revolution. Only I trust nothing I had was the single existing copy. I feel this is my final impertinence to you after my very bad performance with the book. Sometimes, it's impossible to admit one won't or somehow can't do something. Your poetry and probably everything else you have written needs a fresh angle, a new word. I think of Gothic for lack of a better, but this has misleading suggestions of Poe, and old horror novels. A grand style, often very clean and blunt, a mixture of symbol, courtesy, and terror, caught up in history. There's nothing like it, tho I and many others have imitated here and there. When the future reader picks it up, he will pick up your world, its earth and memories.

The attempted praise of Tate's style seems a bit out of place, but Lowell was certainly candid in his understanding of his own difficulty in completing the book. Lowell finished his letter, apparently having settled the matter to his own satisfaction, by cheerily mentioning his trip to Italy and poking fun at Tate's Catholicism: "We leave today for Italy, all three of us, Harriet interested in Venice but certain she'll see as few churches as possible—those stately similar monuments of outworn superstition. Then I go on to Oxford and won't return till late June. Love to Helen and the children. Please forgive me."

Forgiveness this time did not come quickly. Tate, in his reply, invoked thirty years of slights, real or imagined, oddities of behavior, unconscious rudeness, and invasions of privacy. To fuel the misery, Tate implied that his rage was longstanding and had merely awaited a suitable occasion for its expression:

> I have your letter of March 19. I fear I shall come near to insulting you when I say that I can't believe the "Tate" material was lost that

way. I am sure you will understand my surprise at not being able to find anywhere in your letter the wish that somebody else might now undertake to do the book. I didn't keep a list of the pieces I sent you. Some of them cannot be replaced. In any case, it will take five or six weeks of digging in libraries to reproduce the more obvious titles.

At this point I don't think I ought to spare you my annoyance. I never for one moment thought that you would go through with the job, but I couldn't very well tell John Ervin this reservation. It is not irrelevant to ask why you couldn't write anything for my Eliot memorial volume. The same reason in both cases; I know what it is but you don't. I asked Frank McShane to cancel the evening for Tate's 70th, in which you and Red Warren were to participate, because I could not face the possibility of your megalomania getting out of control, either through the condescension of "ranking" me or in allusions to my private life. Your Napoleonic stance permits you to confess other people's lives. I hope that you will not again confess mine.

I have thought all this for many years. A small crisis has brought it to the surface.

Not quite yours as ever. . . .[29]

This is a harsh letter by any standard, and it must have greatly pained Lowell. Unfortunately, it contains a good deal of truth; but it is truth uncharitably expressed. In calmer moments, Tate realized that Lowell's behavior deteriorated only when he was ill and could not reasonably be blamed for his occasionally outrageous comments. What Tate called "megalomania" was plain mania. For years, although clearly disturbed by Lowell's illness, Tate had seemed to accept it as such. Most likely, he was hurt that Lowell had not valued him enough to give the book the priority it deserved.

Lowell's response, written from Oxford in April, was a mixture of apology and chastisement. To appease his friend, Lowell recalled the early days of their acquaintance and suggests that nothing essential had changed in their lives or working habits. He argued that Tate had insulted more with his invective than Lowell had with his carelessness but granted him, as senior, the right to do so:

You have plenty to be sore about. I of course can't excuse my undertaking to do the book, then delaying interminably, then not doing it, then losing the material you sent me. My stumbling block was writing the essay. You claim a mysterious intuition into my motives which I do not possess. But you know why one doesn't write something—the reasons why you didn't write your novel in 1942, or I my Jonathan Edwards book. That good winter. It would be hard to say, but our motives were nothing sinister; neither were mine in again writing poetry and putting off the essay. I could answer all your other accusations (tho none of us can ever be as white as this piece of paper) but I only wish to take up one. I certainly wouldn't have embarrassed or patronized you in New York. You know what you say isn't true.

Ah Allen, which of us has insulted the other more. You have, as is right. I was your student and younger friend. Your letter isn't a good way to keep friends. Please forgive me for the book business, which I trust will come out happily. And forget your diatribe, it's too inspired by half. And please believe that I love you.[30]

It was a stroke of genius to characterize Tate's "diatribe" as "too inspired by half," but Tate was neither easily amused nor mollified, nor did the allusion to the good old days at Monteagle win him over. What did calm him was the recovery of the material, which had not been discarded after all. Hardwick found and returned it, and on 12 May, Tate wrote to Lowell to let him know the anger had passed. Even though he could not resist a further criticism of Lowell's attitude, his desire to prevent a serious rupture seems clear: "As you must know by now, Elizabeth found the "material" and sent it to me. My feelings are, of course, assuaged. What disturbed me was not so much the delay and cancellation of the book (one can live without *that*), as what seemed to me your indifference about the possible duplication of the articles. But now—never mind. On second (or third) thought, I suspect that I could not have edited a book on an old, *and older* friend (e.g. T. S. E.), until after his death; and likewise, say, on J. C. R.!"[31]

The festschrift was not cancelled, however, so the "book business" came out happily at last. Radcliffe Squires's substantial and carefully edited volume appeared in 1972. By then, Tate had begun to suffer the decline of old age, and Lowell, in England, had discarded much of his previous life and entered still another stage of poetic development in which he would find further ways to bring his private and public lives into startling juxtaposition.

Epilogue

Personal turmoil dominated the last seven years of Lowell's life, and Tate's illnesses gradually removed him from the active literary world. Although their friendship recovered from the debacle of the festschrift, the correspondence between them, in these last years, was only occasional and relatively perfunctory. This was an active period in Lowell's writing as well as his personal life, but it is an epilogue to their long and mutually beneficial friendship.

At a London party in Lowell's honor given by Faber and Faber, Lowell met, for the second time, Caroline Blackwood, a journalist and fiction writer who was then married to the musician Israel Citkovitz. Lowell had first seen her in New York three years before, but this time, the attraction was instantaneous and complete. In June, Hardwick, who had remained in New York, found out about Lowell's new affair. By then, his mania had taken hold again, and on 9 July, he entered a nursing home in St. John's Wood. Hardwick visited and found him sedated and under the care of competent doctors, but this time his infatuation was more than a manifestation of his illness. When discharged, he showed no inclination to simply return to his old life as he had done in the past.

In October, he began teaching at the University of Essex, a "new university" in Colchester. He had already begun a new book, another sequence of sonnets. This would be more intensely plotted and completely concerned with the present. *The Dolphin* records Lowell's vacillating personal life during this period, but in a fictionalized and reordered way. Events, places, and people derive from life, but Lowell rearranges and replots to avoid a too strident dramatic effect and a too blunt emotional revelation. Like *Notebook*, *The Dolphin* consists of sequences of closely connected sonnets, but it presents a clearer narrative than was evident in the earlier book. By displacing, to some degree, the order of actual events, Lowell stakes out a claim for art in a book that, like Sartre's *Nausea*, assumes the day-to-day immediacy of the journal to portray the anguish of a confused and disappointed man who finds his life to be far from exemplary. This lack of the sense of exemplary life distinguishes *The Dolphin* and *Day by Day* from the otherwise equally personal writing of *Life Studies* and portions of *For the Union Dead* and *Near the Ocean*. To refuse the exemplary mode of autobiographical writing is to risk triviality, self-pity, or a lack of focus that may characterize life well enough but is rarely suitable for art. The book would be an uneasy mixture of fact and fiction, and this would cause considerable controversy even before it was published.

In late 1970, Lowell's emotional situation was confused, and the outcome of his new romance appeared to be uncertain. His letters to Elizabeth Hardwick reveal his uncertainty about breaking up his marriage, but he was doubtful about his new relationship, unsure whether Blackwood would want to marry him or whether she even wanted to continue the relationship. Lowell already had begun to muse over his situation by recasting it into verse. The process of fictionalizing his life would be more immediate this time, closer to the bone. According to Frank Bidart's account, he had already written more than ninety new sonnets narrating the turmoil of his new life in England.[1] In December, he flew to New York to see his wife and child and to consider his situation. In *The*

197

Dolphin, the account of this journey comes near the end of the book. One of the poems from "Flight to New York" displays some of the problems engendered by this new mode of autobiography. In "Flight," Lowell allows himself to write a poem that only discusses his emotions rather than engendering analogous emotion in the reader:

> If I cannot love myself, can you?   (*Lowell's*
> I am better company depressed . . .   *ellipsis*)
> I bring myself here, almost my best friend,
> a writer still free to work at home all week,
> reading revisions to his gulping wife.
> Born twenty years later, I might have been prepared
> to alternate with cooking, and wash the baby—   (*Lowell's*
> I am a vacation-father . . . no plum—   *ellipsis*)
> flown in to New York. . . . I see the rising prospect,
> the scaffold glitters, the concrete walls are white,
> flying like Feininger's skyscraper yachts,
> geometrical romance in the river mouth,   (*Lowell's*
> conical foolscap dancing in the sky . . .   *ellipsis*)
> the runway growing wintry and distinct.

The reader can sympathize with the speaker's self-deprecatory stance, but the poem offers little ground for empathy. It almost seems inverted in construction. If the skyscrapers opened the poem they might function as a correlative to the speaker's self-directed coldness and withdrawal. By appearing late in the sonnet, after the speaker has established his self-pity, they seem merely gratuitous. "Flight," although it displays the pitfalls of Lowell's journalistic exploitation of an emotion too close for easy fictionalizing, fortunately does not represent *The Dolphin* at its best. It may, however, accurately depict Lowell's state of mind in the confusing and dreary December of 1970. As Stanley Kunitz told Tate after seeing Lowell at this time, "Somebody inside him is pathetically lost."[2] Ironically, during this visit, Lowell saw John Berryman for the last time. His later account of this meeting catches the mood of this period of his life much better than "Flight" does:

Epilogue

I met John last a year or so ago at Christmas in New York. He had been phoning poems and invitations to people at three in the morning, and I felt a weariness about seeing him. Since he had let me sleep uncalled, I guessed he felt numbness to me. We met one noon during the taxi strike at the Chelsea Hotel, dusty with donated, avant-garde constructs, and dismal with personal recollections, Bohemia, and the death of Thomas. There was no cheerful restaurant within walking distance, and the seven best bad ones were closed. We settled for the huge, varnished unwelcome of an empty cafeteria-bar. John addressed me with an awareness of his dignity, as if he were Ezra Pound at St. Elizabeths, emphatic without pertinence, when brownly inaudible.

His remarks seemed guarded, then softened into sounds only he could understand or hear. At first John was ascetically hung over, at the end we were high without assurance, and speechless. I said, "When will I see you again?" meaning, in the next few days before I flew to England. John said, "Cal, I was thinking through lunch that I'll never see you again." I wondered how in the murk of our conversation I had hurt him, but he explained that his doctor had told him one more drunken binge would kill him. Choice? It is blighting to know that this fear was the beginning of eleven months of abstinence . . . half a year of prolific rebirth, then suicide.[3]

During this period of self-doubt and emotional confusion, Lowell no longer had Tate to confide in. Although they had met briefly in June, Tate's coolness and poor health kept them from corresponding about personal matters until the spring of 1971, and by that time, Lowell, learning that Blackwood was pregnant, had finally decided to divorce Hardwick.

On 29 March, Lowell wrote to Tate in response to a rather neutral letter enlisting Lowell's help in nominating Howard Nemerov for the American Academy of Arts and Letters, and he took the opportunity to acquaint Tate with the latest developments:

What a lot has happened since I saw you last June. Caroline and I are going to have a child in October. The months whirl round and the day grows nearer. We are happier than we could have imagined. An eager anticipatory calm.

Lizzie and I are going through the steps of a legal separation, which will be much the same I think as the later divorce. It's all very sad, I

199

have no wish to talk about it now. It could have been much worse. I was in New York over Christmas, will go again in May, then Lizzie and Harriet will come to London for a week or so in June. We've done our best, and at least Harriet won't experience a divorce in which her parents hate each other.

A last thing. Please Allen don't quarrel with me again. You and I have held on to each other for almost thirty-five years. I have always, or almost always, been charmed by you and thought of you with reverence and gratitude.[4]

Since Tate was not in a quarrelsome mood, he replied, "I don't think we've quarreled. We were temporarily at cross purposes." After extolling the delights of "paternity in old age" and advising Lowell to let his forthcoming child "have his chances as a baptized R.C.," he volunteered to be godfather.[5] His dissatisfaction with some aspects of Lowell's behavior lingered, however. On 21 March 1971, Lowell reviewed Stanley Kunitz's new book, *The Testing Tree*, on the front page of the *New York Times Book Review*. The review starts off well and makes clear Lowell's affection for all of Kunitz's work, but after four paragraphs, it digresses to the subject of the "virtues of intelligible and unintelligible poetry."[6] From this point on, the review seems mildly confused but still more or less focused on what Lowell takes to be Kunitz's new style. The penultimate paragraph, though, presents an odd portrait of the poet ("awed and whimsical, perhaps," Lowell says) as "a sturdy, stocky figure, much the shape and height of a *poilu*, the French infantryman of World War I. He carries his sixty or hundred pounds of necessary equipment on his back. He moves forward for a long time, a splattered dim blue haze, marching at a steady pace, with occasional stops and spurts."[7] Lowell never makes clear what purpose this portrait serves. Whether this or the general lack of direction in the review bothered Tate more is hard to say, but he expressed his disapprobation to Kunitz, who responded by agreeing that it was a puzzling and confused piece of writing. Kunitz then complimented Tate on his own understanding of *The Testing Tree*, which acknowledged that Kunitz had not abandoned his respect for craftsmanship in favor of some version of "open form" as Lowell seemed to think.[8]

Epilogue

The fact that Tate expressed his disapproval to Kunitz rather than to Lowell suggests a lingering distance between them. Many of Lowell's friends were, at this time, finding fault with him in various ways. Elizabeth Hardwick was well-liked by Lowell's friends (perhaps more accurately, Lowell's friends were also Hardwick's friends), and understandably, they found it difficult to sympathize with him, whose many infidelities had effected nothing but useless and unnecessary pain.

Still, Tate, like most of Lowell's other friends and regardless of doubts about the new situation, remained loyal. Lowell must have felt the force of their friendship. After Tate wrote to express his willingness to godfather the new child, Lowell responded with praise verging on flattery: "It's your fire that counts. Last term I gave my students a day on sonnets, reading them you, Longfellow and Tuckerman. Longfellow has charming open lines, the Tuckerman something more, a Tennyson turned hard, but their energies are scattered and left me with only haphazard praise to give after reading you carefully. Fury, music and wit, not a word to be dropped or moved in whole poems. I am talking about the Christmas, Subway sonnets. You can afford to nag at criticism, when you have left so much that will stand." [9]

In recent years, Lowell had written more than two hundred unrhymed sonnets, so his praise of Tate suggests that once again his mentor had served as an aesthetic touchstone. "Fury, music and wit" characterize the best of Lowell's sonnets, too (how often poets praise in others what they want to find in their own work), but his willingness to revise, even after they were in print, denies the *Notebook* poems the sense of perfection he ascribes to Tate. On the other hand, since *Life Studies,* Lowell had committed himself to a poetics of process that refused the model of the discrete, highly finished individual poem in favor of the loose poetic sequence or a journalistic series of poems, projecting a more inclusive and immediate sense of a life being lived through poetry. The self-sufficiency and rounded individual closure of Tate's poems of the 1930s and 1940s—as well as of the poems of *Lord Weary's Castle*—may have struck Lowell as static, unyielding, and impersonal, but to replace that earlier poetic with one of process, even though a necessary step away from the conservative modernism of his apprentice years, would not entirely satisfy Lowell. Although he prized inspiration over craft, he could never reject the latter and, in fact, found the role of inspiration problematic in the documentary aesthetic of process he was developing in *Notebook*, *The Dolphin*, and *Day by Day*. Lowell never ceased to expect even the most casually organized poem to project some sense of formal necessity. His complaint in "Epilogue" about the "threadbare art" of his eye is an expression of regret that he had yet to find a poetics capable of effectively mediating between formal and historical necessities, one that would lend the "grace of accuracy" yet preserve forever "each figure in the photograph." Regardless of later reservations about the aesthetic developed in his early years, he never lost his longing for the sense of permanence engendered by strongly realized form. Even at this late date, he could genuinely appreciate the muscular, rigorously conventional sonnets of his mentor.

After discussing the expected child and agreeing that Tate should indeed be the godfather, Lowell concluded with a final apology for the blunder that had sparked their quarrel. His assessment of his difficulty with the preface is candid and accurate: "Again apologies for the festschrift. I was writing all the time, as if I might die before I gave out. Idle time was kept to be idle, and mostly to revise. The difficulties in phrasing strategy etc. for my opening essay. A hundred times I was tempted by strong phrases; when they stopped, I stopped, and fled to the protection of my own work. It would be tactless to thank you for this, it's a little like felony, but I must."

The awkwardness of Lowell's various attempts to apology and the confusions of the Kunitz review may well have left Tate relieved that Lowell had abandoned the festschrift. Now that Radcliffe Squires had the project well in hand, and Tate was assured of its completion, he must have felt in a more expansive and forgiving mood than when Lowell put the project at risk.

In May, Lowell's obsession with dolphins began. Although this interest would determine one of the central symbols of his new book, it also signaled impending mania. Lowell somehow prevented himself from suffering a full-scale attack, but not before he had spent a good deal of money on antique stone dolphins. The dolphin and the mermaid, two closely related emblems of Caroline's personality, would recur throughout the new book. The dolphin, especially, as the mysterious guide and savior of drowning men (and Lowell certainly felt at times as if he were drowning), suggests the mysterious and inexplicable otherness of intelligent life outside of the self. Savior and guide, the dolphin is yet so beyond our ordinary world of reference that communication with it is an exceptional experience. Establishing that communication is one of the problems the book sets for itself. The sonnet entitled "Dolphins" from "Another Summer" suggests how difficult that process is:

Those warmblooded watchers of children—*do not say*
I have never known how to talk to dolphins,
when I try to they just swim away.
We often share the new life, *the new life—*
I haven't stilled my New England shades by combing
the Chinese cowlicks from our twisted garden,
or sorted out the fluff in the boiler room,
or stumbled on the lost mouth of the cesspool.
Our time is shorter and brighter like the summer,
each day the chill thrill of the first day at school.
Coughs echo like swimmers shouting in a pool—
a mother, unlike most fathers, must be manly.
Will a second dachshund die of a misborn lung?
Will the burned child drop her second boiling kettle?

The new life, once celebrated by Dante, is here uncertain in its brevity and painful in its incidents. A dachshund did die of lung problems, and Caroline's small daughter did drop a boiling kettle, as Lowell reported to Tate in a letter of 15 February 1972: "We had a harsh accident. The little six years girl tipped an electric kettle in her lap. Now after a terrible month in the hospital, we know she will be home within a month, scarred from navel to knee, but not unsightly."[10]

By now, Lowell and Caroline shared a child. Sheridan had been born on 28 September 1971 after an uneasy pregnancy. During the previous July, Blackwood and Lowell had moved to Milgate, her country house, and he had been commuting from there to the University of Essex at Colchester. This settled life, to judge from "The Dolphins," Lowell viewed as accidental and temporary. As the sonnet immediately preceding "The Dolphins" concludes, one has to wonder "When most happiest / how do I know I can keep any of us alive?" The accident to six-year-old Ivana, which kept her in the hospital for three months, must have reinforced this sense of helplessness in the midst of relative happiness and calm. As Lowell wrote to Tate, Berryman's recent suicide weighed heavily, and Lowell sensed himself moving toward the close of his career: "I've gathered and finished most of my unfinished poems. And now I look over sheep and orchards into the light gray English winter sky, and feel as empty."

Lowell spent the winter of 1972 completing *The Dolphin* and rearranging and revising *Notebook* into the new sequences that became *History* and *For Lizzie and Harriet*. In the fall of 1971, Hardwick had heard that Lowell's new book would draw upon her letters and conversation, and this would be the most controversial issue surrounding *The Dolphin*. Adrienne Rich would be bitter in her attack on the book as a betrayal of confidences and an attack upon women. Alan Williamson would defend Lowell. Other reviewers would join in, but the most important objections, from Lowell's point of view, were those of Hardwick and of Elizabeth Bishop. To Hardwick, he denied any intention of defaming or harming either her or Harriet. "Poetry lies," he said somewhat disingenuously.[11] *The Dolphin* is plotted, is selective, and so differs from life. The emotions it generates are the reader's, not the poet's, and poems such as "Flight" that attempt to simply depict the protagonist's emotions are not very successful.

A few incidents that had been reported to the public could, even in fragmentary, partly fictionalized form, still hurt those who were affected by the actual events. Also, the use of another person's words, even in distorted, fictionalized, and versified form that cannot be mistaken for reportage, may be plagiarism, which added a literary to an ethical crime. Even in those instances in which Lowell changed Hardwick's language, the intent is clearly to convince the reader that these are her words, not the poet's. The question must be asked as to whether such quotation of another person in a prose autobiography is inappropriate. Certainly the sensation surrounding the breakup of the Lowell marriage made *The Dolphin* of unusual interest, but like George Meredith's *Modern Marriage*, Lowell's sonnets, with their intense emotional appeal, seem somehow even more intimate than a prose version of the same material. Autobiographies of film stars and sports figures appear almost daily, and most of them reproduce the purported conversation of other people, often to their detriment. Yet no other autobiography of recent years has generated the sort of controversy that surrounded *The Dolphin*.

To note this is not to excuse Lowell for including this material or even for writing the book, but it is worth remarking that the book is not inherently sensational; it is the knowledge brought to it by the reader that makes it so painful. In itself, it is a self-portrait of an observant but tired man who is as confused as he is enlightened by his insights. He is balanced precariously between two women, receiving letters from one and trying to come to an understanding with the other. Nowhere does he say or depict anything particularly lurid. Lowell realized, as clearly as anyone else, how painful the material would be for Hardwick, what a violation of privacy it would seem, and he vacillated for some time about publishing it. Bishop wrote on 21 March and urged him not to publish. She admired the book as poetry but was particularly disturbed by the use of Hardwick's words, and even more disturbed that Lowell had rewritten Hardwick's letters. She invoked Thomas Hardy to make her point clear:

> Here is a quotation from dear little Hardy that I copied out years ago—long before DOLPHIN, or even the *Notebooks*, were thought of. It's from a letter written in 1911, referring to "an abuse which was said to have occured—that of publishing details of a lately deceased man's life under the guise of a novel, with assurances of truth scattered in the newspapers." (Not exactly the same situation as DOLPHIN, but fairly close.)
>
> "What should certainly be protested against, in cases where there is no authorization, is the mixing of fact and fiction in unknown proportions. Infinite mischief would lie in that. If any statements in the dress of fiction are covertly hinted to be fact, all must be fact, and nothing

else but fact, for obvious reasons. The power of getting lies believed about people through that channel after they are dead, by stirring in a few truths, is a horror to contemplate." [12]

Hardy's easy distinction between fact and fiction belies the complexity with which biographical or autobiographical writing wrestles with those evasive categories; nevertheless, the ethical point is hard to dispute. Bishop allows Lowell to use his own life as material, but not Hardwick's, even though it would be difficult for him to depict his anguished life at this time without referring, in some way, to his abandoned wife and daughter. Bishop simply does not feel that telling this story can justify what he has done:

> I'm sure my point is only too plain . . . Lizzie is not dead, etc.—but there is a "mixture of fact & fiction," and you have *changed* her letters. That is "infinite mischief," I think. The first one, page 10, is so shocking—well, I don't know what to say. And page 47 . . . and a few after that. One can use one's life [as] material—one does, anyway—but these letters—aren't you violating a trust? IF you were given permission—IF you hadn't changed them . . . etc. *But art just isn't worth that much.* I keep remembering Hopkins' marvellous letter to Bridges about the idea of a "gentleman" being the highest thing ever conceived—higher than a "Christian" even, certainly than a poet. It is not being "gentle" to use personal, tragic, anguished letters that way—it's cruel.

Many poets, after receiving Bishop's measured, uncompromising letter, would have revised to remove the offending material or would simply have abandoned the idea of publication, but Lowell, even though he was soliciting advice from various friends, had already decided. He simply could not leave what he rightly considered some of his best work to remain unpublished. For him art *was* worth that much. If Tate had advised him, perhaps he would have reconsidered further, but to all appearances, he had made up his mind. Whether or not Tate saw any of these poems at this time, he had nothing to say then or later, although the use of such personal material would once have roused him to extensive commentary.

In July 1973, *The Dolphin, History,* and *For Lizzie and Harriet* appeared and began to receive troubled reviews. The most disturbing notice of *The Dolphin* and *For Lizzie and Harriet* came from Adrienne Rich, who had long admired Lowell's work but had become troubled by his apparently callous attitude toward his family. Her outrage was based partly on what she took to be Lowell's sexism, so she chastised him for his "masculinity." She found everything to criticize in Lowell's life-situation and nothing to praise in the book, which she took as merely an extension of himself—a reading the book admittedly invited: "What does one say about a poet who, having left his wife and daughter for another marriage, then titles a book with their names, and goes on to appropriate his ex-wife's letters written under the stress and pain of desertion, into a book of poems nominally addressed to the new wife? If this kind of question has nothing to do with art, we have come far from the best of the tradition Lowell would like to vindicate—or perhaps it cannot be vindicated." [13]

Rich's column in *American Poetry Review* provoked a defense by Alan Williamson but no written response from Lowell. No doubt he had anticipated such reviews—he had had ample warning from his friends—and had steeled himself. Generally, the reviews of *History* were friendly or at least neutral, many reviewers agreeing that the revised sonnets were strengthened, some reviewers decidedly approving of the new ordering, but reviewers of *The Dolphin* and *For Lizzie and Harriet* were distressed by the books' indecisive half-fiction, half-something-else voice. Today's critics, especially those familiar with recent work in theories of autobiography, would find *The Dolphin* more characteristic of its genre than Lowell's reviewers did at the time, but it was almost impossible for anyone in the literary world of 1973 to suspend awareness of Lowell's marital complications and read the book objectively.

Even though Lowell certainly found a number of these reviews upsetting, he had already turned to new work. His sonnet fixation finally exhausted, he had begun to write free verse again. These new poems would recount in autobiographical fashion (that is, in a mixture of fiction and selected fact) the events of his new marriage and, most poignantly, would catch the elegiac tone of an era haunted by the deaths of several friends and the illness and decline of others.

Epilogue

One of these friends was Tate, who, after delivering the annual Christian Gauss lectures at Princeton in October 1973, had collapsed, marking the beginning of his long, final decline in health. Although he would continue to lecture and even write, the last six years of life would constantly try his strength. In March 1974, he lectured on Robert Frost at the Library of Congress and, in November of that year, celebrated his seventy-fifth birthday. By this time, his health had become such a problem that his letters to Lowell discuss little else. In September 1974, he nearly drowned in the bathtub. His last poem was written in 1976 and is a farewell to his immediate family, one stanza for each of his sons and one for his wife Helen. By 1976, he was nearly bedridden.

Despite the lack of contact in these years, Lowell had not forgotten Tate and all that Tate had done for him. In May 1974, he wrote to Tate and recalled once again their time at Monteagle when Lowell was writing *Land of Unlikeness:* "Time, or at least the season, seems to be moving backward since I last saw you. It's so much colder here. We only have fireplace heat, and it's as bad as the windy days during our Monteagle winter of 42 and 43. Nothing could be—I remember going to bed then, and read the three volume St. Simon. Our famous fire must have been a protest against the cold."[14]

Tate's Library of Congress lecture had been published, and Lowell found it admirable: "I liked your Frost essay enormously— I might say I was amazed . . . so long it has been since you wrote an extended piece on one poet. I think somehow it's the rhetoric, the work-up that carries out the feelings of the mind—how you work up to your final conversation with Frost at Yale. It is like a real meeting . . . in words. What is it that Eliot says, Fare forward? So we must."

Tate's essay "Robert Frost as Metaphysical Poet" is one of his last important works of criticism. He finds Frost's work "not entirely sympathetic" but admirable, both in the number of fine poems and for its technical complexity, humor, and narrative skill.[15] Most interesting in the review are its anecdotes, including a description of his first meeting with Frost in London at Harold Monro's flat in 1928. Frost took an interest in Tate's southern

Epilogue

speech, being particularly impressed by his distinct consonants.¹⁶ The final anecdote is characteristic of Frost. Early in 1963, Tate, along with Lowell, served on the Bollingen Prize jury, which decided to award the prize to Frost. It was Tate's duty to call and inform him that he had been so honored: "Would he accept it? I was appointed to telephone him and ask. I did; his feeble voice came through distinctly. 'Is this Allen?' he said. I said, 'Yes, and we hope you will accept the Bollingen Prize for 1962.' After a brief silence he said, 'I've wondered where you fellows stood.'"¹⁷

Frost died in 1963, as did Roethke; Eliot and Jarrell died in 1965; Schwartz in 1966; Berryman in 1972; and now, in July 1974, John Crowe Ransom. He had been a mentor to both Tate and Lowell, and although he was elderly and his death peaceful, Lowell found it one more source of depression. Israel Citkovitz, Caroline's former husband, also had just died, and Lowell must have been in a particularly morbid frame of mind. Peter Taylor, probably Lowell's closest living friend other than Tate, had recently suffered a heart attack. In response to his mood of the moment, Lowell wrote "Suicide," with its powerful but oddly Sylvia Plath-like closure:

Do I deserve credit
for not having tried suicide—
or am I afraid
the exotic act
will make me blunder,

not knowing error
is remedied by practice,
as our first home-photographs,
headless, half-headed, tilting
extinguished by a flashbulb?

Here, as throughout *Day by Day*, the photographic or documentary aesthetic explicitly asserts itself. Because it is committed to psychological association, journalistic accretion of detail, and the chronological structure of the quotidian, this is an aesthetic of process rather than of the formal self-sufficiency of postsymbolist modernism. Despite its attendant limitations, this documentary

209

aesthetic offered immediate response to an engendering emotion and a structural matrix that could support the most mundane facts of Lowell's daily life. The limitations noted here are crudity and incompletion. Lowell's conscious attempts to wield this aesthetic (to make "home-photographs") conjure up the familiar figure of the maimed man, the incomplete ("headless, half-headed") other, the intellectual self so fragile because historical it can be "extinguished by a flashbulb," overpowered by the sudden glare of inspiration. Suicide, this poem speculates, may be the necessary adaptation of an aesthetic so problematic it cannot thrive in this glare.

In writing elegies for his generation—"Our Afterlife," "Homecoming," "For John Berryman," "Jean Stafford, a Letter," "Since 1939"—Lowell found a voice of nostalgia and authenticity, but at the price of allowing exhaustion to creep into his poems. Much of *Day by Day* is about his new life in England, but many of those poems, instead of introducing a note of hopefulness, speak in the same tired voice of the elegies. The effect is disconcerting, especially since a few of the poems ("St. Mark's, 1933," for instance) seem willfully slack. The posthumous air of Lowell's last book suggests that he foresaw his own death, and, certainly, "Home" explicitly predicts the event:

I wish I could die.
Less than ever I expect to be alive
six months from now—
1976,
a date I dare not affix to my grave.

And "Endings" contains the lines now inscribed on his gravestone in Dunbarton: "the immortal / is scraped unconsenting from the mortal."

John Crowe Ransom's death was the immediate issue in July 1974, and Ian Hamilton, later to be Lowell's biographer, solicited both Lowell and Tate for tributes. Tate was uncomfortable with the editorial attitude of Hamilton's journal, *The New Review,* and wrote to Lowell to find out more about it. Lowell acknowledged that the editors (excluding Hamilton) were "careless" but assured

Tate that they meant well and were certainly anxious to have something from Tate.[18] Lowell had already written his piece, which praised Ransom as a teacher and mentor to many: "Randall Jarrell said the gods who took away the poet's audience gave him students. No student was more brilliant than Jarrell, but Ransom had dozens—Allen Tate, Robert Penn Warren, Andrew Lytle, Peter Taylor, John Thompson, Robie Macauley, James Wright."[19] Lowell has something to say about several of the writers on this list, particularly Jarrell, who had been on his mind more or less continually in recent years. The most relevant section of this essay is his comparison of Ransom and Tate:

> There were moments in Ransom's ironic courtesies that reduced even Allen Tate to white-faced finger-twitching, so far had the conversation seemed to fall from reckless sublimity. In a letter just written to me, Tate rightly boasts of being Ransom's oldest living student. But the relationship could never have been this, they were so near in genius, close in age, and different in character. Ransom affected a fear lest Tate, though matchless, prove too strong for himself, he was so close to the danger areas, France, Rimbaud, Hart Crane, *The Waste Land;* he was too eloquent, obscure, and menacingly gallant. Ransom liked to stand behind, and later off from, the agrarian charge, as if he were an anti-slavery Southern commander with liberal friends in the East.[20]

One would like to know in what other ways Lowell saw Ransom and Tate as differing in character. Tate apparently had felt that their differences were not as important as their similarities. The most important difference was that Tate was passionate in his approach to both life and literature. He says of Ransom, "But I was not, like him, cold; I was *calidus juventa,* running over with violent feelings, usually directed at my terrible family. . . ."[21] Finally he admits that this "dislike" of Ransom was his "fear of him."[22] This complex mentor relationship, in so many ways beyond full analysis, shaped Tate's poetry to some extent, just as Tate's shaped Lowell's. One of the common influences on Tate and Lowell that, in each case, helped to alleviate the potentially stifling proximity of the mentor was Eliot. Tate argues that Ransom and Eliot had much in common; undoubtedly Ransom would demur, but fi-

211

nally Tate distinguishes them by arguing, "Eliot's essays will be read . . . for their opinions; Ransom's for their style, regardless of what they say. For Ransom wrote the most precarious, the most engaging, and the most elegant prose of all the poet-critics of our time."[23] He concludes by claiming that Ransom was Virgil to him, reinforcing the earlier statement that Ransom was "cold" and Tate *"caldius"*; as Virgil was the dispassionate chronicler, Dante was the hot-blooded lover who tracked his beloved all the way to the throne of God.

Bouts of mania, a growing discord in his home life, and evidence of a serious physical condition marred the last three years of Lowell's life. In February 1975, he obtained a report on his physical condition from his London physician, a report that was intended not for him but for his Boston doctor to read. The report mentioned high blood pressure, chronic mania, heavy smoking, alcoholism, and, even worse, some heart peculiarities that might lead to more serious difficulties and perhaps require the installation of a pacemaker. Naturally, Lowell was disturbed by this, as anyone might be; but the bad health of others, particularly that of Tate and Peter Taylor, had predisposed him to worry about himself. In the spring of 1975 in New York, he suffered a collapse that might have been caused by an overdose of lithium; the maintenance of proper lithium levels would be difficult from now on.

With his own health problems in mind, he wrote to Tate on 8 May from Brookline (where he lived while teaching at Harvard) to empathize with his mentor's mounting physical problems. He could not resist mentioning Monteagle once again: "Welcome home from the hospital, my hearing of your return was the first I knew that you had been in. I feel near you in a curious way— Caroline and I and Sheridan have had something called the wandering germ or virus. It overcomes antibiotics and wanders from brain to eye to ear, then mostly to stomach. It can return. For a couple of days, my life was all in flakes in my mind . . . among other things our Monteagle in stormy sunlit vignettes."[24]

Lowell has been thinking about a collection of essays and acknowledged Tate as an influence on his prose: "When I was well (yesterday) I leafed through a pile of essays, reviews, tapes etc. to see what could be kept for a small critical book. How often, too often for my vanity, I heard your voice and read your voice in my sentences." The critical book would not appear until ten years after Lowell's death.

Money problems, a trans-Atlantic teaching schedule (he was teaching one semester at Harvard), and long periods of separation from Caroline and the children were wearing. Additionally, he had trouble monitoring his lithium level and apparently, had become more afraid of the manic attacks than he had been in the past. Despite these difficulties, he was writing some fine poems. "The Day," which Lowell may have drafted as early as 1973, ranges over his various moods, opening by simultaneously celebrating the persistence of the natural world and the felicity of perception and association, then linking perception to memory, and closing on a note of regret for the lost day of innocence when love seemed immortal. The poem ends on a paradoxical note:

> as if in the end,
> in the marriage with nothingness,
> we could ever escape
> being absolutely safe.

Mortality is nature, too, and the speaker realizes that he is wedded not only to his beloved but to his own death, the certainty of which is his real safety. Every perception, whether of daily life or derived from memory, even going back to childhood ("child's daubs in a book / I read before I could read"), is "terra firma and transient," but no less fresh and bright for being mortal.

This renewed sense of wonder at perception and the natural world strikes a new note in Lowell's work. Although tinged by emotions of fear, loss, and self-doubt, a few of these poems focus Lowell in a nature that he had never before seen so clearly. Perhaps the relative unfamiliarity of the landscape of Kent has forced him to look afresh:

> these three weeks the weather
> has accreted reek
> like a bathroom mirror:
> hills, cows, molehills,   (Lowell's
> the oceanless inland . . .   ellipsis)

213

the harvest
we whistle from grass.

The struck oak that lost
a limb that weighed a ton
still shakes green leaves
and takes the daylight,
as if alive.   ("We Took Our Paradise")

Lowell spent most of the summer of 1975 at Milgate working on the poems that he had drafted since finishing *The Dolphin*. On 22 July, he wrote his last extant letter to Tate. Lowell praises him for the way he has faced his illnesses, then turns to ongoing literary projects. After praising Tate's tribute to Ransom, he briefly, and for the last time, returns to his favorite subject, Tate's poetry:

> I hate to think of the afflictions the summer may have brought you. Your courage and vivacity shine. Everyone I see who might have heard from you has heard: Peter, Roy Fuller, Red, Stanley. And last year when I was reading at Southern colleges, everyone seemed to know everything about you—with anxious warmth.
>
> Thanks for your encouragement about my critical pieces. There are a lot, but not enough, and not enough order. I despair of more. Each essay [?] cost me more qualms and trouble than any poem—I think it is because prose is a free and open (no hiding places) medium with a deadline. I thought your pages on Ransom almost as good as anything—the lightning of your spirit.
>
> I am trying the *Cimetiere* as you once suggested. I already have good lines but can't keep them and still keep good rhymes and meter. Everyone has this trouble, none of the translations are notable English. I think your Ode somehow did it—a very different, almost opposite historical poem, yet somehow inspired by and answering to Valery. Your Ode and the Ransom prose have the same voice. By the way, is improving on Baudelaire only overwriting? Many thanks for your generous notes on my translations.[25]

Tate denied the link between his "Ode" and Valéry. He wrote to Lowell on 29 July, "My ode could not be in any sense an answer to Valery. I wrote it in 1926. I didn't read anything by him until 1928. This error was first circulated by Edmund Wilson."[26] Lowell never completed his imitation of Valéry's *Le cimetiere marin*. Other

214

projects occupied him, including new poems and the editing of his *Selected Poems,* which he completed by the end of the summer.

Manic attacks took up much of that fall and winter. In November, Lowell was hospitalized in Roehampton, then in Greenways Nursing Home in St. John's Wood. In January, at Blackwood's suggestion, he received acupuncture treatment in Redcliffe Square, and she retreated to Milgate with the children, commuting to London to help care for him. The experiment with acupuncture failed to work, and Lowell returned to Greenways at the end of the month. He was distraught over this prolonged bout of illness, and the poems that grew out of these months are disturbing in their relative artlessness:

> The painter who burned both hands
> after trying to kill her baby, says,
> "Is there no one in Northampton
> who goes to the Continent in the winter?"
> The alcoholic convert keeps smiling,
> "Thank you, Professor, for saving my life;
> you taught me homosexuality is a heinous crime."
> I hadn't. I am a thorazined fixture
> in the immovable square-cushioned chairs
> we preoccupy for seconds like migrant birds.   ("Home")

Finally, by April, he was well enough to fly to New York for a revival of *The Old Glory,* but in September he had to return to Greenways, and even when he arrived at Harvard the next month, he was far from well.

By now his marriage to Blackwell was in serious trouble. She and the children had preceded him to America, and they would return to London without him. Pressed by money problems, she had placed Milgate, much to Lowell's regret, on the market. In January, after an apparently unsatisfactory attempt at reconciliation, Lowell returned to Cambridge alone. Diagnosed with congestive heart failure, he spent ten days in Phillips House, where his grandfather Winslow had died:

> Something sinister and comforting
> in this return after forty years' arrears

215

to death and Phillips House . . .
this irreverent absence of pain,
less than the ordinary that daily irks—
except I cannot entirely get my breath,
as if I were muffled in snow,
our winter's inverted gray sky
of frozen slush,
its usual luminous lack of warmth.   ("Phillips House Revisited")

Lowell read this poem on 23 February at an appearance with Allen Ginsberg in St. Mark's church in New York. This event was followed by an early sixtieth birthday party with Elizabeth Hardwick and their daughter Harriet.

Meanwhile Milgate had sold. Blackwood had taken an apartment outside of Dublin, where Lowell joined her at the end of March. Back in Cambridge after this visit, he believed their marriage had ended. He was uncomfortable with the new living arrangements, and he had had doubts for some time about whether two such volatile personalities belonged together. On his return, he wrote about his visit as if it had been their last meeting:

I meant to write about our last walk.
We had nothing to do but gaze—
seven years, now nothing but a diverting smile,   (*Lowell's*
dalliance by a river, a speeding swan. . .   *ellipsis*)
the misleading promise
to last with joy as long as our bodies,
nostalgia pulverized by thought,
nomadic as yesterday's whirling snow,
all whiteness splotched.   ("Last Walk?")

It was not his last visit, however. In May, he received the Copernicus Award from the American Academy of Arts and Letters, and Blackwood came to New York for the ceremony, but this encounter was unpleasant. Blackwood had been traumatized by Lowell's two years of almost continual illness, and he was afraid to live in Ireland, where he doubted that adequate medical care was available and where he simply did not feel at home.

Hardwick, by now, had forgiven Lowell's betrayal of her and Harriet in *The Dolphin*, and he apparently felt inclined to renew

Epilogue

their relationship on their old terms. After a ten-day trip with her to the Soviet Union as members of the American Delegation to the Union of Soviet Writers, he spent the rest of the summer in Castine working on an essay—actually a series of brief sketches of individual writers—posthumously published as "New England and Further."

In August, *Day by Day* appeared. Many of the poems have not only an air of elegy but of finality, as if Lowell had, at last, settled some old concerns. Most notable is the harrowing poem "Unwanted":

Mother,

I must not blame you for carrying me in you
on your brisk winter lunges across
the desperate, refusey Staten Island beaches,   (*Lowell's*
their good view skyscrapers on Wall Street . . .   *ellipsis*)
for yearning seaward, far from any home, and saying,
"I wish I were dead, I wish I were dead."
Unforgivable for a mother to tell her child—
but you wanted me to share your good fortune,
perhaps, by recapturing the disgust of those walks;
your credulity assumed we survived,
while weaklings fell with the dead and dying.

Day by Day is also notable for those poems in which Lowell reflects upon his own aesthetic and voices a dissatisfaction that, had he lived, might have led to a further shift in style:

Coleridge,
the author of *Dejection*,
thought
genius is the discovery
of subjects remote
from my life.

I cannot read.
Everything I've written
is greenish brown,
as if the words
refused to sound.   ("Wellesley Free")

217

Epilogue

The irony of *Day by Day* distances the speaker-subject from the object, the other human presence, or the symbolic and somewhat alien landscape, usually of Britain. Lowell's consciousness of his irony undermines the central project of his poetry from *Notebook* through *The Dolphin*, which is to forge new links between life and art, if not positively to fuse them. The unreality of this project is explicit even in *Notebook 1967–1968*. Lowell's wry admission of his devotion to "surrealism," later changed to "unrealism" in the "Afterthought" to successive editions of *Notebook*, demonstrates how the self-consciousness of the subject will always intrude to prevent any transcendence of the gap between subject and object. Paul de Man, in a discussion of the rhetorical commonality of allegory and irony, argues that the two are "linked in their common demystification of an organic world postulated in a symbolic mode of representation in which fiction and reality could coincide." [27] Lowell's nostalgia for this organic world shapes poems like "The Day," but by the end of the book, he has demystified his position and recognized the obduracy of his own consciousness. This kind of ironic consciousness, de Man says, "is clearly an unhappy one that strives to move beyond and outside itself." [28] Such a move might forge that link between art and life, but it would do so in the world of the object, not of the subject. To the postromantic sensibility, this negation of the self would leave the poem voiceless, making writing impossible. Further, the poem of the object would lapse into documentary, to which Lowell, in his later years, had been drawn only to understand how "threadbare" the art of observation had become. These are some of the aesthetic misgivings he expresses in such poems as "Shifting Colors" and "Epilogue."

Although perhaps not a dead-end, his recognition of the triumph of irony over art would have forced Lowell into yet another direction had he lived to once more reconsider his poetic. If, as "Epilogue" suggests, he had tired of the "misalliance" of a "snapshot" autobiographical aesthetic that rejected the power of amalgamation that had been earned with such difficulty in his earlier work, he had in some ways tired of his life as well, at least as a subject. Yet, his life—its inner concerns, at least—had served him well

218

through a variety of distinct styles and formal concerns. He explains this in an essay written for a special issue of *Salmagundi* that celebrated his sixtieth birthday:

> What I write almost always comes out of the pressure of some inner concern, temptation or obsessive puzzle. Surprisingly, quite important things may get said. But sometimes what is closest to the heart has no words but stereotypes. Stereotypes are usually true, but never art. Inspired lines from nowhere roam through my ears . . . to make or injure a poem. All my poems are written for catharsis; none can heal melancholia or arthritis.   (*Lowell's ellipsis*)
> I pray that my progress has been more than recoiling with satiation and disgust from one style to another, a series of rebuffs. I hope there has been increase of beauty, wisdom, tragedy, and all the blessings of consuming chance.[29]

The first notices of *Day by Day*, particularly Helen Vendler's front-page review in the *New York Times Book Review*, were perceptive and favorable. The book would win the National Book Critic's Circle Award for Poetry, but Lowell would not live to accept it. At the beginning of September, he flew from Boston to Ireland to visit Blackwood and the children. Even though he had planned on staying longer, he left after ten days in a state of marital indecision and flew to New York to rejoin Hardwick. In the taxi from Kennedy Airport, carrying a portrait of Blackwood wrapped in brown paper, he suffered a heart attack and died.

Lowell's funeral at the Church of the Advent on Mount Vernon Street in Boston drew six hundred mourners, including Blackwood, Hardwick, and most of Lowell's surviving close friends. Allen Tate was unable to attend. Too ill to write or travel, he spent the last two years of his life bedridden, or nearly so, and died in Nashville on 9 February 1979. He had lived into his eightieth year and survived his protégé by a year and a half. Lowell's most chilling lines in *Day by Day* predict his own death in tones of despair and finality, but the third section of Tate's "Farewell Rehearsed," entitled "To my Wife Helen" and written three years before his death, views that foreseeable event with unquenchable earthly affection and a stoic calm:

Epilogue

When I have reached the shady underground
With but sad hope of coming up again,
I shall implore your ghost to hover round
And guide me to a land of lucky men,
Even luckier than the land that I had left
Where love of you was all the air I breathed,
And once I'd left it I was love-bereft,
For with sad hope my empty spirit seethed.

Tate lived long enough to experience some of the reflectiveness old age is presumed to confer, but Lowell died in the turmoil of unresolved personal stress and a changing aesthetic. The lines that Lowell wrote about Berryman in *Day by Day* apply almost as well to Tate as to the generation that the elder poet had shepherded; they stand here as an epitaph to them all:

Yet really we had the same life,
the generic one
our generation offered
(*Les Maudits*—the compliment
each American generation
pays itself in passing):
first students, then with our own,
our galaxy of grand maitres,
our fifties' fellowships
to Paris, Rome and Florence,
veterans of the Cold War not the War—
all the best of life . . .   (*Lowell's ellipsis*)
then daydreaming to drink at six,
waiting for the iced fire,
even the feel of the frosted glass,   (*Lowell's ellipsis*)
like waiting for a girl . . .
if you had waited.
We asked to be obsessed with writing,
and we were.

220

N O T E S

Abbreviations

Austin = Robert Lowell File, Harry Ransom Humanities Center, University of Texas, Austin.

DT = *The Literary Correspondence of Donald Davidson and Allen Tate*. Edited by John Tyree Fain and Thomas Daniel Young. Athens: University of Georgia Press, 1974.

Essays = Allen Tate, *Essays of Four Decades*. Chicago: Swallow Press, 1968.

Hamilton = Ian Hamilton, *Robert Lowell: A Biography*. New York: Random House, 1982.

Harvard = Robert Lowell File, Houghton Library, Harvard University (call 73m-90. bMS Am 1905; access numbers of individual items given in notes).

LT = *The Lytle-Tate Letters*. Edited by Thomas Daniel Young and Elizabeth Sarcone. Jackson: University Press of Mississippi, 1987.

Memoirs = Allen Tate, *Memoirs and Opinions*. Chicago: Swallow Press, 1975.

Princeton = Allen Tate Papers, Firestone Library, Princeton University (all from box 28; folder numbers given in notes).

Prose = Robert Lowell, *Collected Prose*. New York: Farrar, Straus & Giroux, 1987.

Reviews = Allen Tate, *The Poetry Reviews of Allen Tate, 1924–1944*. Edited by Ashley Brown and Frances Neel Cheney. Baton Rouge: Louisiana State University Press, 1983.

221

Introduction

1. Caroline Gordon quoted in Ann Waldron, *Close Connections: Caroline Gordon and the Southern Renaissance* (New York: Putnam, 1987), 208.
2. "T. S. Eliot," Prose 45.
3. "T. S. Eliot," Prose 48.
4. "An Interview with Frederick Seidel," Prose 263.
5. Robert Lowell, *Day by Day* (New York: Farrar, Straus & Giroux, 1977), 127.
6. T. S. Eliot, *On Poetry and Poets* (New York: Harcourt, Brace, 1957), 299.
7. Eliot, *On Poetry and Poets*, 137.
8. "An Interview with Frederick Seidel," Prose 266.

Chapter One

1. "Visiting the Tates," Prose 58.
2. "The Fugitive," Memoirs 33.
3. "A Reading of Keats," Essays 267.
4. "The Man of Letters in the Modern World," Essays 7.
5. *The Fugitive*, April 1924.
6. "The Fugitive," Memoirs 30.
7. "The Profession of Letters in the South," Essays 523.
8. "Translation or Imitation?" Memoirs 199.
9. "Religion and the Old South," Essays 574.
10. "Reflections on the Death of John Crowe Ransom," Memoirs 39.
11. "John Crowe Ransom," Prose 18.
12. John Bradbury, *Renaissance in the South* (Chapel Hill: University of North Carolina Press, 1963), 30.
13. Bradbury, *Renaissance in the South*, 31.
14. "Visiting the Tates," Prose 60.
15. "Tension in Poetry," Essays 57.
16. "An Interview with Frederick Seidel," Prose 261.
17. "Tension in Poetry," Essays 57.
18. Hamilton 43.
19. Manuscript notebook, Harvard 2042. (In quoting from unpublished poetry and letters, I have silently corrected obvious spelling and typographical errors.)
20. "Antebellum Boston," Prose 302.
21. Manuscript notebook, Harvard 2043.
22. Manuscript notebook, Harvard 2047.

23. Manuscript notebook, Harvard 2046.
24. "William Carlos Williams," Prose 40.
25. V. S. Naipaul, "Et in America Ego," *Profile of Robert Lowell,* ed. Jerome Mazzaro (Columbus, Ohio: Merrill, 1971), 80.
26. "William Carlos Williams," Prose 38–39.
27. "William Carlos Williams," Prose 40.
28. "William Carlos Williams," Prose 40.

Chapter Two

1. "Visiting the Tates," Prose 60.
2. Sally Wood, ed., *The Southern Mandarins: Letters of Caroline Gordon to Sally Wood, 1924–1937* (Baton Rouge: Louisiana State University Press, 1984), 209.
3. Lowell to Anne Dick, undated (April 1937), Harvard Autograph File.
4. "Visiting the Tates," Prose 59.
5. Manuscript notebook, Harvard 2046.
6. "Visiting the Tates," Prose 60.
7. "An Interview with Frederick Seidel," Prose 257.
8. Lowell to Charlotte Lowell, undated (summer 1937), Harvard 1530.
9. Tate to Andrew Lytle, 19 May 1937, LT 108.
10. Caroline Blackwood and Robert Lowell, "A Conversation about Ford Madox Ford," *The Saturday Night Reader,* ed. Emma Tennant (London: W. H. Allen, 1979), 201.
11. Manuscript notebook, Harvard 2045.
12. Lowell and Blackwood 201.
13. Lowell and Blackwood 201.
14. Tate to James H. Kirkland, undated (1937), LT 376.
15. *Kenyon Review* 1 (1939): 32.
16. "An Interview with Frederick Seidel," Prose 239.
17. "Miss Emily and the Bibliographer," Essays 143.
18. "Miss Emily and the Bibliographer," Essays 144.
19. John Crowe Ransom to Lowell, 5 October 1945, Harvard 987.
20. "What is a Traditional Society?" Essays 556.
21. Vivienne Koch, "The Poetry of Allen Tate," *Allen Tate and His Work,* ed. Radcliffe Squires (Minneapolis: University of Minnesota Press, 1972), 261.
22. Koch, "The Poetry of Allen Tate," 261.
23. "T. S. Eliot," Reviews 109.

24. Koch, "The Poetry of Allen Tate," 263.

25. Manuscript notebook, Harvard 2047.

26. Lowell to Charlotte Lowell, undated, Harvard 1534.

27. Manuscript notebook, Harvard 2047.

28. Lowell to Tate, 13 May 1974, Princeton, folder 9.

29. "An Interview with Frederick Seidel," Prose 240–41.

30. Unpublished transcript of talk c. 1960, at Harvard, quoted in Hamilton 85.

31. Appendix, Prose 369.

32. Lowell to Tate, 31 July 1944, Princeton, folder 9.

33. Allen Tate, preface to Robert Lowell, *Land of Unlikeness*. (Cummington, Mass.: Cummington Press, 1944), n.p.

34. Tate to Lowell, 16 July 1945, Harvard 1205.

35. Lowell to Tate, undated, Princeton, folder 9.

36. Lowell to Tate, 7 July 1945, Princeton, folder 9.

37. Lowell to Tate, undated, Princeton, folder 9.

38. Barbara Thompson, "Interview with Peter Taylor," *Conversations with Peter Taylor*, ed. Hubert H. McAlexander (Jackson: University Press of Mississippi, 1987), 152.

39. Jean Stafford to Tate, 16 December 1945, Princeton, folder 9.

40. Stafford to Tate, 4 January 1946, Princeton, folder 9.

41. Tate to Stafford and Lowell, 16 January 1946, Harvard 1206.

42. Jean Stafford, "An Influx of Poets," *New Yorker*, 6 November 1978, 46.

43. Stafford, "An Influx of Poets," 51.

44. Eileen Simpson, *Poets in Their Youth* (New York: Random House, 1982), 127.

45. Simpson, *Poets in Their Youth*, 143.

46. Simpson, *Poets in Their Youth*, 144.

Chapter Three

1. John Crowe Ransom to Lowell, 5 October 1945, Harvard 987.

2. Tate to Lowell, 25 October 1946, carbon copy in Princeton, folder 12.

3. Interview with Cleanth Brooks and Robert Penn Warren, Jeffrey Meyers, ed., *Robert Lowell: Interviews and Memoirs* (Ann Arbor: University of Michigan Press, 1988), 39.

4. Brooks and Warren, Meyers, *Robert Lowell*, 39.

5. Worksheet for "At the Altar," Harvard 2096.

6. Telegram, Lowell to Tate, 4 June 1947, Princeton, folder 9.

7. Jean Stafford to Lowell, undated (from internal evidence, shortly after 22 February 1947, the date of publication of "For Her Dead Brother"), Harvard 1157.

8. "A Reading of Keats," Essays 271.

9. Lowell to Tate, 4 November 1947, Princeton, folder 9.

10. Lowell to Tate, undated ("Nov. '48" in Tate's hand), Princeton, folder 9.

11. Lowell to Tate, undated, Princeton, folder 9.

12. Lowell to Tate, undated ("Dec. '48" in Tate's hand), Princeton, folder 9.

13. Hamilton 141.

14. Lowell to Tate, undated ("Dec. '48" in Tate's hand), Princeton, folder 9.

15. Telegram, Lowell to Tate, 1 March 1949, Princeton, folder 9.

16. Telegram, Lowell to Tate, 29 March 1949, Princeton, folder 9.

17. Tate to Elizabeth Hardwick, 30 March 1949, Harvard 1810.

18. Tate to Hardwick, 4 April 1949, Harvard 1812.

19. Hubert H. McAlexander, ed., *Conversations with Peter Taylor*, 152.

20. McAlexander, *Conversations with Peter Taylor*, 152–53.

21. Waldron, *Cross Connections*, 268.

22. Tate to Lowell, 11 October 1949, Harvard 1218.

23. Lowell to Tate, 5 December 1949, Princeton, folder 9.

24. Lowell to Tate, 29 December 1949, Princeton, folder 9.

25. Lowell to Tate, 15 March 1950, Princeton, folder 9.

26. John L. Stewart, *The Burden of Time: The Fugitives and the Agrarians* (Princeton: Princeton University Press 1965), 423.

27. Tate to Donald Davison, 29 May 1965, DT 398.

28. Davidson to Tate, 4 June 1965, DT 399.

29. "An Interview with Frederick Seidel," Prose 250.

30. Randall Jarrell, *Poetry and the Age* (New York: Knopf, 1953), 255.

31. Tate to Lowell, 24 October 1952, Harvard 1226.

32. Tate to Lowell, 24 October 1952, Harvard 1226.

33. Lowell to Tate, 5 November 1952, Princeton, folder 9.

34. Lowell to Tate, 28 November 1952, Princeton, folder 9.

35. Robert S. Dupree, *Allen Tate and the Augustan Imagination* (Baton Rouge: Louisiana State University Press, 1983), 215.

36. R. K. Meiners, *Everything to Be Endured: An Essay on Robert Lowell and Modern Poetry* (Columbia: University of Missouri Press, 1970), 32.

Chapter Four

1. Lowell to Tate, 28 November 1952, Princeton, folder 9.

2. Lowell to Tate, 15 March 1953, Princeton, folder 9.

3. Lowell to Tate, 15 April (1953), Princeton, folder 9.

4. "To Whom is the Poet Responsible?" Essays 27.

5. Tate to Lowell, 28 April 1953, Harvard 1231.

6. Lowell to Tate, 29 April 1953, Princeton, folder 9.

7. Lowell to Tate, 2 December 1953, Princeton, folder 9.

8. Lowell to Tate, undated (Charlotte Lowell died 14 February 1954), Princeton, folder 9.

9. Tate to Lowell, 11 March 1954, Harvard 1232.

10. Lowell to Tate, 15 March (1954), Princeton, folder 9.

11. Typescript of "A [Mad] Negro Soldier Confined at Munich," Princeton, folder 9.

12. Unpublished poem by Lowell, Princeton, folder 9.

13. Unpublished stanzas by Lowell, Princeton, folder 9.

14. Elizabeth Hardwick to Tate, 15 October 1955, Princeton, folder 12.

15. Telegram, Lowell to Tate, 4 January 1957, Princeton, folder 9.

16. "An Interview with Frederick Seidel," Prose 243.

17. "An Interview with Frederick Seidel," Prose 244.

18. "An Interview with Frederick Seidel," Prose 237.

19. Hamilton 233.

20. Hamilton 235.

21. Hamilton 233.

22. Elizabeth Bishop, untitled dust jacket comment on Robert Lowell, in Robert Lowell, *Life Studies* (New York: Farrar, Straus & Cudahy, 1959).

23. "An Interview with Frederick Seidel," Prose 246.

24. Joseph Bennett, "Two Americans, A Brahmin, and the Bourgeoisie," *Hudson Review* 12 (Autumn), 431–39.

25. Tate to Lowell, 3 December 1957, Harvard 1237.

26. T. S. Eliot, *Selected Essays* (London: Faber & Faber, 1951), 287.

27. "The Man of Letters in the Modern World," Essays 13.

28. "A Reading of Keats," Essays 264.

29. "Emily Dickinson," Essays 294–95.

30. Thomas Daniel Young, ed., "Quo Vadimus? Or the Books Still Unwritten: Statements by Tate, Warren, Spender, and Lowell," *Mississippi Quarterly* 38, no. 4 (Fall 1985), 417, 431.

31. Tate to Elizabeth Hardwick, 18 December 1957, carbon copy in Princeton, folder 9.

32. Lowell to Tate 24 January 1958, Princeton, folder 9.
33. Tate to Lowell, 31 January 1958, Harvard 1238.
34. "On 'Skunk Hour,'" Prose 228.
35. Hamilton 237.
36. "On 'Skunk Hour,'" Prose 228.
37. "On 'Skunk Hour,'" Prose 226.
38. Unpublished note on "For the Union Dead," c. 1960, Harvard 2300.
39. Tate to Lowell, 8 May 1959, Harvard 1242.

Chapter Five

1. Hamilton 244–49.
2. Tate to Lowell, 8 November 1958, Harvard 1240.
3. Waldron, *Close Connections*, 361.
4. Waldron, *Close Connections*, 352.
5. Tate to Andrew Lytle, 25 May 1959, LT 274.
6. Noted by Tate on a letter from Elizabeth Hardwick, 1 June 1959, Princeton, folder 9.
7. Tate to Frederick A. Colwell, 30 July 1959, Princeton, folder 9.
8. "Visiting the Tates," Prose 559.
9. Tate to Lowell, 17 October 1959: Harvard 1243.
10. Lowell to Tate, 22 October 1959, Princeton, folder 9.
11. Jerome Mazarro, *The Poetic Themes of Robert Lowell* (Ann Arbor: University of Michigan Press 1965), 126–27, 121.
12. "Narcissus as Narcissus," Essays 599.
13. Thomas Wentworth Higginson, *Part of a Man's Life* (Boston: Houghton Mifflin, 1905; rpt. Port Washington: Kennikat Press, 1971), 131.
14. Lowell to Tate, 27 June 1960, Princeton, folder 9.
15. "Translation or Imitation?" Memoirs 198–99.
16. "Translation or Imitation?" Memoirs 200.
17. "Translation or Imitation?" Memoirs 200.
18. Robert Lowell *Phaedra* (New York: Farrar, Straus & Cudahy, 1961), 8.
19. Lowell, *Phaedra*, 8.
20. George Steiner, "Two Translations," *Kenyon Review* 23 (1961), 714–21.
21. Robert Lowell, *Imitations* (New York: Farrar, Straus & Cudahy, 1961), xi.

22. Lowell, *Imitations*, p. xi.

23. Hamilton 291.

24. Hamilton 292.

25. Tate to Lowell, 26 February 1961, Harvard 1245.

26. Lowell to Tate, 7 November 1961, Princeton, folder 9.

27. Tate to Lowell, 7 December 1961, Harvard 1246.

28. "Translation or Imitation?" Memoirs 207.

29. *Robert Lowell: A Reading* (Caedmon TC 1569 [1978]).

30. Dupree, *Allen Tate and the Augustinian Imagination*, 202.

31. Stafford, *Collected Stories*, p. 31.

32. Lowell to Tate, 9 October 1964, Princeton, folder 9.

33. Tate to Lowell, 2 October 1964, Harvard 1248.

34. Stephen Yenser, *Circle to Circle* (Berkeley: University of California Press, 1975), 227–28.

35. Lowell to Tate, 9 October 1964, Princeton, folder 9.

36. Hamilton 321.

Chapter Six

1. Allen Tate, "Young Randall," *Randall Jarrell, 1914–1965*, ed. Robert Lowell, Peter Taylor, and Robert Penn Warren (New York: Farrar, Straus & Giroux), 1967), 221–232.

2. Robert Lowell, "Randall Jarrell," *Randall Jarrell, 1914–1965*, 112.

3. Tate to Lowell, 7 February 1968, Harvard 1251.

4. Alan Williamson, "The Reshaping of 'Waking Early Sunday Morning,'" *Agenda* 18, no. 3 (Autumn 1980): 47.

5. Tate to Lowell, 15 May 1969, Harvard 1261.

6. Allen Tate, "Postscript by the Guest Editor," *T. S. Eliot: The Man and His Work* (New York: Delacorte Press, 1966), 389–90.

7. "Literature as Knowledge," Essays 105.

8. "Humanism and Naturalism," Memoirs 192.

9. Tate to Lowell, 22 July 1968, Harvard 1252.

10. Lowell to Tate, misdated 14 July ("24?" in Tate's hand) 1968, Princeton, folder 9.

11. Lowell to Tate, 30 July, 1968, Princeton, folder 9.

12. Tate to Lowell, 28 July, 1968, Harvard 1253.

13. David Heymann, *American Aristocracy* (New York: Dodd, Mead, 1980), 481.

14. Tate to Lowell, 26 December, 1968, Harvard 1257.

15. Lowell to Tate, 30 December, 1968, Princeton, folder 9.

16. Robert Lowell, "After Enjoying Six or Seven Essays on Me," *Salmagundi* 37 (Spring 1977), 117.

17. Peter Brooks to Lowell, 14 March 1966, Harvard 277.

18. William Meredith, review of *Notebook 1967—68*, *New York Times Book Review*, 15 June 1969, 1.

19. Tate to Lowell, 15 May 1969, Harvard 1261.

20. Lowell to Tate, 24 May 1969, Princeton, folder 9.

21. Lowell to Tate, 4 September 1969, Princeton, folder 9.

22. Tate to Lowell, 10 September 1969, Harvard 1264.

23. Lowell to Tate, 5 November 1969, Princeton, folder 9.

24. Untitled (on Allen Tate) c. 1969, Harvard 2838.

25. Lowell to Tate, (31 December 1969), Princeton, folder 9.

26. Tate to Lowell, 17 February 1969, Harvard 1259.

27. Lowell to Tate, 31 (December 31 1969), Princeton, folder 9.

28. Lowell to Tate, 19 March 1970, Princeton, folder 9.

29. Tate to Lowell, 30 March 1970, Austin.

30. Lowell to Tate, 25 April 1970, Princeton, folder 9.

31. Tate to Lowell, 12 May 1970, Austin.

Epilogue

1. Hamilton 409.

2. Stanley Kunitz to Tate, 6 March 1971, Princeton, folder 5.

3. "John Berryman," Prose 116.

4. Lowell to Tate, 29 March (1971), Princeton, folder 9.

5. Tate to Lowell, 5 April 1971, Austin.

6. Lowell, review of *The Testing Tree* by Stanley Kunitz, *New York Times Book Review*, 21 March 1971, 1.

7. Lowell, review of *The Testing Tree*, 18.

8. Stanley Kunitz to Tate, 23 April 1971, Princeton, folder 5.

9. Lowell to Tate, 13 April 1971, Princeton, folder 9.

10. Lowell to Tate, 15 February 1972, Princeton, folder 9.

11. Lowell to Hardwick, 29 September 1971, quoted in Hamilton 418.

12. Elizabeth Bishop to Lowell, 21 March 1972, quoted in Hamilton 423.

13. Adrienne Rich, "Caryatid," *American Poetry Review* 2, no. 5 (September/October, 1973): 42.

14. Lowell to Tate, 13 May 1974, Princeton, folder 9.

15. "Robert Frost as Metaphysical Poet," Memoirs 96.

16. "Robert Frost as Metaphysical Poet," Memoirs 97.

17. "Robert Frost as Metaphysical Poet," Memoirs 109.

18. Lowell to Tate, 29 July 1974, Princeton, folder 9.

19. "John Crowe Ransom," Prose 23.

20. "John Crowe Ransom," Prose 22.

21. "A Lost Traveller's Dream," Memoirs 20.

22. "Reflections on the Death of John Crowe Ransom," Memoirs 41.

23. "A Lost Traveller's Dream," Memoirs 22.

24. Lowell to Tate, 8 May 1975, Princeton, folder 9.

25. Lowell to Tate, 22 July 1975, Princeton, folder 9.

26. Tate to Lowell, 29 July 1975, Austin.

27. Paul de Man, "The Rhetoric of Temporality," *Blindness and Insight* (Minneapolis: University of Minnesota Press, 1983), 222.

28. de Man, "The Rhetoric of Temporality," 222.

29. Lowell, "After Enjoying Six or Seven Essays on Me," 114–15.

BIBLIOGRAPHY

Agenda 18, no. 3 (Autumn 1980). Special Robert Lowell issue.

Anzilotti, Rolando, ed. *Robert Lowell: A Tribute.* Pisa: Nistri-Lischi Editori, 1979.

Atlas, James. "Lord Weary: Robert Lowell in Cambridge." *Atlantic,* July 1982: 56–64.

Axelrod, Stephen. *Robert Lowell: Life and Art.* Princeton: Princeton University Press, 1978.

———, and Helen Deese, eds. *Robert Lowell: A Reference Guide.* Boston: G. K. Hall, 1982.

———, and Helen Deese, eds. *Robert Lowell: Essays on the Poetry.* New York: Cambridge University Press, 1986.

Barry, Jackson G. "Robert Lowell's 'Confessional' Image of an Age: Theme and Language in Poetic Form." *Ariel* l2, no. 1 (January 1981): 51–57.

Bawer, Bruce. *The Middle Generation: The Lives and Poetry of Delmore Schwartz, Randall Jarrell, John Berryman, Robert Lowell.* Hamden, Conn.: Archon Books, 1986.

Bayley, John. "Robert Lowell: The Poetry of Cancellation." *London Magazine* 6 (June 1966): 76–85.

———. "The Morality of Form in the Poetry of Robert Lowell." *Ariel* 9, no. 1 (January 1978): 3–17.

Bell, Vereen M. *Robert Lowell: Nihilist as Hero.* Cambridge: Harvard University Press, 1983.

Bennett, Joseph. "Two Americans, a Brahmin, and the Bourgeoisie." *Hudson Review* 12 (Autumn): 431–39.

Berland, Alwyn. "Violence in the Poetry of Allen Tate." *Accent* 11 (Summer 1951): 161–71.

231

Bibliography

Berryman, John. *The Freedom of the Poet.* New York: Farrar, Straus & Giroux, 1976.

Bishop, Elizabeth. *The Collected Prose.* New York: Farrar, Straus & Giroux, 1984.

Bishop, Ferman. *Allen Tate.* New York: Twayne, 1967.

Blackmur, R. P. *Form and Value in Modern Poetry.* New York: Doubleday, 1957.

Bloom, Harold. *The Anxiety of Influence.* New York: Oxford University Press, 1973.

———, ed. *Modern Critical Views: Robert Lowell.* New York: Chelsea, 1987.

Bradbury, John M. *The Fugitives: A Critical Account.* Chapel Hill: University of North Carolina Press, 1958.

———. *Renaissance in the South.* Chapel Hill: University of North Carolina Press, 1963.

Brinkmeyer, Robert H., Jr. "New York on the Poetry of Allen Tate." *Southern Literary Journal* 17, no. 1 (Fall 1984): 107–11.

———. *Three Catholic Writers of the Modern South.* Jackson: University Press of Mississippi, 1985.

Broughton, Irv. "An Interview with Allen Tate." *Western Humanities Review* 32 (1978): 317–36.

Brower, Reuben. *Mirror on Mirror: Translation, Imitation, Parody.* Cambridge: Harvard University Press, 1974.

Buffington, Robert. "Allen Tate: Society, Vocation, Communion." *Southern Review* 18, no. 1 (Winter 1982): 62–72.

Burnham, James. "The Unreconstructed Allen Tate." *Partisan Review* 16 (February 1949): 198–202.

Butler, Christopher. "Robert Lowell: From *Notebook* to *The Dolphin*." In *Yearbook of English Studies,* vol. 8 (1978): 141–56.

Carruth, Hayden. "A Meaning of Robert Lowell." *Hudson Review* 20 (Autumn 1967): 429–47.

Cooper, Philip. *The Autobiographical Myth of Robert Lowell.* Chapel Hill: University of North Carolina Press, 1970.

Corcoran, Neil. "Lowell Retiarius: Towards The Dolphin." *Agenda* 18, no. 3 (Autumn 1980): 75–85.

Cowan, Louise. *The Fugitive Group: A Literary History.* Baton Rouge: Louisiana State University Press, 1959.

Crane, Hart. *The Letters of Hart Crane.* Edited by Brom Weber. Berkeley: University of California Press, 1965.

Crick, John. *Robert Lowell.* Edinburgh: Oliver and Boyd, 1974.

Bibliography

Davidson, Donald. *Southern Writers in the Modern World*. Athens: University of Georgia Press, 1958.

de Man, Paul. *Blindness and Insight*. Minneapolis: University of Minnesota Press, 1983.

Di Piero, W. S. "Lowell and Ashbery." *Southern Review* 14 (April 1978): 359–67.

Doherty, Paul C. "The Poet as Historian: 'For the Union Dead' by Robert Lowell." *Concerning Poetry* 1 (Fall 1968): 37–41.

Doreski, Carole Kiler. "Robert Lowell and Elizabeth Bishop: A Matter of Life Studies." *Prose Studies* 10, no. 1 (May 1987): 85–101.

Doreski, William. "Borrowed Visions: Robert Lowell's Imitations of Baudelaire and Rimbaud in *History*. *CEA Critic* 48, no. 3 (Spring 1986): 38–49.

———. "Robert Lowell's Sonnets on Thoreau." *Thoreau Quarterly* 16, nos. 1 and 2 (Winter/Spring 1984): 68–73.

———. "Dante and the Roman Poets in Robert Lowell's *History*." *Modern Language Studies* 18, no. 2 (Spring 1988): 47–59.

———. "Founding a Literary Friendship: Allen Tate and Robert Lowell." *Southern Literary Journal* 21, no. 2 (Spring 1989): 72–91.

———. "Vision, Landscape, and the Ineffable in Robert Lowell's *History*." *Essays in Literature* 14, no. 2 (Fall 1987): 251–68.

Dunn, Douglas. "The Big Race: Lowell's Visions and Revisions." *Encounter* 41, no. 4 (October 1973): 107–13.

Dupree, Robert. *Allen Tate and the Augustinian Imagination*. Baton Rouge: Louisiana State University Press, 1983.

Eliot, T. S. *On Poetry and Poets*. New York, Harcourt, Brace, 1957.

———. *Selected Essays*. London: Faber and Faber, 1951.

Fain, John Tyree, and Thomas Daniel Young, eds. *The Literary Correspondence of Donald Davidson and Allen Tate*. Athens: University of Georgia Press, 1974.

Fallwell, Marshall, Jr. *Allen Tate: A Bibliography*. New York: David Lewis, 1969.

Folks, Jeffrey J. "Allen Tate and the Victorians." *South Atlantic Review* 50, no. 2 (May 1985): 55–66.

Fraser, G. S. "'Near the Ocean.'" *Salmagundi* 37 (Spring 1977): 73–87.

Fried, Michael. "The Achievement of Robert Lowell." *London Magazine* 2 (October 1967): 54–64.

Gross, Harvey. *Sound and Form in Modern Poetry: A Study of Prosody from Thomas Hardy to Robert Lowell*. Ann Arbor: University of Michigan Press, 1964.

Bibliography

Haffenden, John. "The Last Parnassian: Robert Lowell." *Agenda* 16, no. 2 (Summer 1978): 40–46.

———. *The Life of John Berryman*. Boston: Routledge and Kegan Paul, 1982.

Hamilton, Ian. "Robert Lowell." In *The Modern Poet*. Edited by Ian Hamilton. New York: Horizon, 1968: 32–41.

———. *Robert Lowell: A Biography*. New York: Random House, 1982.

Harvard Advocate 113, nos. 1 and 2 (November 1979). Robert Lowell commemorative issue.

Hass, Robert. "Lowell's Graveyard." *Salmagundi* 37 (Spring 1977): 56–72.

Hecht, Anthony. *Robert Lowell: A Lecture Delivered at the Library of Congress on May 2, 1983*. Washington: Library of Congress, 1983.

Hemphill, George. *Allen Tate*. Minneapolis: University of Minnesota Press, 1964.

Heymann, C. David. *American Aristocracy*. New York: Dodd, Mead, 1980.

Higginson, Thomas Wentworth. *Part of a Man's Life*. Boston: Houghton, Mifflin, 1905. Rpt. Port Washington: Kennikat Press, 1971.

Hobsbaum, Philip. *A Reader's Guide to Robert Lowell*. London: Thames and Hudson, 1988.

Humphries, Jefferson. "The Cemeteries of Allen Tate and Paul Valery: The Ghosts of Aeneas and Narcissus." *Southern Review* 20, no. 1 (Winter 1984): 54–67.

Jarrell, Mary, ed. *Randall Jarrell's Letters*. Boston: Houghton Mifflin, 1985.

Jarrell, Randall. *Kipling, Auden & Co.: Essays and Reviews, 1935–1964*. New York: Farrar, Straus & Giroux, 1980.

———. *Poetry and the Age*. New York: Knopf, 1953.

———. *The Third Book of Criticism*. New York: Farrar, Straus & Giroux, 1969.

Kalstone. David. *Five Temperaments*. New York: Oxford University Press, 1977.

Kelly, Richard J., ed. *We Dream of Honour: John Berryman's Letters to His Mother*. New York: Norton, 1988.

Kinzie, Mary. "The Prophet is a Fool: On 'Waking Early Sunday Morning.'" *Salmagundi* 37 (Spring 1977): 88–101.

Koch, Viviene. "The Poetry of Allen Tate." In *Allen Tate and His Work*, edited by Radcliffe Squires. Minneapolis: University of Minnesota Press, 1972: 253–64.

Kunitz, Stanley. *A Kind of Order, A Kind of Folly*. Boston: Little, Brown, 1975.

———. *Next-to-Last Things: New Poems and Essays*. Boston: Little, Brown, 1985.

Bibliography

London, Michael, and Robert Boyers, eds. *Robert Lowell: A Portrait of the Artist in His Time.* New York: David Lewis, 1970.

Lowell, Robert. "After Reading Six or Seven Essays on Me." *Salmagundi* 37 (Spring 1977): 112–15.

————. The Art of Newman's *Apologia.*" *Kenyon Review* 8 (Spring 1946): 340–41.

————. *Collected Prose.* New York: Farrar, Straus & Giroux, 1987.

————. *Day by Day.* New York: Farrar, Straus & Giroux, 1977.

————. *The Dolphin.* New York: Farrar, Straus & Giroux, 1973.

————. "English Metrics." *Hudson Review* 15 (Spring 1962): 317–20.

————. *For Lizzie and Harriet.* New York: Farrar, Straus & Giroux, 1973.

————. "For the Union Dead." *Atlantic* 217 (November 1960): 54–55.

————. *For the Union Dead.* New York: Farrar, Straus & Giroux, 1964.

————. "For T. S. Eliot." *Harvard Advocate* 125 (December 1938): 20.

————. *History.* New York: Farrar, Straus & Giroux, 1973.

————. *Imitations.* New York: Farrar, Straus & Cudahy, 1961.

————. *Land of Unlikeness.* Cummington: Mass.: Cummington Press, 1944.

————. Letter to President Johnson, *New York Times,* (3 June 1965): 2.

————. Letter to the Editors of the *New York Review of Books,* (29 February 1968): 32.

————. Letter to the Editor of the *Village Voice* (19 November, 1964): 4.

————. "Liberalism and Activism." *Commentary* 47 (April 1969): 19.

————. "Liberalism and Columbia." *Commentary* 47 (March 1969): 4.

————. *Life Studies.* New York: Farrar, Straus & Cudahy, 1959.

————. *Lord Weary's Castle.* New York, Harcourt, Brace, 1946.

————. Lowell Papers, Harry Ransom Humanities Research Center, University of Texas.

————. Lowell Papers, Houghton Library, Harvard University.

————. *The Mills of the Kavanaughs.* New York: Harcourt, Brace, 1951.

————. "Modesty without Mumbling." *New York Times Book Review,* (17 July 1966): 5.

————. *Near the Ocean.* New York: Farrar, Straus & Giroux, 1967.

————. *Notebook.* 3rd ed. New York: Farrar, Straus & Giroux, 1970.

————. *Notebook 1967–68.* New York: Farrar, Straus & Giroux, 1969.

————. *The Old Glory.* New York: Farrar, Straus & Giroux, 1964.

————. *The Orestia of Aeschylus.* New York: Farrar, Straus & Giroux, 1978.

————. "The Pacification of Columbia." *New York Review of Books* (20 June 1968): 18.

————. *Phaedra.* New York: Farrar, Straus & Cudahy, 1961.

————. *Prometheus Bound.* New York: Farrar, Straus & Giroux, 1969.

Bibliography

————. Review of *The World's Body*. by John Crowe Ransom. *Hika* 5 (October 1938): 17–18.

————. Review of *The Testing Tree* by Stanley Kunitz. *New York Times Book Review* (22 March 1971): 1.

————. *Selected Poems*. London: Faber & Faber, 1965.

————. *Selected Poems*. New York: Farrar, Straus & Giroux, 1976.

————. "Three Poems for *Kaddish*." *Ploughshares*, 5, no. 2 (1979): 70–73.

————. *"The Voyage" and Other Versions of Poems by Baudelaire*. New York: Farrar, Straus & Giroux, 1969.

————. "Waking Early Sunday Morning." *New York Review of Books* (5 August 1965): 3.

————. "The Years at Kenyon." *Kenyon College Alumni Review* 1 (November 1977): 22–24.

————. "Yvor Winters: A Tribute." *Poetry* 98 (April 1961): 40–43.

————, and Caroline Blackwood. "A Conversation about Ford Madox Ford." In *The Saturday Night Reader*, ed. Emma Tennant, London: W. H. Allen, 1979: 200–201.

————, Peter Taylor, and Robert Penn Warren, eds. *Randall Jarrell, 1914–1965*. New York: Farrar, Straus & Giroux, 1967.

Lucie-Smith, Edward. "Robert Lowell: 'Waking Early Sunday Morning.'" In *Criticism in Action*, edited by Maurice Hussey, London: Longmans, 1969: 164–89.

McAlexander, Hubert H., ed. *Conversations with Peter Taylor*. Jackson: University Press of Mississippi, 1987.

Mackinnon, Lachlan. *Eliot, Auden, Lowell: Aspects of the Baudelairean Inheritance*. London: Macmillan, 1983.

Mailer, Norman. *Armies of the Night*. New York: New American Library, 1968.

Martin, Jay. *Robert Lowell*. Minneapolis: University of Minnesota Press, 1970.

Mazarro, Jerome. *The Achievement of Robert Lowell*. Detroit: University of Detroit Press, 1960.

————. *The Poetic Themes of Robert Lowell*. Ann Arbor: University of Michigan Press, 1965.

————, ed. *Profile of Robert Lowell*. Columbus, Ohio: Merrill, 1971.

Meiners, R. K. *Everything to Be Endured: An Essay on Robert Lowell and Modern Poetry*. Columbia: University of Missouri Press, 1970.

————. *The Last Alternative: A Study of the Works of Allen Tate*. Denver: Swallow Press, 1963.

Meredith, William. Review of *Notebook 1967–1968*. *New York Times Book Review*, (15 June 1969): 1.

Bibliography

Meyers, Jeffery. *Manic Power: Robert Lowell and His Circle.* New York: Arbor House, 1987.

———, ed. *Robert Lowell: Interviews and Memoirs.* Ann Arbor: University of Michigan Press, 1988.

Moore, Merrill. *The Fugitive: Clippings and Comment.* Boston: privately printed, 1939.

Naipaul, V. S. "'Et in America Ego.'" In *Profile of Robert Lowell,* edited by Jerome Mazzaro. Columbus, Ohio: Merrill, 1971.

Newlove Donald. "'Dinner at the Lowells.'" *Esquire* 72 (September 1969): 3–36.

North, Michael. "The Public Monument and Public Poetry: Stevens, Berryman, and Lowell." *Contemporary Literature* 21 (Spring 1980): 267–85.

Parkinson, Thomas, ed. *Robert Lowell: A Collection of Critical Essays.* Englewood Cliffs, N.J.: Prentice-Hall, 1968.

Pearson, Gabriel. "Robert Lowell." *The Review* 20 (March 1969): 3–36.

Perloff, Marjorie. *The Poetic Art of Robert Lowell.* Ithaca: Cornell University Press, 1973.

Phillips, Robert, ed. *Letters of Delmore Schwartz.* Princeton: Ontario Review Press, 1984.

Pinsker, Sanford. "John Berryman and Robert Lowell: The Middle Generation Reconsidered." *Literary Review* 27, no. 2 (Winter 1984): 252–61.

Pinsky, Robert. "The Conquered Kings of Robert Lowell." *Salmagundi* 37 (Spring 1977): 102–5.

———. *The Situation of Poetry.* Princeton: Princeton University Press, 1976.

Poirier, Richard. "Our Truest Historian." *New York Herald Tribune Weekly Book Review* (11 October 1964): 1.

Price, Jonathan, ed. *Critics on Robert Lowell.* Coral Gables: University of Miami Press, 1972.

Procopiow, Norma. *Robert Lowell: The Poet and His Critics.* Chicago: American Library Association, 1984.

Purdy, Rob Roy, ed. *Fugitives' Reunion: Conversations at Vanderbilt, May 3–5, 1956.* Nashville: Vanderbilt University, 1959.

Raffel, Burton. *Robert Lowell.* New York: Unger, 1981.

Ransom, John Crowe. *Beating the Bushes: Selected Essays, 1941–1970.* New York: New Directions, 1972.

———. *Selected Poems.* 3rd ed. New York: Knopf, 1969.

———. *The World's Body.* New York: Scribner, 1938.

———, ed. *The Kenyon Critics.* Cleveland: World Publishing, 1951.

Bibliography

Rich, Adrienne. "Caryatid." *American Poetry Review* 2, no. 5 (September/October 1973): 42–43.

Roberts, David. *Jean Stafford: A Biography.* Boston: Little, Brown, 1988.

Ronca, Felice C. "My Heart Laid Bare: Some Critical Correspondences among Baudelaire, Poe, and Allen Tate." *Mid-Hudson Language Studies* 9 (1986): 55–64.

Rollins, J. Barton. "Robert Lowell's Apprenticeship and Early Poems." *American Literature* 52, no. 1 (March 1980): 67–83.

———. "Young Robert Lowell's Poetics of Revision." *Journal of Modern Literature* 7 (September 1979): 488–504.

Rosenthal, M. L. *The Modern Poets.* New York: Oxford University Press, 1960.

———. *The New Poets: American and British Poetry since World War II.* New York: Oxford University Press, 1967.

———. "Our Neurotic Angel: Robert Lowell (1917–1977)." *Agenda* 18, no. 3 (Autumn 1980): 34–46.

———. "Poetic Theory of Some Contemporary Poets." *Salmagundi* 1, no. 4 (1966–67): 69–77.

Rubin, Louis D., Jr. "Four Southerners." In *Stratford-Upon-Avon Studies 7: American Poetry,* edited by Irvin Ehrenpreis. London: E. H. Arnold, 1965.

———. *The Wary Fugitives: Four Poets and the South.* Baton Rouge: Louisiana State University Press, 1978.

Rudman, Mark. *Robert Lowell: An Introduction to the Poetry.* New York: Columbia University Press, 1983.

Russo, John Paul. " 'I fish until the clouds turn blue': Robert Lowell's Late Poetry." *Papers on Language and Literature* 20 : 2 (1984): 312–25.

Salmagundi 37 (Spring 1977). Special issue for Lowell's 60th birthday.

Schwartz, Sanford. *The Matrix of Modernism: Pound, Eliot, and Early Twentieth-Century Thought.* Princeton: Princeton University Press, 1985.

Seidel, Frederick. "The Art of Poetry III: Robert Lowell." *Paris Review* 25 (Winter-Spring 1961). Reprinted as "An Interview with Frederick Seidel" in ROBERT LOWELL: *Collected Prose*: 235–66.

Shaw, Robert. "Lowell in the Seventies." *Contemporary Literature* 23, no. 4 (Fall 1982): 515–27.

Simpson, Eileen. *Poets in Their Youth: A Memoir.* New York: Random House, 1982.

Simpson, Louis. "The Critics Who Made Us: Allen Tate." *Sewanee Review* 94, no. 3 (Summer 1986): 471–85.

Spears, Monroe K. *American Ambitions: Selected Essays on Literary and Cultural Themes.* Baltimore: Johns Hopkins University Press, 1987.

Bibliography

———. *Dionysus and the City: Modernism in Twentieth-Century Poetry.* New York: Oxford University Press, 1970.

———, ed. *Sewanee Review* 67, no. 4. (Autumn 1959). Special issue: Homage to Allen Tate.

Squires, Radcliffe. *Allen Tate: A Literary Biography.* New York: Pegasus, 1971.

———. *Allen Tate and His Work: Critical Evaluations.* Minneapolis: University of Minnesota Press, 1972.

Stafford, Jean. *Collected Stories.* New York: Farrar, Straus & Giroux, 1969.

———. "An Influx of Poets." *New Yorker* (6 November 1978): 43–58.

Stang, Sondra J., ed. *The Presence of Ford Madox Ford.* Philadelphia: University of Pennsylvania Press, 1981.

Staples, Hugh. *Robert Lowell: The First Twenty Years.* London: Faber & Faber, 1962.

Steiner, George. "Two Translations." *Kenyon Review* 23 (1961): 714–21.

Stewart, John L. *The Burden of Time: The Fugitives and Agrarians.* Princeton: Princeton University Press, 1965.

Sullivan, Walter. *Allen Tate: A Recollection.* Baton Rouge: Louisiana State University Press, 1988.

Tate, Allen. *Collected Essays.* Denver: Alan Swallow, 1959.

———. *Collected Poems, 1919–1976.* New York: Farrar, Straus & Giroux, 1977.

———. *Christ and the Unicorn.* West Branch, Iowa: Cummington Press, 1966.

———. *Essays of Four Decades.* Chicago: Swallow Press, 1968.

———. *The Fathers.* New York: Putnam, 1938.

———. "Ford Madox Ford." *New York Review of Books* 1, no. 2 (1964): 5.

———. *The Forlorn Demon.* Chicago: Regency, 1953.

———. *The Hovering Fly and Other Essays.* Cummington, Mass.: Cummington Press, 1948.

———. *Jefferson Davis, His Rise and Fall: A Biographical Narrative.* New York: Minton, 1929.

———. *The Man of Letters in the Modern World.* New York: Meridian, 1955.

———. *The Mediterranean and Other Poems.* New York: Alcestis Press, 1936.

———. *Memoirs and Opinions.* Chicago: Swallow Press, 1975.

———. *Mr. Pope and Other Poems.* New York: Minton, 1929.

———. *Poems.* New York: Scribner, 1960.

———. *Poems, 1922–1947.* New York: Scribner, 1948.

Bibliography

————. *Poems, 1920–1945: A Selection*. London: Eyre and Spottidwoode, 1947.

"Poetry Modern and Unmodern: A Personal Reflection." *Hudson Review* 21 (1968): 251–62.

————. *The Poetry Reviews of Allen Tate, 1924–1944*. Edited by Ashley Brown and Frances Neal Cheney. Baton Rouge: Louisiana State University Press, 1983.

————. *Reactionary Essays on Poetry and Ideas*. New York: Scribner, 1936.

————. *Reason in Madness: Critical Essays*. New York: Putnam, 1941.

————. "Robert Lowell." *Harvard Advocate* 145 (November 1961): 5.

————. *Selected Poems*. New York: Scribner, 1937.

————. "Some Influences of Baudelaire." *Bulletin Baudelairien* 5 (1969): 33–40.

————. *Sonnets at Christmas*. Cummington, Mass.: Cummington Press, 1941.

————. "Speculations." *Southern Review* 14 (1978): 226–32.

————. *Stonewall Jackson, the Good Soldier: A Narrative*. New York: Minton, 1928.

————. *The Swimmers and Other Selected Poems*. New York: Scribner, 1961.

————. *Tate File*. Firestone Library, Princeton University.

————. *The Vigil of Venus: Pervigilium Veneris*. Cummington, Mass.: Cummington Press, 1943.

————. *The Winter Sea*. Cummington, Mass.: Cummington Press, 1944.

————, and Herbert Agar. *Who Owns America? A New Declaration of Independence*. Boston: Houghton Mifflin, 1936.

————, and Stanley Kunitz, "Communication and Communion: A Dialogue." *Southern Review* 21, no. 2 (Spring 1985): 404–14.

————, ed. *The Collected Poems of John Peale Bishop*. New York: Scribner, 1948.

————, ed. *Fugitives: An Anthology of Verse*. New York: Harcourt, Brace, 1928.

————, ed. *I'll Take My Stand: The South and the Agrarian Tradition*. New York: Harper, 1930.

————, ed. *The Language of Poetry*. Princeton: Princeton University Press, 1942.

————, ed. *A Southern Vanguard: The John Peale Bishop Memorial Volume*. New York: Prentice-Hall, 1947.

————, ed. *T. S. Eliot: The Man and His Work*. New York: Delacorte Press, 1966.

Bibliography

————, and Caroline Gordon, eds. *The House of Fiction.* New York: Scribner, 1951.

————, Ralph Ross, and John Berryman, eds. *The Arts of Learning.* New York: Thomas Y. Crowell, 1960.

Thompson, Barbara. "Interview with Peter Taylor." In *Conversations with Peter Taylor,* edited by Hubert H. McAlexander. Jackson: University Press of Mississippi, 1987.

Trilling, Lionel. *The Experience of Literature: A Reader with Commentaries.* New York: Holt, 1967.

Vendler, Helen. *The Music of What Happens: Poems, Poets, Critics.* Cambridge: Harvard University Press, 1988.

————. *The Odes of John Keats.* Cambridge: Harvard University Press, 1983.

————. *Part of Nature, Part of Us.* Cambridge: Harvard University Press, 1980.

Von Hallberg, Robert. *American Poetry and Culture, 1945–1980.* Cambridge: Harvard University Press, 1985.

Waldron, Ann. *Close Connections: Caroline Gordon and the Southern Renaissance.* New York: Putnam, 1987.

Wallingford, Katherine. *Robert Lowell's Language of the Self.* Chapel Hill: University of North Carolina Press, 1988.

Williamson, Alan. "'I Am That I Am': The Ethics and Aesthetics of Self-Revelation." *American Poetry Review* 3, no. 1 (January/February 1974): 37–39.

————. *Pity the Monsters: The Political Vision of Robert Lowell.* New Haven: Yale University Press, 1974.

————. "The Reshaping of 'Waking Early Sunday Morning.'" *Agenda* 18, no. 3 (Autumn 1980): 47–62.

————. *Introspection and Contemporary Poetry.* Cambridge: Harvard University Press, 1984.

Wood, Allen Tate. *Moonstruck.* New York: Morrow, 1979.

Wood, Sally, ed. *The Southern Mandarins: Letters of Caroline Gordon to Sally Wood, 1924–1937.* Baton Rouge: Louisiana State University Press, 1984.

Yenser, Stephen. *Circle to Circle: The Poetry of Robert Lowell.* Berkeley: University of California Press, 1975.

Young, Thomas Daniel. *Gentleman in a Dustcoat: A Biography of John Crowe Ransom.* Baton Rouge: Louisiana State University Press, 1976.

————. "Religion and Literature." *Mississippi Quarterly* 39, no. 2 (Spring 1986): 126–32.

Bibliography

———, ed. *Selected Letters of John Crowe Ransom*. Baton Rouge: Louisiana State University Press, 1985.

———, ed. "Quo Vadimus? Or the Books Still Unwritten: Statements by Tate, Warren, Spender, Lowell." *Mississippi Quarterly* 38, no. 4 (Fall 1985): 415–34.

———, and John J., Hindle, eds. *The Republic of Letters in America: The Correspondence of John Peale Bishop and Allen Tate*. Lexington: University Press of Kentucky, 1981.

———, and Elizabeth Sarcone, eds. *The Lytle-Tate Letters*. Jackson: University Press of Mississippi, 1987.

I N D E X

243

Index

Index

Index

Index

249

Index

Index

www.ingramcontent.com/pod-product-compliance
Lightning Source LLC
Chambersburg PA
CBHW060347030726
47497CB00003B/631